CONVICTS CHEER CHANGE!

CONVICTS CHEER CHANGE!

T HANS

PRIMIX
PUBLISHING
THE WRITE CHOICE

Primix Publishing
11620 Wilshire Blvd
Suite 900, West Wilshire Center, Los Angeles, CA, 90025
www.primixpublishing.com
Phone: 1-800-538-5788

Published by Primix Publishing: 08/08/2023

ISBN: 978-1-957676-82-1(sc)
ISBN: 978-1-957676-83-8(e)

Library of Congress Control Number: 2023912090

This outrageous but revealing perspective regarding convicts, Christianity and change was written over a dozen years ago. Today….are we ready for this? Prophetic? Revolutionary? Catastrophe? Lifesaving? Fact or Fiction? You decide!

Convicts Cheer Change!

CONTENTS

INTRODUCTION

The year is 2000. Imagine being on a luxury cruise ship with all its seductions and splendor. This experience highlights the pinnacle of pleasure -- featuring the most beautiful surroundings… and where nearly all desires seem to be within easy reach. Moreover, it's a warm summer evening and the stars above convey a touch of awesome wonder. Everything is right with the world!

Drifting… drifting… drifting. Now you begin to realize the cruise ship has lost its power as it moves aimlessly over the calm water. It soon becomes obvious the ship is not making its way on the high seas but is carried by a gigantic river, which is silently but swiftly pushing the luxury liner and its inattentive passengers downstream. You begin to hear it -- just barely at first -- the low muffled roar of a waterfall. The sound increases, starting to drown out joyful, happy sounds. Thunderstruck, you are riveted to what you are hearing, for your mind tells you there is an awesome danger closing in. Finally, there's no doubt about where you are going. In the midst of one of your most enjoyable moments… in the center of nearly boundless luxury and pleasurable distraction… you and your fellow passengers are without doubt headed for Niagara Falls! Is it too late to prevent disaster?

Drifting… drifting… drifting. Entering a new millenium, we as a nation are drifting along in the lap of luxury. Most of us feel pretty good as we enjoy the benefits of hard work and well-planned periods of relaxation. We assume the "ship of state" is moving along in the right direction and that all we owe is paid in full. It's our right and privilege to enjoy all that lies before us. Our plate is full. But warning signs are beginning to nudge into our consciousness. And apparently, the people we think should be guiding our fortunes are "asleep at the wheel"… or "helping out in the entertainment section."

The people of our nation have historically relied on religion to provide us with a moral compass. It is true that some of our greatest moments out of the past have been spiritually grounded and seemingly divinely inspired. But think more recently about our impressions of religious leaders, institutional programs and so called "spiritual activity". Many popular preachers have been caught deceiving their followers -- looking out for themselves and their own fortunes. Even the average minister in our country seems to be well housed, well paid, well insured and well esteemed… with the comforts of class and privilege. The poor, minorities and the trouble-makers of our society usually live on the other side of the tracks and beg for some crumbs of attention. A good share of institutional programs and fundraisers serve the middle to upper class, whether that focuses on talent displays, intellectual stimulation or comfortable surroundings. "Spiritual exhibitionism" moves us toward the lowest common denominator…

with recent presidential expressions of "God bless America" and millionaire sports heroes showing off their "give God the glory" gestures. Where is all of this taking us? Certainly not to the cutting edge of moral enlightenment for the twenty-first century!

Let's look for religious or moral enlightenment in our society today. It may well be true that the basics of our religious convictions have a tendency to show up in our politics -- in the things that occupy our minds and voices as well as in the actions of our daily business. Take people on the political right for example. Publicity makes clear their positions on…"right to life", advocacy for military build-up, prayer in public schools, rights to have guns and desire for legislative power. On the other side is the political left, which appears to reject spiritual truth, explicit morality, the accountability of the individual and the value of local political control. Even "the middle" seems to encompass a mushy mess of unclear thinking and impractical proposals. All of this is a reflection of religion and politics gone bad -- stale and stinking to high heaven for their worthlessness. Our moral compass is hard to spot in an era of selfish materialism. We go in circles trying to find happiness and elusive security.

It's shocking to say we are afraid. Yet it's not strange we are uncomfortable when we lose what we love -- prestige jobs, national dominance, political prominence, suitable neighborhoods, spotless churches and even distant children. Who is satisfied with present wealth, power, control, leisure, entertainment or anything else that advertising attempts to sell us? We are lost in the struggle for personal success and afraid we won't get enough of everything that's available. This is the perfect set-up for a troubled and vulnerable future.

In days gone by the story was told about a "fortress built on a hill". In the 21st century that fortress turns into an upscale house, with a fence erected around the property and protected with the latest security devices. "Our people" then head out to acquire whatever we might want to satisfy our ever-expanding desires -- all at the lowest possible price! We admit "it's a jungle out there" but affirm that's just the way the system works. Another way of putting it... is to speak of our world as a family, where the big, fat older brother grabs nearly all the food and takes off in the car, while the newborn baby girl and rest of the family go hungry. So what's a parent to do in such a case, especially if the ground rules have not been clearly established?

The world of "the jungle" tells us that the only rules to live by are the ones implemented by the powerful ones. Essentially then, the only options available are violent solutions... except, of course, where the answers are clearly in the interests of the big boys. Maybe that's why our society love's violence so much. We know the rules of the game. Most of our sports are violent and increasingly so. Races, fights, demolition derbys and the like seem to attract the most attention and excitement when the most violence occurs. Video games that draw a good deal interest by children seem to be ones where there is a great deal of destruction and bloodshed. Practically all television programs insert violent scenes to attract fascination and appeal. Such programs are not limited only to the Jerry Springer type shows. Our love affair with guns and the hunting mentality transfers violence into the most mainstream activities. All this is to say nothing about crimes of violence, how we treat serious offenders and the terrorism that becomes the eventual answer to counter the most forceful "winners". To say that the violence in our society and culture is not learned... is to suggest the absurd. We have been told, "You've made your bed, now sleep in it!"

Terrorism may be the most frightening development of "business as usual" in our culture. Naturally it's the most troubling, because it seems to be the least predictable and controlled outcome of our entertainment and indoctrination. The truth is that practice makes perfect. We learn very early how to upset one another. Our brains and emotions -- from the smallest children on up -- are prepared (through many aspects of life today) to demonstrate the means and method of responding to disappointment and challenge. From childhood we are taught to use whatever talents we have to "beat the competition". It's not far fetched to feel the desperation and panic of the doe in the woods when the hunt begins. People react too. Be assured... terrorism is at almost everyone's disposal and it's not out of character for hurting people to "shoot back" indiscriminately!

It's no wonder that crime and drug use are chosen methods for coping with a very challenging and dangerous system. Many "less capable" individuals may well feel that they have little or no choice when they start out at the back of the pack and feel a lot of "growing pains." Because crime and many forms of lawlessness are so easy to get into... and examples are "a dime a dozen" in our age, it's almost considered normal to do what is outrageous and detrimental to the welfare of the majority. To make matters worse, both getting caught and not getting caught reinforce anti-social behavior. Punishment without rehabilitation as well as advanced training by fellow convicts in jail merely sends the convicted one on to more sophisticated acts of violence and desperation. Not getting caught rewards the individual with a feeling of payback, reinforces bad behavior and through "the excitement" stimulates more imaginative acts of terror. Is it at all surprising that criminals and drug addicts seem to have little chance of escaping a life of injuring and backsliding?

The important question is... "How will the majority react to this "muffled roar" of almost certain tragedy ahead?" There are at least three possible reactions -- two of which will do nothing to turn our society away from disastrous consequences. The first bad choice is the easiest to make and therefore the most likely to happen. The masses of our well-pampered citizens will decidedly ignore any potential danger signals. Messed up individuals -- no matter how great their number and no matter how serious their crisis -- will be left at the side of the road with little attention while the general population hurries along to places unknown. It's easy and seemingly less risky not to pay attention to what we might think are little problems along life's highway. It's none of our business and it might cost us, we say to ourselves. Furthermore, we have developed the habit of looking out for number one -- taking care of our own interests and happiness, generally without regard to the personal welfare of any unrelated people. The only real exception might be when someone gets in our way. Then we might lose our apathy and react! Apathy is the choice of the vast majority of people in our society and culture today and probably will remain number one while the good times roll on.

The second bad choice may be showing up with more frequency as we begin to sense some signs of trouble now… and more on the horizon. A growing number of people are beginning to panic, becoming even more aggressive and making a critical situation even worse. Where have we heard people advocating longer sentencing, stiffer punishments, bigger defense budgets, lower levels of foreign aid, isolationism, shutting off immigration, expulsions from schools, tax cuts for the wealthy and the like? People all over are uneasy, upset and propose any number of simplistic, immature and disastrous solutions to complex, serious problems. Accentuating this disaster, the news media (in simply their reporting) reinforce a lynch mob mentality among the masses. Where are we headed?

Maybe it would be good to consider the scope of any possible disaster ahead. Here again our instincts may lead us astray. Our first reaction might be to envision the whole ship of state going down in one big grand finale! Certainly that possibility does exist, since there seem to be any number of ways our nation as we know it could meet it's fate. When we are sent into a tailspin with Y2K -- with concerns about the chaos a small date chip can cause, think about how vulnerable we are economically, politically, morally and spiritually. Considering solitary future terrorists… all the way to the masses of deprived third or fourth world people, there are plenty of baffling, tragic endings for us to imagine. Yet the more realistic and sad disaster is the loss (one by one) of individuals caught in the grinder of our country's material success. Who doesn't want to have it all? But who is capable of getting it? And even in getting almost everything imaginable, who is capable of handling it? The road rage of daily business activity hits close to home. Many are hurt in the speeding road race… physically, mentally and spiritually. The dull roar seems to be growing louder and more threatening to us -- both individually and corporately.

We quite naturally respond to the sights and sounds of trouble and turmoil in our society. The two choices -- of trying to ignore obvious problems…or starting to panic when we sense some danger -- are not in our long-term best interests. Usually significant problems don't just drift away; and secondly, we don't want to make matters worse by reacting badly. There is a third response, which is a bit more challenging but is light years ahead of the other two for moving us toward quality living in the future. This choice presses us to seek out the root causes of our immediate and long-term danger and then change course before it's too late. That's the subject of this book -- "Vision 2000." It is critical to not only look back and see where we have been and where we have gone wrong, but also to attempt to seek out new ways of carrying out the business of living together in harmony on this shrinking planet.

In order to enable the reader to grasp my personal perspective in this book -- where it originates and where it might be leading, it seems imperative that I lay out some important turning points in my own life, personally. Who knows whether my experience and insight will adequately move the reader toward understanding and enlightenment. Certainly each person considers what words or actions will imprint the mind or move the heart toward newness. Moreover, clearly it's a very complex issue to know what motivates change. Yet change we must… if we are to survive, say nothing about living in peace, security and happiness. Put candidly, "my story" is about the need for change.

As the oldest of six children, I was strictly disciplined in a "Christian home" and decided that I wanted to be a minister at the ripe old age of nine. Needless to say, I was strongly influenced by my family and never seemed to go through the "rebellious stage." After four years at a Lutheran Church college and four years of seminary training, I entered the parish ministry and served approximately 14 years in three different places before deciding to leave. It was my conviction that I was not cut out to "grease the gears of the middle class." Before leaving in 1982, I wrote a 19-page "statement" voicing my concerns about the structured church in the United States. "Should I Leave the Parish Ministry" was sent to the District Presidents of The American Lutheran Church throughout the U.S. as well as to four seminary presidents. Below are a few excerpts from that paper.

As the Good News Bible introduces the Book of Amos -- "It was a time of great prosperity, notable religious piety, and apparent security. But Amos saw that prosperity was limited to the wealthy, and that it fed on injustice and on oppression of the poor. Religious observance was insincere, and security more apparent than real." It may well have seemed to this Judean shepherd that he was living in "the best of times, as well as the worst of times."

> For Amos, there was a crisis brewing. Events had become critical. He was caught up in a scene where the rich got richer, and the poor got poorer. Since Israel controlled trade routes, rulers and merchants shared increasing affluence and built elaborate homes for themselves. Land was taken out of the hands of small farmers so that large estates could be developed. Wealthy citizens believed the nation's prosperity was a sure sign of God's favor; and the religious leaders benefited so much from the

generous offerings... that they were not inclined to say or do anything which might depress the happy, confident, self-righteous mood of the upper class.

We live in a materialistic age, yet we would not admit to being the cause. We know there is increasing evidence that people are caught up in the idolatry of "looking out for number one," yet in daily competition to get ahead, we neglect to face our first priorities. There is little commitment to "the least of these" in sacrificial giving, yet we imagine that we must be doing our share. There is a general feeling that "politics" is a dirty word and that politicians are corrupt, yet we do not feel compelled to exercise our rightful responsibility to influence legislation or to speak out for more than what is in our own self-interest. As Nathan said to David, "You are that man!"

In looking back, clearly our nation has been blessed beyond the dreams of most men. We have become the managers of a great land -- "blessed to be a blessing" as God's stewards. Through the years, we have enjoyed the fruits of awesome natural resources, unprecedented political power, increasing social strength and stability, as well as a spiritual heritage radical enough to change the face of the globe. In the last three decades, our power, prestige and influence has been the envy of the world community. Yet we have not been satisfied. We have desired and grasped for more. If not actively involved as individuals, we have turned our backs in complicit ignorance and apathy. Who cares where the stolen goods come from, as long as they are ours! And we "possess them" as David took Bathsheba. Such is "a sign of the times" -- a day and age not unlike the one in which Amos lived.

The most tragic aspect of the book of Amos is that the people to whom he spoke believed that they were on the right track with their religious rituals. They "worshipped," sang songs, praised God, thanked Him, celebrated great religious festivals, "sacrificed" their tithes and gifts; and they most certainly took care of their worship / education centers... as well as the needs of their own "families." But to God it was all words, words, words! Theirs was nothing but a man-made religion that claimed authenticity by way of superficiality. The radical nature of His Will was overlooked. Although their practices made them feel "spiritual," the Lord said, "I hate your religious festivals; I cannot stand them!...Stop your noisy songs; I do not want to listen to your harps."

God speaks the above words to us. The "churches" throughout our land are for the most part "social clubs" -- where the rich care for the rich, and banners and flowers grace the altars; where bazaars build budgets by selling fattening foods and materialistic trinkets to those who have too much; where pastors and laity conspire with one another to justify increasing take-home pay and security benefits;

where leaders "play it safe" to keep the membership statistics climbing and the money flowing, and professionals are paid to keep "the stockholders" happy; where buildings and conveniences expand to impress even the most worldly among us; and the examples of such successful business techniques would seem to flow on forever.

How can those who are truly poor and hungry be "comforted" as they come to the doors of lavish churches and homes where gigantic cost overruns demand captivating interest payments? In a society where approximately 6% of the world's population consumes nearly 50% of the world's resources, while spending billions to trillions to protect its "investment," how can "the least of these" be moved to embrace a God of love? No, "the medium is the message" we are told; and the medium is mammon.

Take, for example, our traditional American Christmas celebration. Perhaps in some year long past, Christmas provided a special time of joy to those poor who saw Jesus in a humble manger and received a tangible expression of love from those who had more than enough. But today the poor are far away (at least so the saying goes) -- out of sight and out of mind. Meanwhile, our capitalistic society goes on a binge for nearly two months -- a pagan festival the likes of which the world has never seen. So-called "Christian families" go on shopping sprees to try to pacify the gluttonous appetite of those made fat by rampant consumerism. Drug habits among the nation's worst abusers would seem less addictive than those hooked on the Christmas hedonism. Year after year, gifts given (by those who can buy, to others who can pay back) insure that "the rich get richer, while the poor get poorer."

Are we afraid and insecure? To be sure! We are afraid of being robbed, of getting sick, of not having enough insurance, of losing our job, of not having enough to eat, of getting left out, of being laughed at, of losing a loved one, of rising taxes, of getting bombed, of just about every worldly thing imaginable! Line that up alongside of how placid people are about what those Bible passages really mean for life… or how to carry out that Biblical admonition to "sell all that you have." In fact, regardless of the reality that we as a nation are more materialistically endowed than any other people in history, still, it seems a sure thing that we are the least secure. Yes, we have laid up our riches on earth, and there is no way we will ever have enough food, clothes, insurance, security devices, bombs or military might to satisfy and protect ourselves. We make a mockery of God and imprint on our coins, "In God we trust," as He dies 10,000 deaths a day in those who are his starving brothers.

What inspires an election where the popular candidate is overwhelmingly swept into office by promising less interference in personal profit-taking, lower taxes, and sharply increased "defense expenditures?" What but greed and insecurity produces tax breaks for the rich and powerful, sharp cutbacks for the poor and powerless, accelerated military spending and arms sales, renewed support for racist South Africa and unwavering determination to ward off the call from underdeveloped countries for a new international economic order? As Senator Mark Hatfield has said, "The world spends $17 billion for arms every two weeks. With $17 billion, we could feed every person, clothe every cold person, house every person, and provide medical assistance for every person in the world for one year...."

It is clear that the so-called Christian populace in these United States is responsible and will be held accountable for the American lifestyle. The Church is not helpless to speak out or to act in defiance of powerful capitalistic paganism. Yet in her conformity to the world, she favors soft-spoken <u>words</u> to radical action! As a beneficiary of our materialistic society, she knows (like the rich young ruler) that if she is to <u>act</u> on God's will, she will have a lot to lose. And therein lies the crux of the matter -- for Amos' day as well as ours. It is the matter of whether we "play at religion"... or, sacrifice our lives to "carry out the radical will of God."

Word, words, words! Amos shouted at the people of his day that their religion was hypocrisy! They went through all the gestures beautifully -- they celebrated (they carried out the feast days with a flourish), they sang beautifully, they performed on fine instruments, they quit buying and selling on the Sabbath, they undoubtedly prayed and recited the Word of the Lord, they even gave their tithes, sacrificed their animals and bragged about their extra offerings. In short, their religion would have been considered "a fine performance" by anyone but Almighty God. He knew that their primary concern was to save their skins and pat their fat, while the poor went hungry and injustices were perpetrated on the weak without so much as a pang of conscience.

It is our general identity as American church-people that we have either "emotionalized" or "intellectualized" the Gospel. We have either been "touched" and led to private experience or "persuaded" and led to intellectual pursuit. We have had our testimonials, our altar calls, our healing services, our prayer services, our Bible studies, our conventions, our seminars and our retreats. We have read the Word, interpreted the Word, discussed the Word, debated the Word, prayed the Word, preached the Word, sung the Word, confessed the Word, visualized the Word, play-acted the Word, touched and tasted the Word, translated the Word, rationalized the Word and repudiated the Word. We have done just about everything possible with the Word, except practice the Word and live out its radical imperatives!

How many times have you heard at the conclusion of a sermon or service, "What shall we do, brothers?" No, the preachers and proclaimers would probably be so taken off-guard that they would be speechless (for once)! As church goers we are programmed by tradition and by social conformity not to act -- not to get carried away! In fact, in many congregations, spectators do not even use their mouths or voices well. When was the last time you attended a worship service where you went "to work" -- to carry out the radical Word of God in reverence of his Holy Name? Such worship services are not well attended, for one reason and probably one reason only: We "play" at our religion; in fact, we are spectators who have become so apathetic that in most cases we do not even do good copycat cheering.

John the Baptist was a radical! Yes, now there's a man who got carried away in pointing the path toward Jesus. There was a preacher! Part of the problem in today's church rests with the preachers! Every Sunday we go through our "monkey in the cage" routine, and every Sunday people come up with blank stares or encouraging smiles or cute compliments. Have you ever noticed in the zoo... how the spectators love to watch the monkeys perform... and how usually the monkeys do those tricks that get them the treats... and how unchanged the spectators are as they leave the viewing area? Does "a monkey in a cage" personally challenge your life-style, or act different than a monkey should, or quit doing those things that get him compliments and incentives? Not if he wants to be in the limelight and move up in the world! He is a captive of his environment and trained to do the spectator's bidding. How effective are the rich -- those who pay to see the show and hold the bags of peanuts!

No more Christmas celebrations! That indeed is a bitter thing, for it hurts us where we feel it the most. It cuts into our materialistic life-style, it hurts our greed, it hinders our pleasure, it denies our pride, it troubles our thinking. But Jesus would have it stopped! He was that baby born in a humble manger, who today walks among us with no place to lay his head. And His Father in heaven is repulsed and angered to the core of his Holiness as we yearly commit this sacrilege of "Christmas" and smear his Son's Name before the peoples of the world. We give to those who pay us back and walk pietistically past those beaten unto death by the side of the road. Imagine! Crucified at Christmas!

Remember, all of the above was written back in 1982. From the beginning, the Christian Church was meant to be the Body of Christ in the world... bringing forth newness of life -- change! And change has always been at the root and center of Christian theology. In fact, the Bible is a book about change -- from beginning to end. To put it bluntly, daily change should be an integral part of every Christian life and fundamental to every Christian church. So approaching the end of the 20th century, should it be so shocking to propose the need of a new reformation? One seminary professor suggested early in 1982 that the manuscript contained issues that should be discussed among the clergy and other leaders. After presenting my paper at a conference pastor's meeting, the comment in response that shocked me the most came from a pastor who apparently spoke for many -- "What can we say? It's all true!" Yet generally the silence from the churches was deafening... and still is! Once again tradition clashed with change... and tradition won in a landslide.

In April of 1986, in response to a letter informing me that my name would be removed from the clergy roster, the following paragraph was included as a part of my comments:

Having "worshipped" in many churches (mostly ALC), it has become increasingly obvious to me that most of us as U.S. church members are fatally materialistic, dependent upon ourselves and our country for our security, seriously hopeful only about human accomplishment and addicted to a comfortable if not luxurious lifestyle. Are we not known by our "fruits"? It hardly needs to be said that such priorities go exactly contrary to "the way of the cross"! Dead in the water, drifting on a storm-tossed sea, looking to ourselves for consolation; and I don't see many, if any, willing to "rock the boat" for the purpose of seeking new direction!

Should there be anything more troubling to disciples of Christ than to watch the institution of today's church turn away from change and newness of life? It's no wonder the church has strayed so far away from its intended mission! We observe that our proud "promiscuous body" represents little more than the status quo. How bad and sad!

What a beginning point! Crucified at Christmas. What a point of departure! If change is to take place, then something must be left behind. And for all the badness and sadness that is part of our past and present as a people, we must acknowledge that newness is the answer... and necessary for our survival. Christians believe the event of Christ's crucifixion was "that point in time" where new life for all people was born... and is born, even today. So it's not so strange we need to take a long, serious look at where we have been and even how in the world we got there. It's a hard and humbling thing to do but not impossible for any person or any people of any time or place. The purpose, of course, is to get us ready to charge off with a different purpose for our lives.

As months moved into years, there was a need to recognize a change in mission for my own life. Thankfully, I was given the gentle assignment of providing a good example to my two wonderful, school-age sons. My wife's employment gave me quality time to spend with them, trying to influence, inspire and instruct. Also, it became increasingly obvious -- "It's the little things that count!" I recall two of those "little things" clearly. Many times our boys asked about doing the same things as the other kids -- whether that involved going places, buying things or staying out -- and I needed to remind them of our opportunities to learn to "go against the grain" or "turn against the tide." I also remember the evening when my high school age son and I came to a mutual decision as to the appropriate time for him to return home. He was about two or three minutes late that night. We had a long discussion about caring, faithfulness and responsibility. As I remember, he was never late again... without letting us know the reason in advance. Together, we all learned how to change, hopefully for the better. I had my own struggles, of course. Many years had passed since I had confronted an aspect of my personality I didn't like. It was evident I needed to focus my attention on a way to change that deep part of me. I felt profound satisfaction it did happen... slowly but surely... over months and then years.

The question arises, "If we truly desire to change, how can we enable that change to take root and bear fruit? No simple yet comprehensive guidelines for change were apparent in my studies. People we might consider authorities on the subject -- teachers, psychiatrists, doctors, ministers and others -- seemed to be very casual and indecisive about workable guidelines. Had any profession taken into account the whole person --

mind, body and soul? And finally, if a conclusive way to bring about change existed, why was almost nothing being done to enable it to happen in the most important places -- in a prison, for example? It became critical for me to take an extensive look at any information available about change. Material came from all directions -- from theological institutions to villages in the Third World, from AA groups to marriage counselors, from general information sources to daily newspapers. Individuals around the world had a lot of insights concerning "change", but little had been provided to focus this mountain of resources on getting human beings to the places they wanted to go in their lives. At minimum, I felt the need to take "a little step of my own" to consolidate some of the general insights that seemed helpful to me.

A series of "change booklets" was the product of a period of digesting and meditating on the material I had been absorbing over the years. Personal experience played an important role in my presentations, although the desire was strong to make understandable and practical what I was learning. Could I start to bring together the beautiful and varied "colors of the rainbow" of beneficial change? Would I be able to help others know and enjoy change intimately -- as a friend? All people should be able to enjoy the benefits of personal power... over bad choices and addictions... over personal weaknesses... over family and cultural ignorance... over troublesome feelings... over simply poor training and other such things. Insights confirmed that healthy change could be accomplished in an enjoyable and interesting way.

If individuals in our society could begin to pick up the tools to make desired changes in their own lives... and in finding success could begin to pass those same tools on to others, we could quite literally experience a social and cultural revolution. Imagine the potential of a recycling of the whole person -- body, mind and spirit! And who in their right mind wouldn't want to be involved? Potential for human goodness could be an endless process toward divine standards. Moreover, the power in every living soul to change would reassert the fantastic potential of every human being.

The "change booklets" began to take shape in late 1994 and were finally finished and printed in 1997. They covered the territory from introducing change to motivating change and were simply written for the average curious reader. Here are the titles with their subtitles: "Change... From Grief to Joy" (Probing For Health And Happiness); "To Choose To Change" (In the Spirit For Christian Survival); "The Success Stories" (Inspirations For Desirable Change); "Checking In... To Change" (A Playbook For Winning); and finally, "Motivated For Change" (Challenged For a Better Life). The frustrating truth was that practically all the printed copies were boxed -- never to be used. After printing up my business card -- "The Change Agent" -- Fun Change... To Easy Success!" -- right or wrong, I concluded it would be too risky for me to start counseling without extensive "liability insurance." I never made the move into "business" to offer assistance to needy people. Did I fall back into "the status quo" of my old life (avoiding change) or was I put on stand-by for greater things to come? Since I can't answer that question, I guess only time will tell.

Absorbing ideas, wrestling with my inner self, writing down thoughts to pass on -- in the midst of all this, how could I effectively minister to people in need, even if that was without pay? Struggling from weeks to months to years, I read some letters to Ann Landers (in the newspaper) that moved me to respond with my own suggestions of interest and concern. After all, wasn't Ann a popular, knowledgeable person who might be able to help… and who might be the foremost "change agent" in our country?

On January 13, 1995, I sent Ann Landers (in care of the Chicago Tribune) the following letter:

Thank you for revealing more of "the whole picture" to your readers and to Burned Up in Connecticut. Certainly frustration with our justice system is understandable, and as you say, there are no simple answers. However, in response to your comments… "criminals might be rehabilitated" and "suggestions please", may I offer two radical, workable, interrelated and yet mind boggling proposals. Both of these come out of the same heart and spirit.

> First, my answer to the baseball strike: Owners and players simultaneously propose that all players earning over $100,000 /year take cuts of 50%, all owners and management take identical cuts in

pay and profits, all prices for baseball tickets are cut 50%, and finally, all players can become "free agents" every year. Motivation would come from a spirit of thankfulness rather than greed… and from salary comparisons with those who have less rather than with those who get more. A two- page proposal was sent to Commissioner Selig last September. If the strike is settled according to the above terms, I would present....

My second proposal: I believe that almost any person can be changed through basic behavioral modification. What is needed over time is an effective correction and reward system… with more focus on the latter. The most unproductive part of our society can become the most productive! Moreover, crime and drug use can be reduced significantly!

I propose that most criminals serving time be given opportunity to volunteer for rehabilitation. After being prepared for a new life, they would be paid by federal or state government to cut down criminal activity in high crime areas. They would work for a living wage in teams of two with the understanding that they would be monitored for results. If either one broke away from being "a model citizen", both would go back to prison. With insight into the path they took to prison, criminals could be our best experts in preventing future criminal activity.

Contemplate some of the potential benefits.

Liberated, hopeful people would be prepared and paid to cut off crime at its roots. Criminals wouldn't be going back to a life of crime after serving time. Less money would be needed for incarceration and for building prisons. Working with criminals would be uplifting rather than depressing. Society would demonstrate a constructive way to handle anti-social behavior. Ponder the wonderful advantages for families of criminals. Then consider the vast savings in human and economic resources. So what are the chances of something like this ever happening, Ann?

Clearly Ann Landers receives so many letters that she can't possibly respond to or print even a small faction of them. I wasn't surprised my letter was set aside. A little over one year later I read another letter in Ann Landers' column. She was still looking for suggestions. This time I became a lot more specific. On February 21, 1996, I sent Ann a one page letter (along with a seven page enclosure) detailing my proposal...

Dear Ann Landers:

Recently, a letter to you from Hartford, Conn. concluded, "Our justice system stinks... it's a revolving door and does nothing to discourage crime." I am writing in response to your comment -- "I welcome suggestions...."

Our nation needs some creative ideas to deal with

increasing crime and overflowing prisons. Here is one, sound, beneficial, inexpensive and exciting way to begin to reduce both our crisis with crime and our prison problems. However, it requires that we look from a new perspective.

Our prisons today are full of VIP specialists who could be recruited for a national "war on crime." With careful correction and adequate incentives, criminals could be encouraged to switch sides and become crime fighters. Criminals know well the roots, progress, temptations and hazards of crime. And convicts with the hope of a fragile "new life" could find incentives appealing… and corrections valuable.

Criminals can be changed! However, for lasting change it is important to use the best ideas that rational thought, science and religion have to offer. Utilizing a "holistic approach" -- in a sense, consensual brain washing, behavior modification and spirit cleansing along with practical and proven methods from groups such as AA -- a new way of life can be "programmed" and implemented one step at a time.

My proposal is this: Test the process by permitting approximately six convicts to begin a unique rehabilitation / training program for the explicit purpose of being paid to fight crime. Specialists would work with convicts until approved by an evaluation committee. "Crime fighters" would work in teams of two... knowing that without personal growth as well as career achievement, both would be dismissed and return to prison. Teams would be aided by daily checks of short and long-term goals. This program would greatly benefit both prisoners and society as a whole.

The incarcerated crowd -- what many see as that "garbage pile" growing by leaps and bounds -- is a valuable community resource. If we will be open-minded, efficient and caring, many "throwaways" can be picked up and found to be credits to our morality and health as a democratic society.

The enclosure was introduced: Re: Proposal for dealing with crime and criminals

I have mixed feelings writing to you. After your comments on criminals and crime early in 1995, on January 13th I wrote in response to "some suggestions, please." Since I realized my letter was a bit radical, although entirely practical and sincere, I really didn't expect attention to my proposals.

On the other hand, I feel pressed once again to respond to "I welcome suggestions...." Having read your column for many years, I believe my "suggestions" are not only what you are looking for but also present a sound and reasonable way to **begin to deal with crime and criminals.**

The big barrier is... that my "solution" has not been

tried and would be a radical departure from what the general public considers to be an "appropriate solution" to this troublesome problem. My quandary over speaking out is this: Should I take the "baby steps" of going through all the proper channels… or wait and hope for a more enlightened age… or contact Ann Landers? Well, you asked, so here is a mere "moonbeam" into the darkness of despair we face as a society. I only reflect to you what I have received over many years.

You wrote: "Dear Hart: Many prisons not only do nothing to discourage crime, they are "graduate schools" where neophytes learn the real tricks of the trade. I welcome suggestions on what can be done to cure this sick and costly problem."
I completely agree and feel the need to contribute.

Here are half a dozen other statements which I believe are just as accurate: We live in the "dark ages" of managing crime and guiding criminals for the health and well-being of our society. About the only redeeming aspect of our criminal justice system is that we sometimes, temporarily stop criminal behavior. We need to consider the **total** damage of crime to society -- not only to injured victims, but also multiplication of hate, abuse of criminals, family guilt and shame, wasted resources used for prosecution and incarceration, ruthless revenge, deterioration of personal and social moral standards, decline of community security, etc. There is no evidence to show that punishment produces thoughtfulness or that hate inspires love. We generally do not understand what we teach or how we teach; it is the little things that count... at the earliest possible time!

This may be the most shocking statement of all: The cause of our greatest national distress -- the convicted criminal -- can become our greatest national benefactor in fighting crime. Only approval of a small but concentrated effort by a few people over a short period of time is needed to reap big rewards. Ann, I believe you can be an important part of the enlightening process.

You mentioned prisons as "graduate schools." Speaking of schools and learning... I was running past our fine high school last summer and noticed the large amount of trash which had accumulated. After my run, I decided to go back and pick up some of the litter around the school, which I did for approximately five hours -- for the fun of it. You maybe can imagine the questions and comments I received from students and adults alike. But the bottom line was, "We have kids serving detention who do that!" I asked, "You mean no one picks up trash for the fun of it?" There was a shocked negative response. Our society as a whole is suffering from the consequences of what we have been teaching -- from throwing litter to enjoying destruction and carnage. And with regard to captured criminals, we have no idea what to do but to throw them! Wow! Have we ever accumulated a pile of "litter!" How about a little "recycling?"

My "suggestions" for changing criminals into crime fighters is based on the best ideas that rational thought, science and religion have to offer, plus practical methods from groups such as AA. I use a "holistic approach" -- in a sense, brain washing, body/behavior modification and spirit cleansing -- to bring about desired change… using as many or as few "tools" as an individual is willing to permit. Three "D's" -- Departure, Desire and Destination -- help focus as much correction, desire and incentive as seems to be appropriate for each situation.

Briefly, permit me to use an example of how to bring about radical change. Let's suppose someone has committed a crime, which will soon be found out if the behavior is not stopped. Change is desired because of fear and/or incentive. First of all, there is discussion about when, where, why and how the behavior got started and progressed over time. The criminal is the specialist. The goal will be to depart from the behavior, one step at a time, as fast or as slow as is practically feasible. A checking system is established as well as very short and long-term goals.

How can the "criminal / addictive behavior" be turned around? Focusing on the most feared negative consequences as well as on the most attractive incentives, the desire for change is significantly increased. As with "brain washing", when almost any "escape to freedom" becomes highly desirable, then almost any tool for correction is welcome. At this point, relatively enjoyable small steps away from "addictive behavior" become extremely attractive. When appropriate and/or applicable, this process is used with the mind, body and spirit. Finally, the path to change may be **slowed**, in order to heighten desire and insure progress toward long term goals.

In this process, both counselor and criminal become agents of change and are strengthened through interdependency. Through an enjoyable process, they will try to trick the mind, body and spirit into a new reality of behavior (by whatever means it takes… even if that means "faking it" in the beginning). Moreover, the strongest incentives will focus on the hardest first steps, with less concentration needed on each successive step as the whole person becomes familiar with the new pattern of life. This is an ongoing, victorious, self-fulfilling, fun filled process -- each day establishing a new record for success and achievement.

Now, thinking about all this, who would be better equipped to understand the roots and hazards of crime than the criminal? And who could do a better job of warning others about the pitfalls? Our prisons today are full of VIP specialists who could be recruited for a war on crime wherever it was rampant, say nothing about prevention of criminal activity in the future. Consider what might motivate the criminal to change sides, so to speak -- freedom from addiction, incarceration, low self-esteem, etc., payment for valuable work in "their field," opportunity to show acquired skills among their peers, and the list could go on and on! Moreover, the turn around for each individual would start out in such small increments that the success rate would surely be near 100 per cent. Both criminals and society would see hoped for goals becoming realities... quickly!

Here is a concise statement of my proposal: Within a single prison, approximately six convicts would be permitted to volunteer to begin a unique rehabilitation / training program for the explicit purpose of receiving pay for fighting crime. Knowledgeable specialists who are paid no more than reasonable wages from charitable grants would work with these convicts as long as needed to prepare them to be approved by an evaluation committee composed of interested community professionals. Personal as well as vocational goals would be formulated and carried out from day one. Convicts turned "crime fighters" would be required to work in teams of two individuals with the understanding that without personal progress as well as on the job success, both would be dropped from the program and returned to prison. These "teams" would be aided by daily evaluation from various community monitors or checking agents.

In determining which prisoners would be the first to try out such a proposal, it might be beneficial to "test the process" by working with those who the prisoners themselves feel might be the best candidates. The understanding would be that if the program worked, more prison inmates would have opportunity to work as "crime fighters". On the other hand, if the most promising among the prison population failed in their vocation, the experiment would be stopped. Obviously, great pride and peer pressure would come into play to help insure that these rehabilitated "change agents" could make a worthwhile difference in areas of high crime.

Monitoring the work of previous offenders would be extremely important. First, working by two's, obviously it would be critical that team members watch one another closely... to see that progress was continually being made toward their goals... as well as to see that neither member has "slip-ups" or regression into past criminal behavior. On the positive side, starting pay would need to be adequate for a decent standard of living... with incentives for length of service as well as outstanding service. From the beginning of rehabilitation all the way to fighting crime on the streets, both members of the team would understand the importance of supporting, encouraging and monitoring their companion and co-worker.

At least initially, this plan would be of very little cost to taxpayers and risk to society, since charities would provide funding and the plan would have to prove its success to continue. The fundamental philosophy would be operable here -- one small step at a time... with immense incentives and careful corrections. The speed of overall implementation could be as slow or as fast as professionals, officials and politicians think workable. Monitoring for progress and success would be extremely important... but naturally handled by teammates, correction officials, community leaders, and especially peers in prison. Probably the most critical need early on would be the cutting of "red tape." On the other hand, the potential benefits for society as a whole would be tremendous!

Obviously, "behavioral modification" would have to play a key role in the success of such a plan. "Change Agents" would need to spend adequate time with people in prison to help them change and prepare to be a credit to society. The work with these incarcerated individuals would pay high dividends in nearly every case, however. In doing something for inmates, law abiding citizens would be doing something for themselves... remembering that 95% of those incarcerated will someday be back on our streets. Hopefully, with positive publicity, there would be adequate incentive and encouragement from appreciative communities.

<u>Some of the benefits for rehabilitated prisoners would include:</u>

1. Convey to them a sense of hope.
2. Motivate them to be "model prisoners"... since they might have the opportunity to be released, find "meaningful employment" and repay their debt to society.
3. Inspire them to "thank society" for another chance, for in receiving "a pardon" they would be receiving a great gift.
4. Promote in them an elevated sense of self esteem, since in understanding the "regretful past" they would be led into preparing for a highly regarded future.
5. A chance to receive helpful rehabilitation and a perspective on how they could live with purpose and dignity... as well as improve their lives with beneficial change. (Currently, 70% of ex-offenders in Wisconsin return to prison within one year of getting out.)
6. Find fulfillment and joy in becoming friends of society -- helping others avoid falling into rebellion, deterioration and ultimate incarceration.
7. Learn how a person travels the road to prison... as well as learn how to stay out of prison in the future.
8. Reaffirm and strengthen the capability of sticking

with the new way of life… by continually renewing and repeating their anti-crime message.

<u>This anti-crime program would yield far-reaching benefits for society:</u>

1. Offer the people of our country some progress in the fight against increasing drug addition, violence and crime.

2. Encourage all members of our society to be less dominated by fear, hate, insecurity, frustration and hopelessness.

3. Heal society by attempting to "give another chance" to those who may have "fallen through the cracks" of our capitalistic system.

4. Cut back the widening gap between rich and poor through financing… and have a chance to break down divisions across our land.

5. Root out a major source of our society's internal disease and deterioration by hiring caring, healing people to enhance the welfare of all.

6. Reclaim vast amounts of money from the "rat hole" of staffing, maintaining and building prisons. Also receive a better sense of security with a feeling that something constructive is being done with our resources.

7. Learn about how change in human lives can be accomplished and how society can work toward correcting basic social problems.

8. Experience within our culture and nation a

concrete application of the power of forgiveness, caring and love.

<u>What could "Crime Fighters" do in areas of high crime to change social deterioration into healthy community living? Here are just a few ideas</u>:

1. Work in schools talking to not only delinquents but also to entire student bodies about healthy habits… and about how to turn away from hurtful addictions and simply poor daily priorities.

2. Spend time with parents who have difficulty raising their children, pointing out new ideas and speaking from experience about what doesn't work.

3. A courageous team might "work the streets or back alleys" in search of areas where criminal activity is being practiced or promoted. The team might seek out gangs or criminals and try to discourage or stop such activity. The goal would be to diminish criminal activity, not primarily to incarcerate new criminals.

4. Show skills as "educators"… letting communities know how people become vulnerable to crime or "fall through the cracks" to unproductive living. Insight could be directed to progressive legislation, therefore enhancing community security and productivity.

5. Act as counselors for individuals who have committed crimes in the past and who might be tempted to repeat criminal activity in the future.

6. Work directly with police to understand the

criminal mind, prevent criminal activity and deal with it in the most creative, honest, and constructive way, when it has occurred.

7. Research criminal activity in all of its various facets: Progressive steps leading up to crime; methods of "reaching criminals" before they are prosecuted; ideas for legislation to deter crime and enhance community security; tips to help average citizens reduce their vulnerability; even conceptualizing new ways to fight behavior detrimental to healthy community living, etc.

Since this proposal initially sounds very radical, it might be wise to have a university verify that behavioral modification is almost completely predictable, given adequate "motivational stimulation." There should be special focus on rewarding positive behavior over an adequate period of time. A second critical step would be to convince legislative leaders that such a plan would be not only workable, but also extremely beneficial to all of society. Also, our citizens would need to be convinced that this "new idea" could work effectively and would be "worth the risk," considering all the present and future advantages. The present prison system and increasing crime rates is simply not acceptable.

I have before me a news report dated Oct. 19, 1995 entitled "Thompson wants prison alternatives". The article says that Wisconsin Gov. Tommy

Thompson... "wants a study commission to find alternatives for handling the record flow of criminals that is overwhelming the prison system... Thompson said he soon would name a blue-ribbon commission to explore alternatives to the high cost of incarceration, which now exceeds $22,000 per inmate a year." Thompson went on to say that "the state must find new ways to deal with non-violent offenders, which make up 2,000 of the state's prison inmate population of nearly 11,200. Given the high cost of incarceration, as a society, we also have to look at other options... We must find other, more cost effective ways to sanction non-violent offenders and still protect the citizens from criminal behavior."

The program I am proposing might best be funded by a grant from religious and business organizations… and ideally would not be of great cost to anyone. As benefits are realized, hopefully money from community and state resources could be utilized to move forward as rapidly as possible, so as not to jeopardize the plan's long term success. As "Crime Fighters" would be released from prison to work in areas of high crime, their salaries might be provided from the money which was used to incarcerate them.

One of the most critical questions about this whole idea is this: How much time would it take to adequately prepare an incarcerated individual for service in the community…so as not to have a unreasonable risk to that community? I believe that both "The Change Agent" and "The Offender" would need to indicate when the individual (and then the team) was prepared for their new challenge in the outside world. Possibly a panel consisting of legislator, minister, business-person, parent, etc. might evaluate the team before the formal date of hiring. Obviously there would not be absolute certainty of success with any member or team, as this would be similar to the complete healing of an alcoholic in the program of AA. However, it would seem that necessary preparation could be accomplished in a matter of weeks or months, given the proper motivational tools. After all, the selected individuals already have the important "expertise" necessary for their job, developed over many years. They would only be called and motivated to "change sides!"

Well, Ann, that in a "nutshell" is my proposal -- some suggestions, but probably much more than you had in mind. Still, I feel it is my responsibility to at least "sow the seed."

Early in my letter, I mention my mixed feelings and my quandary about laying it all out… even to you. The one opportunity that drives my effort and that pushes the slim chance that these words will be taken seriously is this: If you and your authorities think this idea merits attention, you would be our nation's best media expert at making it palatable for public consumption.

"Criminals becoming crime fighters" is quite a different way of thinking... and training... and teaching. It has implications all the way from parental responsibilities to political priorities. For example, what would be more radical for thankful living than for each person to check out those who have less rather than those who have more? And consider "the least" becoming "the greatest"! Will the likes of this only be known in a new age? You and I hold the key. There is risk, to be sure, but there is almost nothing significant to lose and almost everything beneficial to gain! Really, the welfare of our nation is at stake here. What we may need more than ever today is for true leaders to lead... and not "wimp out" when mere popular approval and financial gain are risk. Tell that to some our preachers and politicians!

I guess that's about the best appeal I can make for a better way to begin to deal with the "sick and costly problem" of crime and criminals. Certainly the incarcerated crowd -- what many see as that "garbage pile" growing by leaps and bounds -- is a valuable national resource. However, it is necessary for us to be willing to open our eyes and look at them in a new way. Criminals can be changed! They can be picked up and "recycled"... to be a credit to our morality and health as a democratic society.

We only need to be open-minded, efficient and caring!
Thanks for asking... and for listening...

I wasn't holding my breath waiting for some kind of response from Ann Landers, although I must admit I did watch the papers for the suggestions she was seeking. Sadly, I didn't read any proposals or new insights dealing with crime, criminals or our justice system. Did Ann Landers forget about her request? Did she draw a blank from most of her readers? Would certain kinds of suggestions rub readers the wrong way? Was she looking for some "magical" solutions? Or is it conceivable even Ann Landers might not want to lay out extraordinary solutions to shameful problems? In any event, where we need the best creativity the human spirit can muster, we confront silence instead. We seem destined to go over the cliff of moral decay. Apathy leads us into the chaotic destiny we so desperately fear. The momentum of our present life together increases the tension of our lives and highlights our frailty. Truly these are the best of times for some but also the worst of times for many.

We are ripe for change. Some of us who have a sense of happiness and success in our lives undoubtedly control the wheel as we speed down the road into the future. Most people are probably not aware of what our human race can accomplish or of our present momentum toward a terrifying fate. Most are too busy trying to survive their immediate dangers. "Vision 2000" is about how people who sense danger signals can make a world of difference to the many others who are terribly vulnerable. Put in another way, those who begin to be thoughtful about change -- when to change and how to change -- will need to be the first to change for the sake of others. There is no bliss in ignorance or in going down to defeat together. Responsible, caring, hopeful people know that our reform will enable others to reform for everyone's mutual happiness and security. We know that some favored people not only have certain powers of control but also a personal perspective of coming dangers! Many of the readers of this book are those "favored ones".

While in the midst of partying, it's not so easy to see problems, pitfalls and perils around the corner. We wouldn't expect the wealthy and powerful elite of our nation to see much beyond themselves. Their near-sightedness and obsession with the things that consume them prevent their awareness of how and where they are leading the rest of us. How long can entertainment satisfy the basic needs of manipulated people? How long will human beings watch in apathy as their brothers and sisters fall to the side of the road in weariness and hopelessness? And how long will ignorance of the root causes of our mutual predicament keep us inflicting violence on those who all too often have known tragedy and injury in their lives? Without insightful change, the longer risky activities go on, the closer we come to realizing our ultimate decay and destruction.

How will others be lifted up or turned around? It's good when a society or a people are given good things -- like a crisp, sweet apple or a delicious orange. But what happens when life gives certain individuals or groups a sour lemon? The person who gets a bum rap does not usually think of the possibility of making lemon-aide. How can a sad soul find his or her way out of a feeling of being wronged? It's not so easy, especially when a person feels deserted and lonely. Show me a wealthy person (with abundant resources) who can change and enjoy being poor, and I will show you a poor person (with few resources) who can change and enjoy being rich. Beyond all that, to make "lemon-aide" one might need certain limited resources... and a marketplace... and a good sales technique. The bottom line is that we need some inspiration to "change"... and a few good tools to do the trick wouldn't hurt either.

How will others be lifted up or turned around? Here's another final consideration. We have learned from our infancy "monkey see, monkey do." That's really getting back to our roots! When changed people exhibit the joy they find in their own powerful life-giving change, that good news will become evident to others. In that shared blessing, a sense of security and happiness will bring about mutual admiration. There is hope in creative change! In taking action to get at the roots of some of the disturbing trends we see around us in our society, we take steps to avoid disaster for individuals and possibly our country. With a new program of insightfulness, our country still may well be the best option for our planet in the 21st century. But it is time for many of us to quit partying! We must change course before it's too late!

Convicts Cheer Change!

CHAPTER 1

"The Beauty of Change"

I have a spellbinding question. Who has experienced or witnessed real confession recently? Did it die with the "confessional" in the old Roman Catholic Church? If I remember correctly, it takes shape something like this: As an English major in college, I received an "F" in one of my courses… in part for plagiarism. Here's another personal one: I often get "turned on" when I read about sexual episodes -- even criminal ones. And finally, this is a more public confession: I supported Bill Clinton as President of the United States. As you might guess, I'm not very comfortable writing out these three confessions. Moreover, I doubt that I have much to gain by admitting them.

The last confession above maybe deserves some special explanation. As President Clinton began his run for the presidency, I believed that he represented… the best hope for poor people to get much needed help… a departure from the "military mentality" in coping with foreign affairs… an outsider's approach to overcoming "business as usual" in Washington… and a friendly, common man appeal "up close and personal". The bonus was that he had charisma. What more could I want in a president?

After he was elected, over time I became disillusioned by President Clinton's priorities and perspectives. My ultimate disappointment was in listening to him deny his "affair" in the White House. It was difficult to watch and listen to the defensive tactics of one who had been caught in an embarrassing situation. "Slick Willy" was struggling to run away from his responsibility; and yet he was "setting the hook" the more he tried to escape.

I felt sadness for President Bill Clinton, as well as for his wife and daughter. They all were hitting an emotional low point in their lives. Surely almost all of us have made serious mistakes... and there's a good chance we have even regretted them. On the flip side, if we are to assert the value of confession (and possibly forgiveness), certainly there was a way for President Clinton to take the high road -- in fact, there was a good chance for him to attain a revered place in history. Yet it would require taking a path not well traveled... and admittedly... terrifying to the ego of powerful and popular people. If he chose the more difficult course, the beauty and simplicity of confession and then "change" for a new way of living could be spectacular! I couldn't resist conveying my feelings to this beleaguered man in a letter -- August 21, 1998...

Dear President Clinton,

I feel bad about your present predicament! You still have such awesome potential for a positive impact on national and world events. I would guess you understand that critical choices are yet to be made even in your personal life -- choices that will be beneficial or detrimental to all of us. If only each of us could know how to choose our paths wisely. Sad to say, many of us in this wonderful country are in a rather sorry mess -- from the most common people among us to the most influential -- from Washington, DC to unpretentious Eau Claire, WI.

My sympathies to your wife, Hillary, your daughter, Chelsea, and to your whole family.

We really are awfully interdependent aren't we!? Community is at the center of our lives... for good and bad... for justice and injustice. In community we hurt others and feel ourselves hurt... we set out to heal others and find ourselves healed. Only at our own peril can we neglect to look out for the welfare of "the whole body."

I want to write to you a note of good news! You can still accomplish almost anything good you truly desire. Surprisingly enough, your past may give you some assistance. Only the path leading to the destiny you yearn for may seem strange as you encounter change. I can say this with complete confidence, because I know that even criminals can become crimefighters! What today is regarded as the lowest "scum of the earth" -- those who bring us grief and heartache -- can in a literal sense become our most valuable citizens. Could the moment soon be upon us when we open ourselves to the understanding of how this can be done? Could your "blunder" be the stepping stone to the healing and renewal of our national community? Yes, this is <u>possible</u>, but I must admit <u>not probable</u> given the natural flow of events in our world today.

Who am I... to write to you... and to make such outrageous suggestions? I believe I am one who is trustworthy and creative, as Almighty God has given me life and breath. I desire to be used according to His purpose. If anything I have written seems to provide you with even the least glimmer of light, I invite you (and your closest friends and family) to check me out. At the moment, I care for my elderly parents and function as a father and househusband. I have simply given some years to research and to write about change. May "The Spirit" lead you.

It was my hope that President Clinton would face his guilt, make a complete confession of his past errors, accept the judgement of the law and the American people, throw himself on the mercy of the court, learn how to change his bad habits and then lead our country into carrying out change and renewal. Was that too much to expect? (Maybe we should ask if *anyone* could take that rigorous path of self-examination, confession and renewal?) What an inspiration a changed leader might be to all of us. Certainly in the final analysis, we are all, in our own way, like the vulnerable man,

Bill Clinton. On the positive side, in overcoming our weaknesses and bad habits we can be shining examples of rehabilitation to others. Instead of being caught on the defensive in claiming innocence and propriety, we can set all that nonsense behind us, learn what got us into our messes and move on to help others avoid the nasty pitfalls of our common life.

Watching President Clinton over the last few years, the public perception is that nothing has changed. I would guess that disturbs him greatly. However, in his words and actions he has given us the feeling that he wants to either overpower our negative image or at minimum make us forget his weaknesses. He wants to succeed from a position of power. Yet in that process, he merely comes across as a manipulative man who insists on his own way. He also wants us to see Bill Clinton as he would like to see himself. So is anyone fooled? No, we are not deceived by a weak approach we have used far too often ourselves. Power and knowledge and wealth and privilege usually capture our attention and make us think we will get what we desire; so we go with the flow... not realizing that we will be hurting ourselves down the line. But that's the weak way -- downright disgusting, ugly and shameless!

The beauty of change is -- it succeeds where we fail. It's not too hard to admit that all people are imperfect. Yet how hard it is for us to admit any specific failure and the need to do things differently. Maybe the real difficulty is that we want to be winners and proud. We believe that losers are the ones that need to eat humble pie and find a way to change. Could that be it? Could that be the reason we miss out on quickly correcting our mistakes? What would happen if "change" was "a friend" that quickly came to our side when we first began to sense a problem? What would happen if we were acquainted with how to get ourselves moving in a new direction? What would happen if our weaknesses could become our strengths? What would happen if we could warn others about where we had gone wrong... and furthermore, that they would be sincerely interested in receiving our guidance? What would happen if in seeing the benefits of change, people would begin to seek out change, find accomplishment and turn away from mistakes? What would happen if indeed criminals could become crimefighters? Yes, the beauty of change is -- it succeeds where we fail!

CHAPTER 2

Probing For Health And Happiness

"Change... From Grief to Joy"

Introduction

In the following pages it is my intention to probe a bit into the mysterious depths of the timeless concept that has earthshaking implications for every human being -- change. The fear of change has probably "paralyzed" nearly every person at one time or another. On the other hand, the inevitability and necessity of change is as certain as night and day. In our day and age, we are awed by how fast change has pushed us to new levels of demanding and complicated living. It moves us moment by moment. We cannot escape it!

Clearly, all of creation continually responds to changing circumstances.... with consequences -- for better or worse. It is also clear that as we come to more fully understand the deep mystery of change and how it affects us, we are better able to act and react in ways that have significant and positive impact on our destiny and quality of life. Young and old alike can learn to appreciate and cope with change as well as utilize change to reap rich rewards. It is my hope that through this probing examination, we can know the opportunity and privilege of orchestrating change in a way that will transport us from defeat to victory -- from grief to joy!

What Is Change?

The word **"change"** is a relatively simple, small, familiar word that **carries a lot of weight** in our world, and especially as we enter the new millennium. Many people often talk about change in the world at large as well as in their own personal circumstances; and most people today acknowledge that we have to live with a lot of change whether we like it or not.

Maybe this word "change" is a bit **like the word "love"** -- in a sense we think of these as simple terms, yet in another sense, both words are **filled with great depth and complexity**. The dictionary defines "change": to put or take (a thing) in place of something else; substitute; to give and receive reciprocally; exchange; to cause to become different; alter; convert; to put on other clothes; to pass from one stage to another.

Thinking of **synonyms** -- **"change"** denotes a making or becoming distinctly different and implies either a radical transmutation of character or replacement with something else; **"alter"** implies a partial change, as in appearance, so that the identity is preserved; **"vary"** suggests irregular or intermittent change; **"modify"** implies minor change, often so as to limit or moderate; **"transform"** implies a change in form and now, usually, in nature or function; **"convert"** suggests more strongly... change to suit a new function.

We note **other single synonyms** for "change": merge, alternate, diversify, fluctuate, **shift**, transfigure, warp, remodel, revolutionize, **regenerate**, turn, temper, qualify, inflect, substitute, diverge, **evolve**, deflect, translate, reduce, recast, reconstruct, restyle, reorganize, **reform**, denature, disguise, vacillate, transpose.

Obviously the above gives broad definition to the word "change" and helps us to understand why change is **hard to totally comprehend**. This is especially true when we consider that, as human beings, **we are creatures of habit**; we tend to want to resist change -- doing that which is distinctly different.

Still, most of us recognize that in a very basic and simple sense **we are all in the process of change** every day of our lives. For example, from conception, a child is continually growing and thus changing; then, after a certain number of years, an adult experiences deterioration, until death finally occurs. As human beings we are continually involved with change, even though for the most part **we are unaware of it**. In fact, it may be this unawareness of most of the change we go through that causes us the most difficulty.

So have we changed? We look in the mirror day by day and we see essentially the same person. We think about our political outlook on life and we recognize it as very close to the outlook we had last year. We take account of our habits, and they fit us like an old shoe. Our morality and spirituality seem to remain quite constant in our relationship to others. Then how have we changed? That's not quite so easily analyzed or defined, because generally **it happens so slowly** and seemingly inconsequentially. We change one aspect or another of our life without knowing when or how we got there.

The opposite of "change" is **"to remain the same."** The question arises, "If we are absorbed so much in the process of change, why is it that we recognize ourselves as such creatures of habit?" Think of the hundreds if not thousands of routines or repetitions that we all go through day after day. In fact, if we could not rely on our routine habits, we could not survive. From taking steps and making sounds to buying groceries and driving a car, we can easily be made aware of the many things that we do during our lives that remain pretty much the same. Essentially then, we are **kept alive by opposite dynamics** or tendencies working within us moment by moment. So which is best -- changing or remaining the same? Both tendencies are not only valuable to quality living but also necessary for happy, fulfilling life in the twenty-first century.

In the final analysis, change is as necessary to us as the blood flowing through our veins. **We should embrace change as our confidant and friend.** It stimulates us and urges us on to be all that we can be. Yet change is almost as invisible as is our life-blood. While it sustains us, we usually take for granted that it moves and strengthens us. It usually functions so quietly, slowly and unobtrusively that we hardly know it is a part of us. Sometimes we may be so ignorant of the presence of change in our lives that we think we do not need it or want it. On the contrary, all people need to embrace "change" as a confidant and friend.

The Fundamentals of Change

The beginning of **change is in creation**. As newborn babies we enjoyed a comfortable, pleasurable and secure environment; we were content with a warm place to sleep, plenty of good food and lots of attention to meet our personal needs. Everything had changed, yet much seemed to remain the same. As time went on, however, we moved further and further out into our surroundings and found that **we needed to adapt or change to find happiness** in our daily experiences. Much of the time, these experiences gave us good feelings. Sometimes, however, inadequate attention to our basic needs or a withdrawal of love or a wrong step would alert us to change that made us feel pain. We began to resist as best we could those situations which hurt us the most.

Today, the word **change signifies something that many of us fear**. Growing up in a fast moving, complex, insensitive and threatening age has meant that a vast majority of people have run into change that **has been hurtful**. Think of what the child who has been "advantaged" has had to struggle with, as that child has faced vast changes in the home environment, changes with moves, changes with education and changes with basic health and development. Then consider how **much grief** the "disadvantaged" child, youth or young adult might feel after finding that very little of what is good and valuable and rewarding remains constant. Carry these thoughts on to today's average adult and contemplate what divorce, job loss, crime, drug addiction, immorality, anonymity, disloyalty and stress have in common with the radical change that has gone on around us, and there are not many sane human beings among us who have not **"had it" with change**.

We are a people who are **looking for a return** -- a return of health, caring, nourishment, fulfillment, leisure, community, morality, happiness, peace and love. In the very search we are admitting that we have **lost that for which we seek**. The change which has brought us to the brink of chaos in our lives is what we want to avoid at all costs. **But how will we get back** to that which is desirable and worthwhile **without** again being able to venture through **the turmoil of more change?** This is the difficulty we face. Shall we remain in the chaotic jungle of our daily living where we are continually threatened with more difficulty and hurt or shall we once again step onto the unfamiliar path of change... that we might hope to secure a better future?

The key to our dilemma is found in looking at the change which has caused us pain. Two characteristics stand out which we should zero in on. First, the change that has been **the hardest for us to bear** has been that which **has been the most hurtful** and has taken place **over the shortest period of time**. The loss of a parent or a job, having to move or face a disaster, harming someone or losing a valuable asset -- these kinds of changes make an immediate and usually negative impact on our inner beings. We are shocked and our good life is terrorized. Like touching a hot stove, we try to separate ourselves from what we think injured us, whether that is in our long term best interests or not. It seems far better to be "a creature of habit" no matter how boring or damaging, than to get too close to a quick, radical change, which upsets the personal world we have tried so hard to hold secure.

Second, the change which usually has been the **most destructive** in our lives is that small but significant change which over the long term leads us down a disastrous road. For example, look at the long term effects of that first cigarette on the person suffering from lung cancer, or the consequences of that initial killing of a small animal on the person arrested for first degree murder, or even the terrible waste of sitting in front of the T-V on that teenager who is bored and flunking out of high school. Such examples illustrate those usually **small, rather innocent changes**... that turn into trends... **that often lead us to tragic endings**. Such changes were merely the first "baby steps" down a bumpy road leading to a tragic end we never dreamed we would find.

This points us to an **answer for the dilemma** we face. Not many grown-ups remember those very early days of our lives when as babies or toddlers we seemed to reach out and yearn for change. Change seemed to feel good; it was exciting and promising and fulfilling! We always wanted more -- more new steps, more new intellectual challenges, more new friends, more new experiences. Why? Because it never really overwhelmed us in those days. For the most part **we could stop change anytime we wanted to**... and go back to what was familiar and what felt good. We probably felt secure, and **we got just a little** -- just the right amount -- at one time. All of this was quite different from the rapid, gigantic leaps expected of us as we faced the rough and tumble adult world of competition and complexity.

A few helpful facts stand out then as we investigate change in our basic experiences. It is obvious that we are most **comfortable when we have some direct control** over change and when it comes in doses that we can easily manage. It is also understandable **we like change that** interests us in the present as well as **gives us benefits we desire for the future.** The bottom line is that we must carefully choose to embrace change which improves our quality of life, while resolutely rejecting the change which tears us down. The secret of being able to **differentiate between destructive** change (which hurts us in the short and long term) **and beneficial change** (which gives us a more wholesome, fulfilled and happy life) is clear. It is in understanding our reactions to our past experiences, evaluating our present circumstances and what we want for the future and being inspired to use change to our short and long term advantage. We can feel good about the change we choose. And we should go for it!

Resisting Change

The kind of change that is desirable is often not easy to accomplish. There are several reasons for this. First of all, **we intuitively resist change**, even if changing something seems necessary or in our best interests or the obvious thing to do. Most of us as human beings tend to set ourselves, including all that we say and do, at the center of the universe. It has been so since we entered the world and became aware of ourselves. We have always wanted attention and we have done almost everything but stand on our heads to get it. Moreover, from the beginning, our words and actions have been just as important to us as our physical bodies. They have been a part of our identity; and we have done everything we could... to not only control our own lives but also the environment around us. Not to have done all this would have been to negate our self worth and even to have given up our drive for survival. Essentially then, **every part of our identity is vitally important to our sense of self** -- whether that is the way we talk, the things we do each day, the habits we have developed or just the space we live in. To give up any significant part of our past -- even a bad habit -- is giving up an important part of ourselves. We intuitively resist.

A second reason we resist change is that momentum usually is what carries us on down the road we travel in our lives; and that same **momentum hampers striving for doing what is different**. Think of how difficult it would be to run a mile, if declining exercise made a person "puff" going up a flight of stairs. Consider the challenge of speaking in front of a crowd, if an individual had learned to be a loner over the years. And how easy would it be to do some simple math on paper, if you had only learned to use a calculator? Most people have established a certain momentum... in sleeping on the same side of the bed, sitting at the same spot at the table, reading the paper the same way, greeting people with the same mannerisms, etc. You get the point. **Most of us need to have a very good reason to change** any of our personal habits, simply because we've "perfected them" over a long period of time.

A third reason we may resist change is that **we are not at all sure we will be happy with it**. The future is always unclear; and that's especially true if there's a chance we might make it even more unpredictable by changing something we have counted on. We know from our past experience that any change we have gone through has at least in the beginning made us **feel a bit uneasy and disoriented**, if not downright "out of control". We want to play it safe. Is changing worth it, if I find myself unhappy? What if I end up losing more than I gain? Our sense of happiness is very important to each and everyone of us. And that vague sense of happiness, if we feel it at all, is dependent upon a lot of intangible inner feelings which have connections to all that we do and all that goes on around us. It's very hard to tell someone else how to be happy. This is **something we need to find for ourselves**; and what we choose for our future has a lot to do with it.

One last reason we resist change is that it may make us feel separated or alone. All of us are social beings -- we need our friends and family, if not the equivalent -- and changing something in our life can often make us feel cut off from people we care for. Interestingly enough, **we often don't want to be in charge or strike out on our own.** We naturally gravitate toward those who give us a sense of belonging and security and importance and power, etc. We do this because they have been a part of our past experiences, and in fact, may have been a part of reinforcing much of what we have done. That makes it **risky** to strike out on one's own -- **to do the new thing!** Reaching out for change can be a little like being a pioneer -- its exciting! But when we start imagining the personal challenges we may well face, and if we begin our venture without encouragement from those we are dependent upon, the trail into the wilderness is certainly a special challenge, no matter what the reward is at the end! Obviously, it is not at all strange that we resist change.

The Cost of Change

Is the cost of change too high? Sometimes we would have to agree it is. **Change** that is **out of our control**

and that has great impact on us can sometimes take us to the very limits of our endurance -- to the very brink of destruction. Most of us would say that the cost of this kind of change is too high. The tragedy is that we may have no choice but to pay the price. In this case our only acceptable alternative may be to **accept the change and make the best of it**... i.e... try to turn aspects of it to our own short or long term benefit. A couple of examples: The loss of a loved one might be overcome by developing a number of new friendships; going through a heart attack might be the inspiration to gain a new appreciation of the simple joys of life. The main consideration here is that **we do not let change dominate** or overwhelm or discourage us from useful, productive living. Then we will not have paid too high a price.

Confronting change that is beyond our control, at minimum, usually causes us stress. **How we manage that stress determines**, in the long run, **how high a price we pay**. Taking good care of ourselves physically, mentally and spiritually has a lot to do with handling this task. Eating right, getting enough sleep, maintaining good social relationships with family and friends, keeping priorities straight, taking time off, practicing **healthy moral and spiritual rituals** -- these are the kinds of big, "little things" that **help us weather the storms** of the stresses that are unavoidable over a lifetime. Spending our time and using our resources wisely in day by day activities will certainly save us the cost of the big ticket item when the bill is due on stress.

Even change under our control requires us to pay a certain amount. There is a certain amount of **risk in any change**. We have no guarantees everything will work out alright. That costs us. Leaving behind what is familiar and comfortable -- that costs us something too. We pay for the energy it takes to turn around and go a different direction. There is even a significant cost for admitting we want to change from what we have done in the past. A little **ego has to be left behind**, and that may hurt. What about having to **let go of some "sheer laziness"** if we choose to take off in a new direction? With all of this accumulated cost, is it any wonder that not many people want to buy into change? But we shouldn't be discouraged. There aren't many of us that will have to pay a lot for any of the above. If we've handled our lives reasonably well, **the rich rewards** we will reap from change **will far exceed the costs!**

Why Change?

Why not just avoid change? This is a question we often ask ourselves unconsciously if not consciously. Since we are the most comfortable with what we have done the most often in our most recent past, it is natural that we ask ourselves this question. **Why should I do anything differently** than I have done it in the past? Wasn't my life satisfactory an hour ago or yesterday or even last year for that matter? If not, doesn't that imply there's something wrong with me or with my decision making ability? So who's to say that the way I've been doing things has been wrong? **Who's in charge here?** If it was good enough for me this morning it should be good enough for me this afternoon. After all, I'm alive... and I'm surviving pretty well. So often this is the argument and the reasoning for sticking with the familiar. And it does make some sense, especially when we are so good at justifying ourselves.

Looking at the above argument, it's easy to see why we are such creatures of habit. We go from one thing to the next with **little thought to the ultimate consequences**. What harm could one more little potato chip do? Why shouldn't I watch just one more half hour program? The effects are not obvious in the least. In fact, we usually don't even ask ourselves, "Why not?" We just roll on along, **until we meet enough resistance** to stop us for the moment. This is why habits play such a big part in our lives and why today we often drift on down the least challenging path. We just don't run into much resistance, and we feel good in those old familiar experiences.

However, when practically unnoticed change begins to lead us toward deterioration and pain and a declining lifestyle, our ignorance or **inattention to detail should be cause for alarm**. Most of the social problems we confront in our day and age, whether caused by individuals or groups or institutions, have their origin in what appears at first to be almost totally insignificant detail. Yet this little detail, rather than being a creative force like the raindrop, turns out to be **what ultimately hurts us** and often others -- a destructive power... more like a cancer cell. We maybe don't even take notice, until we have to get a "check up" and find out we are about to die.

Once in a while we get a glimpse of **another possibility**, much like the small child who experiences that first step. We say to ourselves, **"What if...?"** What if I could walk to Mom? What if I did some exercise rather than watch T-V? What if I didn't buy any more cigarettes? What if I decided to obey the traffic signs? What if I decided to make a budget and cut spending? What if I spent that time with my children? What if I decided to go to the marriage counselor? The questions are endless. And they are endless because as human beings we sometimes get **glimpses of newness** and better opportunities and what we might be, if only... we did it differently!

Why change? Sometimes we get **tired of the old routines**. Again the example of the baby comes to mind. Crawling just doesn't "make it" after you've gotten that vision of walking. Can't you just hear those inner thoughts -- if only I could reach some of those things way up there; if only I could get over there faster; if only my knees weren't so sore; if only I could get around like Mom and Dad. Yes, whether we are babies or senior citizens, we sometimes get downright tired of doing things the old way. We desire change because **we are pioneers... and explorers...** and creators... and inventors... and trailblazers... and pacesetters... and instigators, that's why!

The Process Of Change

The process of **change can begin as spectacularly as "a bolt out of the blue" or as subtly as "a rain drop** falling on parched soil". Most of the change we experience in our lives can be most closely compared with the latter. We hardly notice most of the change happening to us on a day by day basis; and inasmuch as change improves our opportunities and quality of life, subtle, unnoticed change is not at all bad for us as busy human beings.

As important as unnoticed change has been in our lives, this is not something we should either applaud or worry about in the present. Why? Because by very definition it is part of our past, it has been "unnoticed", and we can override it if we wish. We need to **focus on that kind of change which we can initiate and control** for an improved future. How does that "bolt out of the blue" or fragile enlightenment arrive? Maybe we are inspired or maybe our creative intuition gives us insight or maybe we just "bottom out" and get sick of the old pattern, the increasing pain or the road to disaster. In any case, we see that there just might be another option for us, and we have a kind of "yearning" for change. This might well be the hardest part of change to come by, because it needs to originate from within -- a bit like the natural talent which an athlete possesses that just can't be coached. **We really need to want change**, personally, in order to enable change to occur.

If we have a desire to change, we usually face **a big barrier** almost immediately. In our day and age, we as members of "the great society" are very often impatient people. We want our solutions and our answers now, just like we want many forms of pleasure and gratification now. To put it bluntly, **we want the "quick fix"**. But change is often difficult to accomplish in large quantities, habits usually affect us deeply over a long period of time and insight is often fleeting. It is not so simple to get the kind of "change we want" done immediately. And so the end result is that **we fail to change** and drift back into our old patterns.

If we persist in wanting to do things differently, a second part of the process is in not only **finding out what we want to leave behind, but also** in figuring out **what direction we want to go.** This is a significant step because it forces us to come to grips with not only our past but also with what we want for our future. What is the best option at this time? What personally will be the short and long term results? What will be the consequences for those people who are immediately affected by the changed direction? And last but not least -- Is this really what we want or is this only something that someone else wants? It is no small thing to **come to grips with what we want** to do with change, if in fact we really do want it!

A third step in the process of change is in setting in motion or **executing change**. At the point where we attempt our first motion toward the goal, we confront a major challenge to any success for which we might hope. Anything significant enough to want to change in our lives is undoubtedly ingrained deeply enough to be difficult to escape. We are set up for difficulty if not failure. Here is where we must **set ourselves up for success**, if we want to keep on track toward our goal. It is incumbent upon us to make change easy on ourselves -- we need goals easy enough to carry forward; and with proper understanding of our capability and tenacity, we can find accomplishment.

Each person's unique characteristics come into play as we enter this critical stage. **Whenever we move into new territory we are very prone to feel uncomfortable**, if not even afraid of whatever is ahead. The future is in itself frightening enough. When change is added, we are often stymied from making any progress. Each of us also has to wrestle with our experience of whether or not we feel we can accomplish what we set out to do. **Will we mess up once again?** Then again, maybe even if we do make progress, those around us will not be happy with how we have changed. A lot of doubts and questions can enter our minds, as we attempt to reverse a large part of our past.

If by careful decision and action we make it through the mine-fields of our surroundings and personal weaknesses, we break into the openness of **exciting opportunity**. We feel satisfaction and happiness when we have even small successes which are not expected of us. **A taste of success is good**, and there is nothing like it to encourage more. This does not mean that the first positive movements in a new direction secure the future we so desperately desire. What it does mean is that like "the little engine that could", we may well have overcome the most difficult challenge... and can **look forward to building momentum** toward ultimate success... if we stay on track!

Being a Change Agent

It's fun being an agent of change. It's like being an artist or engineer or designer or writer. There's newness and creativity involved... and excitement! Being an agent of change is being involved in change -- doing it, carrying out the nitty gritty of it.

Moreover, an agent of change can also be **one who nurtures** the idea of change **and encourages** the implementation of it. The definition of an "agent" is... a person or thing that performs actions or is able to do so... an active force or substance producing an effect... a person, firm, etc. empowered to act for another. The root of the word is "to do, act; to drive." Here is a word that implies force and movement and power and impact. Put that word agent/**"action" together with** change / **"newness"** and you've really got something!

An agent of change should be a little **like a mother's womb**. Here is an image that conveys warmth, security, protection, care, sustenance and even love. It's a place to begin and grow and evolve. Interestingly enough, it is also a comfortable familiar sort of place. So an agent of change is awed by the opportunity as well as the responsibility... to nurture what is small and tender and precious. Change, after all, is vital to life and health. It gives us power to overcome that which is less than desirable and opens the door to new options and opportunities. The thought of change for a human being could mean something as great as "hope" in a dark and painful world. And that thought could be as important as a decision for life (in the face of death). The womb, of course, has always represented **the source of new life and blessing**. Likewise, an agent of change.

The word change by itself, however, does not convey to us any sense of what is right or wrong, creative or destructive, practical or impractical, valuable or worthless. It only indicates movement in a different direction. It may be safe to say that usually we are not interested in changing anything that, by our standards, is headed in the right direction. So an agent of change only tries to nurture and **encourage "inspired change" of that which is painful** or hurtful or hinders abundant living. It only makes sense that an agent would not want to participate in or speak for any misdirected change... but would support and applaud any change which seems worthwhile and good. **What is critical is that all agents** involved with "a single change" **work as a team** to help that change take root and grow... to fulfillment. Such teamwork involves great insight, careful planning and patient persistence.

Facing Change

Maybe **the most difficult thing** we ever have to do in our lives is **to face change that is overwhelming and hits without warning.** How we handle that "crisis" determines whether or not we survive successfully in our environment... and whether we are "happy or bitter"... "at peace or at war"... in the deep inner recesses of our souls. This is no small thing -- facing change. And the rather unfair part is... that how to handle this challenge (which all people sooner or later face) **has to be taught!** It is not something that comes naturally from within. This could be the reason that few people today are really well equipped to deal with the kinds of changes that confront us in our time and place.

It is well understood that people who are leaders have very little difficulty in handling that which is new and different. In fact, leaders have been taught to **treat change as a challenge**. Usually they are not confused or troubled by it, nor do they try to get away from it. They often try to bring about change... so that something under their influence might be improved or perfected. Being close to change, **leaders try to use change to their advantage**, deflecting those aspects which might be most harmful or hurtful and latching onto others which benefit them and their purposes. Furthermore, leaders have **learned and developed a "positive attitude"** which attempts to deal with whatever crisis hits them. They look at change as an opportunity ...and this developed outlook or skill makes them successful.

It is not necessary to be a leader, however, to be able to face change successfully. **We all can** learn how to deal with major upheavals in ways that **minimize the sufferings. Learning to manage our negative emotions** is a big step in the right direction. Why do we feel certain emotions? Can we use our intellect to act in a way that puts away bad feelings inside? **Staying cool, calm and collected is especially helpful** for dealing with what can disrupt us... or make us afraid... or hurt our security. People who seem to "fly apart" or "lose it" whenever something unforeseen happens are very vulnerable to unpredictable change. While learning to master our emotions or feelings is not one of the quickest or simplest of challenges, there is no doubt that we can make significant progress in this area too.

Preparing ourselves ahead of time for change can be very valuable. For example, working on our "emotional stability" is a worthwhile project over a long period of time, since our emotions are deeply ingrained and not easily modified. When we begin to **plan for the unexpected**, we can begin to formulate in our minds a way to get through the challenge. This may not be too different from the kind of planning a team goes through to win a victory over a formidable opponent. We will not be winners very often if we do not understand and **take into account** whatever has the power to penetrate **our weaknesses**. So we plan **and practice** and formulate in our minds a successful encounter with change; and we can come out on top -- as winners!

It is important to **consider the many resources** we can use in dealing with distressing change. Almost all of us feel comfortable with certain **assets we have at our disposal**. Some people are good listeners; others are good speakers. Some individuals are sensitive to feelings; others are intellectually blessed; still others are physically strong. All of us have strengths that we can employ to wrestle with what would overpower us. Even our basic senses can come into play and be used to our advantage when we are disturbed. At that moment, we might sit down to a delicious meal... in a romantic setting... and listen to pleasant music... while feel a loved one's caress... and smell a wonderful fragrance. In this example, all of **our human senses help distract us** from painful change and overpower what pulls us down into the dumps. In choosing a path around what hurts and hinders us, **we learn to** be rulers of our own destiny and learn to **find joy instead of suffering.**

In the final analysis, maybe just **letting out the child within** would be as good **an antidote** for uncontrolled change as almost anything. We know that a little child shows a kind of free flowing creative response to all that it encounters. A child goes about looking for and testing newness in every way possible. It is not anxious or put down by what changes outside of its control. So for us today **that fresh, new perspective** is what can handle difficult change in a positive way. Today our brains need to be stimulated and stretched for healthy interaction with the world, if we want to have some control over our environment. Consider that new perspective! Be free! And **think of the fun** we will have as we break away from the old... for fresh insight, power, confidence **and excitement!**

The Rewards of Change

It's safe to say that **the rewards of change are almost too good to be true.** Change, after all, seems to be a part of normal, quality living... every day of our lives... from birth to death. Even people who don't want to change do so. But they are the unfortunate ones, because they fight what is inevitable; and rather than reap rich rewards, they only gather unhappiness and pain.

Consider the simple **benefit of just getting out of a rut**. Most of us have at least some desire for **freshness and excitement.** Breaking out of a bad habit certainly provides what we are looking for here. The old habit, even if it does give us a kind of comfortable feeling, still yields a big dose of sameness and boredom and possibly even frustration and anger. Getting out of that quagmire of what tends to slow us down and restrict us from true happiness is a great benefit indeed. We are thankful to be free!

When we make a good choice in our lives -- as when we control a move in a direction we really want to go -- **we are rewarded at the deep level of our self-esteem.** Any action we might take that we know is good for others or for our environment or even for ourselves is to be applauded... especially in an time when we are so much aware of our shortcomings and mistakes. We need to give ourselves a pat on the back (on a regular basis) when we choose right. It's good for us to know "we deserve it." It helps our self-image. It affirms we can and do make good decisions. And it also **sets us up for future success**.

Changing some aspect of one's life is a bit **like winning twice.** When we realize that we are doing something that we don't like, that action hurts us, and often hinders more than one facet of our living. When **we put that negative behind us and** are freed, we have profited greatly and are certain winners. Second, when we then move on to a better way of living or a new positive action, we **are lifted to a new level of freedom** and opportunity, we develop our creative talents, and we win again! In the putting down of the adversary within us and in the raising up of what we want to be, we are in a very real sense doubly rewarded.

There is also significant pleasure to be gained by **showing the world** (or at least those people who are close to us) **that we are in fact winners**... and that we can achieve what is difficult -- change. Examples abound of people who fail to accomplish what they set out to do. In fact, we begin to assume that certain things cannot be changed and that we just have to live with them and that there's just no hope. We surely surprise ourselves and those around us, then, when we take up a certain challenge and come out on top... with an "upset!" **Our win can even be inspiring** to those around us. Knowing the struggle, we relish the victory; and those who watch us, cheer!

An often unnoticed reward **we should become more aware of** is the **ripple effect** of positive change. From childhood we have watched with great interest ripples of water moving out in ever widening circles from the point of an object impacting the water. Depending upon the size of the object, those ever enlarging circles reach out to uplift, move or change even those things that are some distance away. Life is a lot like that impacted, rippling water, because everything in life is connected to something else. So also change. Whenever one thing changes, a lot around that thing changes too. Making a personal change -- making that impact of an action that stirs up the status quo -- that **change reaches out to touch and influence** other people and things... probably far **beyond our understanding**. If we would become more aware of the far reaches of our influence when we make a good solid change in our lives, undoubtedly we would be wonderfully blessed.

The **above rewards are far-reaching** in the implications they have for our immediate and long term happiness. Moreover, there may well be **spin offs** of each of them **that multiply the joy** and satisfaction. In any case, the rewards of positive controlled change can usher us toward divine pleasure and perfection. We can indeed be in the process of turning grief into joy!

CHAPTER 3

A Playbook For Winning

"Checking In... To Change"

Imagine for the moment you are on a trip and you have arrived at your destination motel—you are "checking in" as they say in the travel business. All the arrangements have been made in advance and you are relaxed, curious and prepared to soak in your surroundings. There are a lot of good feelings about reaching a place you have dreamed about going for some time. Congratulations on finally arriving! Enjoy "checking in"... and then checking out a whole new adventure.

At this very moment you have started to take a peek at some new surroundings — you have started "checking into change." Believe it or not, this is a great place to be. You should be congratulated on successfully arranging a great trip to arrive right here -- right where you are. Checking out "change" involves looking over some territory that not many people have had the courage to discover. "Change" is often pretty awesome... and downright scary. Not too many people want to schedule a trip to change, and then settle down to look around.

But believe me, this will be one of your best "get-away" excursions ever!

The odds are pretty good that you are a leader, for after all, you have taken some good initiative to even get to where you are now -- reading this book. Whether out of curiosity or inner pressure or maybe even a wish for a new experience, you have decided to take a stab at trying to find out more about the unknown and how that relates to the good times you hope to experience.

It's surely true that no one can know the future. Furthermore, when it gets right down to it, change seems to be hooked up with everything; for when one thing changes, everything else also changes. No wonder most people feel like helpless pawns in the hands of cruel fate. Yet we need not be so controlled; for in having a better understanding of change, we can play a much larger, satisfying and exciting role in laying out our own destiny.

Still feel good? I hope so. A good feeling inside will help as we take a look at the landscape of change and how that will affect our future happiness. The attitude we carry with us will determine the resources we have at our disposal as we respond to what lies ahead on life's path. Have you come checking into change out of curiosity... or might you be facing a problem you would like to change... or could it be something else about change that interests you? Whatever the reason for "checking in", have fun checking out five techniques for accomplishing change and getting to your goals.

Full "3-D"—Departure, Desire, and Destination

Picture the ideal vacation. Isn't a vacation for the purpose of getting away from the undesirable and getting to a place that's desirable? In other words, vacationers want to escape from the negatives and get to the positives. And desire is the key to making that move.

The state of Wisconsin has advertised for tourists with the phrase, "Escape To Wisconsin!" People in big cities like Chicago, who long for the rural, quiet lakes and campgrounds of northern Wisconsin are attracted by this slogan. They certainly do want to escape! But many who experience the bitter cold and danger of northern winters have different thoughts about a place to go. In contrast to the stressful, hazardous, chilling Midwest winter, advertisements for a restful, pleasurable, warm Caribbean Cruise is very desirable. Maybe the extremes -- the contrasts -- heighten the desire for a change in scenery, so to speak.

Going through change is much like the process of planning to go on vacation. The full "3-D" picture is departure, desire and destination. With change, we first need to have a good look at what we want to escape or get away from -- our place of departure. Probably the more unattractive that looks to us... the more we want to get away... and the deeper our desire. In addition, our desire is also dependent upon what the future holds for us. If that's very attractive -- like the Caribbean Cruise -- we will do almost anything that needs to be done to arrive at our destination. Departure, desire and destination show us the full "3-D" picture of how to make enduring change work. We must remember that we will only have the necessary desire to change, if we have done our homework on all the reasons for departing (the negatives of our past experience) as well as on all the attractions of our destination (the positives of our hoped for future). Yes, it's good to put on those "3-D" glasses to arrange for change.

A Renewing Lifestyle—Step by Step Progress

When most people finally start thinking about change, they usually are at a place they don't want to be in their lives. They may have simply drifted into that spot. As an old preacher once put it, "You get way out yonder without knowing how you got there." If we give this a little thought, however, we must admit that as human beings we are creatures of habit; and many things we drift into become bad habits. Most of our bad habits are really "addictions" -- as the dictionary tells us -- "habitual inclinations." Just think of all the bad habits or addictions evident in our society today: alcoholism and other drug abuse, uncontrolled spending or shopping, over-eating, gambling, smoking, excessive use of television, bondage to work or play, and now obsession with the Internet... to name only a few. Almost everyone has some place in their lives from which they would like to escape. But how?

Figuring out how to change (or how to escape) becomes relatively simple as we check out the method by which we have become addicted. How does an alcoholic or gambler or smoker become "hooked"? It's not just on that first drink, bet or cigarette, although that indeed is the beginning. (No one ever has become addicted without taking that first step.) But the experience becomes ingrained as little by little, step by step, we increase focus and interest on that which has attracted our attention. Since there is almost never any comprehension of where the steps are leading, and since we often move quite slowly and almost unconsciously, we are rather like the frog in warm water slowly brought to the boiling point. Yes, we are "way out yonder without knowing how we got there." Neither our minds or our bodies recognize the danger, until we really are in a bad spot! Our bodies and minds have been fooled into thinking "everything is all right" every step of the way to the point of disaster. It's all quite unintentional. As the bumper sticker warns us: "What is bad... happens!"

For the fortunate people who reach (or have not yet reached) "the boiling point" of their addiction... and decide that they do not want to go further down this uncomfortable path, there is a way out. And the way out is the same as the way in -- little by little, step by step. Generally, people are no better than frogs at adjusting to extremes -- going from boiling water to cold water or from gluttony to starvation. There's just too much shock to the system! We may try the extreme, and sometimes we may even be successful; but more often than not we fail and slip back into the old comfortable routine, no matter how harmful. Maybe it's because learning comes slowly... or because we like the security and comfort of habits... or because we live in gradual cycles, in any case, it's tough to fool the body into a big change. The bottom line then is to slowly but surely, step by step, reverse the bad habit and move away from the addiction. The conscious decision to get away from what is harmful or unpleasant is what is critical to success. While it's true that usually getting into trouble just happens, finding a way to freedom or newness takes a conscious decision and good planning.

Step by step progress away from anything that hurts or hinders us and toward any truly desirable goal can certainly be realized. "Renewing our lifestyle" is refreshing and exciting for those of us who want to thoroughly enjoy our lives. We understand that we not only make our own beds, but we also sleep in them. Our actions certainly do have consequences. So the idea is to plan the progress to one's new destination in steps that are easily accomplished. In some extreme cases, maybe steps away from what is undesirable will be as prolonged as the steps we have taken getting into trouble in the first place. As we have said before, what is necessarily different is that while getting into a bad spot was probably quite unconscious, now getting out will have to be very deliberate.

The wisdom of slow progress which never stops or retreats is that it can change anything! Taking those "first steps" or turning around the momentum is the most critical, for once the pattern of newness has been set, further steps will get easier and may well get faster on down the road. Remember, we are creatures of habit, whether for our own personal destruction or for our own long-term happiness. Essentially, we trick ourselves into gradually moving toward that place which will make us truly satisfied. Step by step progress -- yes, that's the secret. As they say, the only way to eat an elephant is one bite at a time!

Enjoying the Process -- No Instant Win!

Accomplishing difficult change can be a bit like eating a whole elephant. It's a lot to handle and probably something most people would want to avoid. Like, what do you do with that overwhelming task of trying to single-handedly tackle a week's worth of really dirty dishes? Walk away. Put it off. Don't look. Beyond that, not only is the project perceived to be too big, but it is also no fun! That last reason not to check into change is "the killer" in our day and age; for we surely have gotten acclimated to having fun.

If we want to get going with change or get change going, in this case at least, I think we need to take the easy way. A person who is going to change really needs to want to change. So if we are going to sell anyone on change, accomplishing it had better feel pretty good. We are indeed fortunate, because change can be fun. Look at the little child going through all kinds of change... and see if that child is having fun. You bet! It's all a matter of the child's perspective.

As with the lottery, with change there is no "instant win" for most people. Consequently, we have no other option than to deal with "the process of change." This can be an enjoyable experience. Since healthy change is rather natural and enjoyable, no one needs to fail with change. The problem is that as a society we have gotten used to instant gratification. We want relief from pain now. We want to win it all now. We want to satisfy our desires now. We want to reach our goal now. But that's hard to do. So we give up trying to change. The answer is -- the day by day "process" of getting to our desired destination can be a lot of fun. It's simply a matter of our way of thinking of how we go about getting there.

Have you ever noticed how that cross country or marathon runner just really enjoys running? Doesn't that fitness expert relish the workouts? Or how about the great weight lifter and mountain climber? They too are enthused about their practice. Their work becomes their play or pleasure. Now that does not mean that any of the above have it easy, so to speak. In fact, most of us might almost literally die trying to reach their achievements. What they have done is to mold their minds to make easy what most of us would find very difficult and overwhelming. It can be noted that the consistently best cross country team in the nation has as its motto -- "run for fun and personal best!" Not only do these high achievers enjoy each day's difficult activities, but they also enjoy the final results. How can they lose when they enjoy the whole process?

Every one of us can discover fun change to easy success! We only need to think positively about the route we take to our goals. There may be times when we even have to "fake it" in order to move forward. That's "mind over matter" or using our brains to convince our bodies to travel down the new road. We know where we want to go and so we are willing to use every method available to move toward our daily and long-term destinations. What is at stake here is nothing less than our present and future happiness. Enduring happiness is a whole lot more important than a quick success or even winning the lottery!

Checking Agents—Increasing The Odds

There certainly are times in our lives when we desperately want to achieve a particular goal. For example, think about the high school basketball team that has won most of its games throughout the year. Members of the team desperately want to play their best in tournament competition, so that they can continue to move on toward the state title. They undoubtedly would be open to suggestions from the coach, extra practices, extended strategy sessions and maybe even a change in eating habits, in order to minimize their mistakes, feel good and play up to their potential. Chances are that almost any checks on their team's performance would be welcome, in order to have a better opportunity to take home the title.

Maybe another way to consider the importance of

checking agents is to think about the young teenage driver who likes to get to his destination in a hurry. Imagine he has gotten so accustomed to "speeding" that he has received a number of tickets and is in danger of losing his driver's license. This young man feels that it would be terrible if he lost his license, so he looks for any help he can get... in order to counter his tendency of driving too fast. What are his options? For one thing, he can encourage passengers in his car to warn him about speed limit signs... or tell him if he is driving over the limit. He might seek information about how slower driving makes for safer driving. Another strong deterrent to speeding might be to think about the embarrassment of getting pulled over or of not being able to drive. Finally, he could even decide to do some walking, biking or riding with a friend in order to lessen his chances of getting another ticket.

Like this young man, certainly there are times in our lives when most of us not only personally want to check on our own behavior so that we accomplish our goals, but we even may be willing to look for outside checking agents to help us. In some cases, we might be willing to sacrifice past "freedoms" to increase the odds of attaining something we want much more. Since changing some habits or tendencies is perceived to be quite difficult, it deserves repeating that often most of us will be more focused on where we want to go, if we really are willing to be held accountable to ourselves and others. That is simply having good understanding of our human condition.

Usually, the more checks we have on our behavior, at least in the early stages of change, the better our chances are of succeeding. "Good intentions" are easy to acquire. However, it's not so easy to carry them out, if we have a lot of baggage standing in our way. We must admit that our strong tendency to repeat past behaviors is a big barrier to change in our lives. Therefore, at those times we are really serious about getting turned around, we need to be mindful of acquiring checking agents... to increase our odds of being successful.

The Whole Person—Mind / Body / Spirit

The above four techniques for accomplishing change can be adequate. But there is still more! We can look over an even greater influence on our achievement, if we desire. In a sense, this last technique is the one that can carry us to a whole new level in checking out change. We get a glimpse of a new, inspiring, amazing perspective. Maybe this is a bit like looking down and viewing our globe from a space ship; or maybe it's like looking into the depths of the sea -- a place where we witness a whole new way of living and the source of all life. In any case, we might just call this perspective "living in the zone" -- it all looks and feels and is just right! It's getting the ultimate "big picture" together with "the answers"-- getting everything to work together and flow harmoniously for excitement, contentment and peace! Change not only works, but it is "the answer" and "the design" for our living as it grants us the miracle of healing and wholeness.

Again, let's go to the sports arena to get a feel for what I'm talking about. Teams in competition definitely have a goal when they really want to excite their fans... and that goal is to win. But how can they win? Sometimes great teams go after the best offensive players. Offense definitely can carry a team a long way toward winning. Other teams focus their strategy on building the sport's best defense. Great defensive players can also give a team tremendous potential for success against any opponent. Finally, a few teams seem to zero in on coaching as their ticket to success. There aren't many knowledgeable sports fans who would argue against the importance of having an excellent coaching staff for domination in a sport. But now what happens if a team is fortunate to be able to put together all three -- a fine offense, defense and coaching staff? Now you've got something special and undoubtedly a team that'll go a long way in winning!

Three similar components are critical to being effective with change. As offense, defense and coaching are important to winning in sports, mind, body and spirit -- these three are significant influences on whether or not we attain our goals. Yes, change can be accomplished by basically mental concentration, just as offense can be dominant. Our bodies too can be conditioned to move us in certain desired directions... pretty much apart from the other two. And certainly the spirit has had a dominating place in altering our destiny as human beings, just as coaching has proved its value to top teams. What really helps manage change is when we concentrate the mind, body and spirit on getting to our intended goals. That's when we realize we've really got it "made in the shade!"

The basketball player who is having that career game and is in that "can't miss" mode is certainly envied. He or she is, as they say, "in the zone" and hitting on all cylinders. Now picture "the mind" firmly focusing all of its attention on getting change accomplished, whatever way possible. Think of "the body" being cleansed of whatever holds it back from its intended destiny and then being nourished and stroked into new physical health and wholeness. Last but not least, consider "the spirit" free from past bondage and restrictions, inspired and yearning for a more meaningful, exciting and happy future. Put those three together, and what do we have? We experience a person "in the zone", seeing the big picture as well as the creative details, knowing where to go, feeling good, and ready for the future. In the end, we know a person in the process of change who feels the miracle of healing and wholeness. What an exciting and rewarding way to live!

Putting It All Together

We started out by envisioning ourselves "checking into change." Many of us may be studying this concept for the first time in our lives. Others may be returning to somewhat familiar territory for a new look... or a new future. Hopefully, our surroundings around change are inviting, pleasant and comfortable, for if they are, we will be led to find lasting joy in the promises and benefits. What we have studied while checking into change could mean as little as a sideways glance or as much as an exciting, new way of life. Obviously, it's a very personal choice. There's not any single "get away" journey for everyone.

If we like these insights about change, we can become winners by organizing and applying the above techniques to our life's challenges. As we look back, certainly a good place to start is to become immersed in that big "3-D" picture -- departure, desire and destination. We all need to take a long look at where we have been... before laying out where we are going. It's like learning from history. Ultimately, the yearning or desire we have (to leave the past and strive for the future) will determine our progress. Reversing the momentum of what we have been through, we will open our minds, bodies and spirits to the enjoyment of a step-by-step process toward freedom and healing. That will mean letting those detrimental aspects of our lives fade away as we focus on our new life goals. In the end, the checking agents that we initiate and welcome will help to focus our attention on the attainment of our hopes and dreams.

Checking in... to change. Now it's time to check out... what we want to do... and what we want to be... on down the road of life. We can be in control of our destiny! Living doesn't need to be fatefully restricted, because we don't have to be bound by our habits or our past. Maybe the best we can do now is to make a commitment: Today we will take the time to determine our destiny tomorrow. We'll certainly do all right for ourselves in checking out "fun change to easy success." It's like... "We have a liftoff!" The powerful engines ignite and the surge comes propelling us upward. We are carried safely toward that ever-changing, far out, spectacular view. This "zone" is for you!

CHAPTER 4

Challenged For A Better Life

"Motivated For Change"

Whether we like it or not, we as individuals and as a society are rapidly moving into the new millennium. Many of us may be thinking we are moving too fast toward the future. A large part of our lives seems almost out of control and that which is familiar, stable and secure seems to be slipping away. What in our lives isn't up for grabs? It's tough for the most successful among us to remain calm and cool these days in the midst of a world "exploding all around us!" Understanding the unprecedented difficulties we face in our time and place, it is my conviction that probably the biggest challenge we face is the challenge of change. Here are a few thoughts about this challenge.

Wouldn't it be great if the major problems we face individually and corporately were not getting any worse? Consider global ills -- exploding world population, depletion of forests and cropland, terrorism, chronic disease, loss of species, climate change and political instability. On a national scale, think of how nice it would be... if our national debt wasn't a burden, if drug addiction was controlled, if our natural resources weren't declining, if pollution wasn't getting more serious, and if... well, you get the point. Change is happening way beyond our comfort and control.

Similar questions could be asked, moving all the way down the chain to the individual and his or her immediate problems and concerns. Think about it. Wouldn't you be pleased... if increasingly we didn't have to worry about getting laid off or be concerned about more violence in our communities? Wouldn't it be good if taxes, addictions, time demands and pressures at work were not all escalating? It would also be a blessing if our health would hold up and if our children wouldn't have to face more and more competition and less and less security.

You and I know these items just scratch the surface of the decline around us. That's change... for the worse... and we can't do anything but try to deal with it. What a challenge! How can it all be handled? But what's hard to digest is -- that's only the half of it!

Maybe the most difficult half of change is the up-side of it -- how to get better at what we do, how to improve what we don't like within ourselves, or how to be creative with our everyday activities. This too is change that needs to be handled in the best way possible. The good news is that most people have done a pretty decent job of handling a certain amount of needed change in their lives. Most of us have learned to adapt; and we are successful survivors -- alive and well, even if we don't quite know how we did it. Yes, most of us are doing adequately because nature has forced us into a certain amount of change.

So how do we get those New Year's Resolutions accomplished... and all those other "break out" things we know we really should do on a daily basis? More simply put, how do we really go about being the kind of people we want to be? We are such creatures of habit -- it is so easy to slip back into the old or to give up on trying the new. That's the other half of a gigantic challenge before us... probably forever! What we learn about change and how well we put that knowledge into practice... is absolutely essential for our survival as human beings... as we head on into this century and millennium on spaceship earth. The title of this chapter -- "Motivated For Change" -- may well be the keystone for getting necessary and desirable change accomplished.

Heading In The Wrong Direction

The challenge of change might not be so overwhelming if generally we as a society were not heading in the wrong direction -- changing for the worse or for a more detrimental lifestyle. Assuming this is the case, we can be pretty sure that many of us as *individuals* also are heading the wrong direction in many aspects of our lives. The increase of violence, drug addiction, abuse, racism, divorce, immorality, pollution, health problems, greed and carelessness, etc. is concrete proof that we are not holding our own and are heading the wrong way! Unless we begin to stop this hurtful change, it's just a matter of time before our personal and corporate destruction is assured.

There may be those among us who feel that they are above or beyond the reach of harmful and hurtful change. But even wealth and power cannot separate individuals or governments from risk... or eventually from the common misery of the masses. Spaceship earth has its limits and history teaches everyone that we are interdependent and can only ignore what surrounds us at our own peril.

It's worthy to note here, without much comment, two key influences on our decline into chaos -- two important principles which we have forgotten, relating to every problem area of detrimental change. They are both so simple that they are overlooked and/or forgotten: Number one -- "It's the little things that count!" And number two -- "We need to take good care of ourselves and one another on spaceship earth." Since these two are so difficult to absorb, let me elaborate: First -- "Since *every word and every move* counts for change, everything needs to count for the welfare of all." And second -- "If we neglect to be concerned about the interests of our adversary or enemy, he or she surely will be motivated to see us eliminated from the race."

Let's begin with a simple example. Imagine a man, having little more than a gun, who finds himself without food and water while living in a dessert. We also live in this dessert, but we control the water and food supplies.

Eventually the man becomes very thirsty and hungry. On the other hand, we don't want to give up our power or resources. Survival is tough for every individual! Now the question is this: What normal human being would not use whatever he has at his disposal -- a gun for example -- to try to get what he wants and desperately needs? Be certain of this fact: He has enormous motivation!

Consider the situation in many of our deteriorating inner cities or rural communities today. The conditions for many people become desperate and seemingly quite hopeless -- unhealthy food, ramshackle housing, inadequate income, bad working conditions, loneliness, insecurity, injustice, empty morality, poor education and the list goes on. What person among us, who is backed into the corner of such terrible and intolerable conditions will not use whatever is at his or her disposal to try to escape? Many people in a tight spot can become motivated even to terrorist activity if their options seem extremely limited. The whole human race has a great drive for survival, and everyone of us seeks to be satisfied... realistically, by whatever opportunity is available. Honestly thinking about the terrible stresses and strains applied to people in our society, it is not hard to understand why we are heading downhill in a hurry.

Maybe the most obvious illustration of apparent human failure and destructive change is evident in our booming prison population today. In Wisconsin we can't build prisons fast enough. The decision is made to try to take care of the problem by paying other states to take offenders off our hands. Other suggestions are -- to pack prisoners into cells a bit more tightly, to make conditions within jails "less attractive", to legislate longer prison penalties, to "throw away the key." Meanwhile, many advantaged individuals wonder why convicts who are let out of prison "haven't learned their lesson"! It hardly occurs to us that offenders who have been released... essentially have been motivated in prison to perfect and even expand their law-breaking and corrupting techniques. As outcasts and students of crime they have little to lose. So society's situation becomes just a little more desperate.

Finding ourselves "heading in the wrong direction", we have to accept the consequences of our inattention to detail. We should remember that with either positive or negative change, "It's the little things that count"! Moreover, we can see the results of not caring for one another as interdependent members of our communities. In the human body we would understand that if one of our members (body parts) is hurting, the whole person suffers. Admittedly, not many people today even know *what is happening*, say nothing about *why* everything seems to be falling apart. After all, who has the time to study why we have so many difficulties? Where are the resources to get at the roots of society's problems? We are far too absorbed with looking after our own rights... and letting everybody else take care of what we consider the "little details".

Drifting… Hopeless And Helpless

In many respects, it seems we are "wandering" and "in danger" and unable to understand the consequences of our words and deeds as a society. Yes, we are drifting… and seemingly pretty much hopeless and helpless. This is not what we really want to hear. What we want the most is to feel that we are in charge… that we can run our own show… that we don't have to answer to anyone! But where has our independent self-interest taken us? Into a situation where we are "hopeless and helpless" in finding our way into a better world for ourselves and our fellow travelers on spaceship earth. Either we will learn to care and be concerned about all of our fellow passengers… or we will eventually go down in flames with no survivors.

I am reminded of the story about the busy, wealthy father who couldn't understand why his wife and children never loved him. He worked hard to make money -- probably for power and prestige and pleasures for himself and his family. He was good enough in his own eyes to give his wife and children almost anything they wanted. He figured he had everything in hand and everything under control. But he ended up without anything of lasting value, because he didn't have any time for his family. Essentially, he put nothing into his relationships… and so essentially, he got nothing in return. Since he was led away from the important details in his life, he became unaware of critical change that caused him to be a big loser.

Many of us in this country are quite a bit like the wealthy father. Basically, we just don't seem to find the time to take care of what's really important! We don't really know what our children are doing. We hurry around trying to accumulate more and more material things. We cast judgments on those who are unlike ourselves. We are into defending what we consider our own turf. And finally, we find ourselves a long way from home without knowing how we got there. Have we even thought about our motives? The little but important things have eluded us. We are lost in destructive change, drifting hopelessly and helplessly toward a bitter end.

How in the world did we get to this sad state of affairs? The answer is really quite simple: We have drifted down the "exciting but dimly lit alley" of technological change with very little vision and moral courage. We are beginning to recognize that there are consequences to individual and corporate carelessness -- our inattention to basic goals, our confusion about stewardship and ownership of the planet, our forgetfulness of the interdependence we need for survival, and maybe most important of all, our neglect of considering the motivation available to begin corrective and constructive change. It all makes a lot of sense, if we begin to seriously look around at our problems and seek some honest answers. True, we will not be able to just drift, or make excuses, or give up, or be selfish, or take revenge, or forget the details. On the other hand, we will find an escape from hopelessness and helplessness... and be on our way to enduring health and happiness.

Vision For A Better Life

It is important to think about how we as human beings are motivated to drift into harmful change and how we are carried along by it! At some point, that information may help us stop whatever hurts us... or at least slow it down. But it is also important to think about how individuals can be motivated for healing, healthy and corrective change. Just as the thirsty man in the dessert probably did not decide to use his gun when he first became thirsty, and just as the youngster in the inner city did not begin to sell drugs the first time he felt deprived and persecuted, so we as individuals usually do not get to where we want to go with the first sign of positive motivation. The smaller stimulants or motivations often really need to pile up.

A forceful illustration: Many of us know someone like this particular addicted smoker. He has heard all the public health messages and all the rational discourse against smoking, but has never been motivated to give up his habit. A family member points out the smoke stains around their house and then suggests he think about what a mess is being made in his lungs. The smoker acknowledges all this, thinks about it for a moment, and then instinctively lights up another cigarette.

Down through the years, there has not been one overwhelming way to get people off their smoking habit. We must admit that mere words very rarely are the most effective motivations, and so in this case. The cancer that this man eventually was diagnosed with could have killed him, if he had not quit smoking and received long-term treatment. Through many months of radiation and chemotherapy he battled nausea and unbelievable fatigue. More than once he had setbacks and things became desperate, but he prevailed. After several years, his cough has gone away and his illness is still in remission. Sometimes he thinks he'd like a cigarette, but the memory of coming so close to death makes him stop short. "You have to have motivations," he said. "Mine were radiation and chemotherapy... dictated by cancer!"

Almost anything under our control can be changed, if somehow we get the vision of a better life and find adequate motivations. As with the smoker, much successful motivation has been connected to the "escape from disaster" kind of thinking. Along this same line, there have been times in the past when we have heard of "brainwashing" in connection with change. Sadly, this has usually been associated with something terrible... like torture in war or religious fanaticism. Extreme measures have been taken to accomplish the desired change, and the motivations usually succeeded in producing the intended results.

Now consider the power of a *desired and healthy* kind of "brainwashing" for the purpose of serving an individual's personal goals or desires! Imagine using whatever agents might motivate a person the most -- all appropriate, effective and tailor made to bring about desired change. If an individual was especially stimulated by money, power, pleasure, food, friendship or whatever, one or more of these might be prescribed for specific results. Increases or decreases in "dosage" would be determined by the need or the speed of recovery. There is little doubt that this kind of well-planned behavioral modification could bring about wonderful results in the life of almost any individual. Three simple steps could guarantee change: First, finding the desire to change. Second, accepting a vision for a better life. And third, acting with motivation to change direction.

You have heard all kinds of people say it: "I'd do anything to... you name it -- loose thirty pounds, have a happy family, succeed in business, win the lottery!" And many of those same people are willing to sacrifice a lot for what they so desperately desire. They have a kind of wishful "vision". The only trouble is, many of them really don't know how to go about reaching their goals, say nothing about coming up with goals that are something other than frivolous and fruitless. The next problem they face is that their environment doesn't let them succeed. Obviously, a teenager is going to find it tough to get better grades, if his friends only like to drive around, cause trouble and party. When a person has drifted into detrimental change, it's not very easy to come up with a vision about how to achieve a better life. On the other hand, this not-easy vision is "the only game in town."

"Outlaws Becoming In-laws"

Probably the best thing we could do as a society heading into the new millennium is to find a way to foster or generate productivity out of what is unproductive and what is hurting us. This applies to both our individual and corporate lives. Whether we are talking about our national debt, consumption and pollution, people in poverty, a wayward teenager, or our criminal justice system, we need to find some ways to bring about a more wholesome and healthy way of life. And that means making wise use of all the resources around us.

Down the road a bit, it can happen that we erase our federal debt... that we live in harmony with our environment... that the needs of all people are met... and even that "outlaws become in-laws." However, it will demand resourcefulness and courage for us to turn the tide. We will need to be *motivated* to change. And how we are motivated may well shape whether the results are good or bad. Is our society ready for this -- personal change and corporate change for the benefit of all? Are we ready to take chances for change? For example, are we willing to think about new, healthy ways of dealing with the criminal? In a way, the element of crime in society is rather symbolic of the detrimental behavior we all demonstrate. Both problems need long-term solutions if we really want enjoyable living in the future.

Isn't the real core of our problem (in making any kind of change) the troubling idea that we simply have to turn around our thoughts and actions!? It's the same for "outlaws becoming in-laws." But that's good and right... and will be productive and healthy, if we can only get started. Thinking about dealing with crime and our own detrimental behavior, check out a few of these "turn around" kinds of statements:

We live in the "dark ages" of managing crime and guiding criminals for the health and well-being of our society. About the only redeeming aspect of our criminal justice system is that we sometimes, temporarily stop criminal behavior. There is no evidence to show that punishment produces thoughtfulness or that hate inspires love.

> We generally do not understand what we teach or how we teach; it's the little things that count... at the earliest possible time! Our society as a whole is suffering from the consequences of what we have been teaching -- from throwing litter to enjoying destruction and carnage. And with regard to captured criminals, we have no idea what to do but to throw them! Wow! Have we ever accumulated a pile of "litter!" How about a little "recycling?" And this may be the most shocking statement of all: The cause of our greatest national distress -- the convicted criminal -- can become our greatest national benefactor in fighting crime. Remember these statements?

> For argument's sake, let's assume for a moment that the above statements are true. Wouldn't they constitute some massive motivation for a change

in the way we deal with both crime and criminals? On the other hand, if the above are false, why are we continuing to be so overwhelmed by this social problem? Why are the answers so hard to come by? The truth is, almost anyone is capable of change given the proper motivation. What an excellent strategy it would be... to do our utmost to encourage the lawbreaker to switch sides -- from outlaw to one who is in step with the law! Think of the benefits... for everyone!

Considering incarcerated people have become specialists in crime over an extended period of time and have a great feel for the environment in which it thrives, who would be better equipped to understand the roots and hazards of crime than the criminal? And who could do a better job of warning others about the pitfalls? Consider what might motivate the criminal to change sides, so to speak -- freedom from addiction, incarceration, low self-esteem, etc., payment for valuable work in "their field," opportunity to show acquired skills among their peers, and the list could go on and on!

Obviously, "behavioral modification" would have to play a key role in the success of such a plan. "Change Agents" would need to spend adequate time with people in prison to help them change and prepare to be a credit to society. In doing something for inmates, law abiding citizens would be doing something for themselves.... remembering that 95% of those incarcerated will someday be back on our streets. Hopefully, with positive publicity, there would be adequate incentive and encouragement from appreciative communities.

The Carrot And The Stick

Most people in today's society probably think that the above proposal is purely idealistic or maybe even "crazy." It's not so surprising we think this way, for we also lack understanding about why we can't get difficult things changed in our own lives. Moreover, we are informed time and again that there aren't any simple answers to the problems we face in our day. It's true that much of life is just very complicated.

Since so many of us are distressed and on the run, there are a number of *reasons* we resist healing and healthy change. First, we have become less rigorous and decisive in our morality as well as less able to understand just where that morality is leading us. It's not easy for us to admit and reform our careless ethics and sloppy self-justifications. Second, we don't really want to take the time or put in the effort necessary to "turn things around"; we would much rather go about "the quick fix" or simply offer an ultimatum. Third, we are much more comfortable with being accusatory and dispensing punishment than accepting responsibility and understanding forgiveness. Fourth, there can be upsets with other people and our environment when we finally take the courage to change course in our lives. And finally, there is usually quite a bit of personal and corporate risk in trying anything new, especially if we believe that it may end up in another failure or embarrassment for us. There even may be other reasons we tune out on proposals for significant change.

Yet no matter how skeptical we are about the possibilities of changing what has been going wrong, we also know (at least in the back of our minds) that certain motivations can do the trick. Consider the positive motivation of a million dollar lottery, an Olympic gold medal, a Super Bowl ring, even fifteen minutes of fame, or the best score in a game. We have already explored how hurtful threats can motivate -- the fear of death or terrible pain, the loss of family or friends, restrictions of freedom or self-esteem -- here the list of punitive motivations can be as far reaching as our bad dreams. These and other similar sources of motivation can be what it takes to change nearly any behavior known to man.

As we live out these last years of the 20th century, apparently our society considers some human beings to be beyond hope of change... or at least beyond anything but punitive motivations. The consensus seems to be that prisoners should be "taught a lesson." This kind of thinking goes far back -- undoubtedly as far back as the man who tried to motivate his stubborn mule. The mule wouldn't move; and sometimes it wouldn't move even when he beat it with a stick. So he hit it as hard as he could to "teach it a lesson." But still he was rarely successful.

Somewhere along the line, the frustrated man came up with a new idea. He would try dangling a carrot out in front of the mule to encourage it to go forward. This solution was much more successful, especially when the mule was hungry. Finally, using the two motivations -- both the carrot and the stick -- the man with the very stubborn mule was able to accomplish almost all of the work he needed done.

Basically, even though we are advanced, sophisticated and cultured members of the human race, we still share with the mule (and the rest of creation) our basic instinct of needing to be motivated by the carrot and the stick. Even our spiritual heritage -- maybe that which has carried us on to the greatest of human aspirations -- has adopted similar kinds of inducements to move or change us. At least several thousand years of inspiration confirm that a divine scheme of correction and reward directs our attention to heaven and hell -- basically, the carrot and the stick. I guess this might be one more indication that we just have to have incentives to be what we were meant to be and do what we were meant to do.

Let's take another look at what undoubtedly is one of the most stubborn problems we face in our generation -- the problem of how we should deal with crime and criminals. And let's consider how to implement this scheme of correction and reward. Hopefully, as we work our way through this "model for change," we will begin to more clearly understand how we can apply this example for change in our own lives.

The heart of our interest is in what *motives* actually change the "criminal /addictive behavior." First, we focus on the most feared negative consequences -- unpleasant prison conditions, fear for personal safety, loss of freedom, lowered self-esteem, worry about future success and limited social contacts, to name a few. For a lot of offenders these punitive measures may well hurt as much as touching that hot stove or painful treatment as a result of cancer. As with concentration camp "brain washing," when almost any "escape to freedom" becomes highly desirable, then almost any tool for correction is welcome. Even the *thought* of hurtful things can be awesome motivations; that's because many first time lawbreakers are rational human beings and are not "as stubborn as a mule."

It is sad that today, for the most part, there is little opportunity for criminals to change the direction of their lives before they are sent to prison -- before society applies "the stick." The long-term negative consequences of imprisonment are maybe even greater for society than for the incarcerated individual, when the total costs are added up. How wonderful if the resources of wayward individuals as well as of society could be freed up to advance the far greater good of all.

Undoubtedly even more important than the feel of "the stick" is the hope for "the carrot." Imagine the attractive incentives that our society could use for encouraging productive behavior. Generally, prisoners have received very few beneficial motivations in their lives, and so in essence are starved for healthy enticements. Recognizing what is at stake with correction and reward incentives, the desire for change is significantly increased. At this point, relatively enjoyable small steps away from "addictive behavior" become extremely attractive. When appropriate and/or applicable, this process is used with the mind, body and spirit.

In this process, both a counselor and criminal become agents of change and are empowered through interdependency. Through an enjoyable process, they will try to gently force or seduce the mind, body and spirit into a new reality of behavior. Moreover, the strongest incentives will focus on the hardest first steps. There is less concentration needed on each successive step as the whole person becomes familiar with the new pattern of life. This is an ongoing, victorious, self-fulfilling, fun filled process -- each day establishing new highlights for success and achievement.

Appropriate Incentives

We have been examining many aspects of the motivation needed for moving a person to change behavior. But we have not given much consideration to *appropriate motivation* for any particular person or problem. Since it is almost impossible to deal with specific situations in this analysis, by necessity, suggestions will be quite general.

Probably the most obvious point to be made about appropriateness is that neither the penalty nor the reward should exceed the minimum of what is necessary to attain the desired change. There are several reasons for this. Considering the fact that we live in an environment of limits, all applications of what we have at our disposal should be allocated as wisely and fairly as possible. No one should get more than enough... for any purpose, because there would then be cause for jealously and bitterness as well as misunderstandings of prominence. Another reason not to exceed what is minimally needed has to do with every person's ability to adjust up to higher expectations with no greater results: The wealthy man always seems to be able to spend a higher salary just as the mule always seems to be able to accept more blows. One additional reason to apply the lowest appropriate level of incentives has to do with the need to sometimes prescribe a new and higher level of motivation, when there is obvious failure to accomplish necessary change. These and other reasons give evidence that we need to use prudently both the carrot and the stick.

Appropriate motivation is especially important with unusually difficult change and also with how quickly that or any other change needs to be accomplished. When it is advantageous that behavior is slowly modified over an extensive period of time, then obviously a lower level of incentive may be adequate. Extremely difficult change may demand not only more powerful incentives but also application over a longer period of time. In all of these cases, however, it is expected that the earliest steps into new behavior will be the most challenging and also will require the greatest degree of motivation.

Some question may be raised as to if and when it is appropriate to use either negative or positive motivations exclusively -- the carrot or the stick. This question may be resolved as the person to be changed reveals his or her needs and desires. Certain individuals may require being motivated purely by penalties... or maybe only by rewards... to attain the results that they want. But in most cases, a combination of both -- possibly emphasizing one a bit more than the other -- will yield the most successful motivation for change. That is probably due to the fact that almost all of us are very responsive to both pain and pleasure. Running from pain toward pleasure is almost always the fastest route to a victory with change.

Proper motivation for any individual is always dependent upon not only what is acceptable to that person but also what is acceptable to the community in which the person functions. For example, most of us would agree that within our democratic society, usually no one should be forced into behavioral modification without his or her consent. We know that people do need to be *restrained* for the welfare of society as a whole, but the idea of forcing unwanted change is in many minds close to murder. It is necessary that any individual not only cooperate in the process of changing his or her own behavior, but even better, earnestly desire and actively seek that change. Obviously, then, personal preferences for incentives are first priorities. For broad social support, it is also important to use motivations that are generally acceptable within each community. Clearly, the social standards of society should not be violated, or else a great deal of unfavorable resistance will tend to block favorable results.

One last point should be made about what is or isn't appropriate in changing behavior. We should be clear about the fact that any newness brought into a person's life might turn out to be the first step toward a dominant result. It's obvious then that any incentive for change should not end up being more detrimental in a person's life than what is being left behind. What a waste if a person went through an extensive process of rehabilitation... only to end up with a problem as large or greater than he or she had in the first place. When considering any change in an individuals' life, it is very important to think about the desirability of the potential result. Everyone wants change... but only for what is better!

Implementing With Checks

There's an interesting challenge in working out appropriate motivations to help turn a person's life around. But all that effort and ingenuity goes for nothing if those motivations are forgotten or left behind. That's why there's another essential element in the process of finally getting change accomplished. Just as there are very few people who would not change without adequate motivation, so also there are very few people who can make significant changes in their lives without some method of checking up on their progress.

For illustration's sake, lets go back to how convicts can become productive citizens... or how "outlaws can become in-laws." Probably the most important key to actually getting any change accomplished is this: Use all available resources to appropriately and carefully plan and implement a method of watching, guiding and assuring progress. We certainly have noted -- it's the little things that count! This is especially true with such challenging cases as convicted criminals.

Here then is a modest proposal... with checks... for altering criminal behavior: Within a single prison, approximately six convicts would be permitted to volunteer to begin a unique rehabilitation/training program for the explicit purpose of receiving pay for fighting crime. Convicts turned "crime fighters" would be required to work in teams of two individuals with the understanding that without personal progress as well as on the job success, both would be dropped from the program and returned to prison. These "teams" would be aided by daily evaluation from various checking agents.

Monitoring the work of previous offenders would be extremely important. First, working by two's, obviously it would be critical that team members watch one another closely... to see that progress was continually being made toward their goals... as well as to see that neither member has "slip-ups" or regression into past criminal behavior. On the positive side, starting pay would need to be adequate for a decent standard of living... with incentives for length of service as well as outstanding service. From the beginning of rehabilitation all the way to fighting crime on the streets, both members of the team would understand the importance of supporting, encouraging and monitoring their companion and co-worker.

The basic understanding concerning the above proposal is that corrective and healing change must be carefully monitored in order to be successful. It may well be true that the more carefully behavioral change is monitored, the higher the degree of long-term success.

The average person seeking behavioral modification for personal health and happiness has many options for monitoring or checking his or her progress. Some of the simplest ways involve self-accountability, such as a signed and dated commitment sheet, a check off progress report on a daily basis, verbal and/or mental repetitive reminders at predetermined times, pre-planned sessions with an inspirational audio or video tape, *measuring or testing* physical, mental or spiritual health -- these are just a few methods of checking on accomplishment.

Other than counting only on oneself, a family member, associate, relative or even neighbor can be helpful for insuring progress toward a goal. This person might be an inspiration, a guide to success, a counselor, a record keeper, a "cheerleader" or even a chosen critic. Certainly telling other people about personal goals could be an internal reminder of the mission to be accomplished. Also, community professionals are usually very qualified to help monitor progress if the need arises. If any person truly desires healthy change, there surely are many creative ways to certify the relatively pleasant transition to a better way of life.

It can turn out that even the simple *use of checking agents* (apart from the change itself) can be beneficial... and bring a certain richness into living. When people learn to rely on one another for close and lasting relationships in their lives, they begin to feel fulfillment. When individuals find that they can use certain tools to better their lives, they find new satisfaction and meaning. And finally when people can discover workable principles that bring optimism into their lives, they are filled with contentment and peace.

The Process And The Joy

Implementing change with healthy incentives and helpful checking agents can be an extraordinary experience. Moreover, the process can be a lot of fun, especially if changing the harmful into the healthy is carried out like playing a game. Don't we really seem to get motivated when we get into fun competition? The success of change all rests on how a person mentally approaches the challenge of behavioral transformation. Today, when most people in our society enjoy games, sports and physical challenges, and when very difficult activities are considered enjoyment, it's not hard to understand that overcoming many different kinds of challenges in life can be exciting! A person can experience offense and defense. There can be "rules of the game." Attentive "officials" can watch the play carefully to insure that the final results are achieved. And a lot of people can be cheering for "the good side" to be a winner.

Think for a moment about the preparation that goes into working out the change of any behavior. First we need to be willing to put ourselves into *a competitive team mode...* for the chance of excitement... for the challenge of competition... for the sake of team goals... for personal accomplishment and for the thrill of victory. Is the person who is having "some difficulty" willing to take a new look and give change a chance? Sometimes it takes some humility, or courage, or real risk to take the plunge into the battle of behaviors. But the great rewards are definitely out there if the first step is taken and the player intensely wants to do it. Wanting to get into the action of change is the biggest step there is, because once the burning desire flares up inside... the rest is relatively easy.

When a person accepts the challenge of change and really wants to be part of a winning team, the practice begins in earnest. People who never get to this stage consider *the practice* to be a lot of pain and agony; but team-mates know this is not the case. Good practice for winning the game becomes an enjoyable process. It's full of newness and strategy... and the satisfying development of skills and teamwork. Each practice session can be an additional step in a pleasant process toward a kind of hoped for "super bowl victory"! With every step along the way being an enjoyable one, there are simply no losers. That's because players as well as change agents always find more days ahead to improve. And they never back off from receiving more challenges in the future.

Finally, there is the experience of actually playing the game. This is really the center of satisfaction and meaning for great competitors. Working hard with good friends and teammates toward a clearly defined goal is fulfilling and exciting. Think what it means, personally, to start to carry the ball with change and to be in the process of winning the battle.

When one gains some momentum with a little accomplishment, there is the strong desire to *keep on going* so that all that has been gained is not lost. One careful play or day at a time (while following the rules) is at the heart of consistently moving toward the final goal. Many people would give a lot to be a perpetual winner -- having power over and putting away some dreaded adversary. This desire, in itself, could be enough to encourage a great number of individuals to be motivated for change.

As we consider the competitive nature of change, our real opponent or adversary is our lesser self -- our destructive behavior. Through a joyful, exciting and satisfying corrective contest, it can be defeated and put behind us!

Results And Rewards

Motivated for change and playing out the game of challenging bad behavior, people in our society can come to realize that there are countless, far-reaching results and rewards for all of us individually and corporately. Such results and rewards are also, in their own right, ongoing motivations. We have come to know... when one thing changes, everything else around it also changes. It follows then that when a person changes for the better, many other individuals around that person are also changed for the better. Water ripples (moving outward on a lake after a force impacts the water) give evidence of this principle.

Members of our society, who are attracted to the challenge of changing their own detrimental behavior for more health and happiness... are obviously richly rewarded personally. They might well have been motivated for change in part because they clearly understood what the results could be in reaching out for new possibilities. Still, very few individuals can grasp the full societal impact of one simple but radical change. If only we had the vision!

Part of the mystery of society's deterioration is due to the fact that we don't understand that this same principle is also true for harmful behavior -- it reaches far out and multiplies even beyond our comprehension. Whether change for the positive or for the negative, the results and rewards are by no means merely limited to personal gain or loss. As we race into the new millennium, increasingly we are coming closer together and so more deeply and radically affecting one another's lives... for better or for worse. Yes, we have vast power to improve our individual and corporate behavior, if we dare to comprehend the interpersonal influence that exists among all of earth's inhabitants.

> Interestingly enough, these thoughts bring us back to those two key contributors or principles that affect change... past, present and future. First, it's the little things that count. And second, we need to take good care of ourselves and one another on spaceship earth. Undoubtedly, forgetting these two principles has brought us down, not only as a nation but also as travelers with others on spaceship earth. Yet it is equally true that with an understanding of how change happens and then a willingness to move toward newness of life, many small positive changes will lead us toward a more kind, caring, healthy and happy world. Our individualistic, insecure, hurting cities can give way to inter-related, confident, healing "families".

As we monitor results and rewards, it would be good for us to take a look at how carefully motivated change among criminals could affect all of us... as well as how profoundly inspired change among us could affect them. Criminals turned crime fighters could yield far-reaching benefits for everyone -- benefits rising and rippling outward even to distant places around the world. We all need one another on this planet for many reasons. And we all need one another to be at our best. For everyone that means some change. Since I know that I can change for the better, I need to be confident that others can change for the better too. To get the job done right, we all need to be willing to think and act differently!

As we begin to grasp what a tremendous impact thoughtful change can have -- going from what is hurtful to what is healthy for us, both individually and corporately -- it's both proper and productive to get excited! The results and rewards can give us a sense of hope. They can even be *stimulants* for new and greater commitment to the meaningful but pleasant process of the challenge of change.

Conclusion

We began this discussion with the suggestion that probably the biggest difficulty we face today is the challenge we call change. Clearly, change is not optional for us individually or corporately as we move toward the future. We are moved over time -- for what is better or worse. Sadly, without much effort at all, we tend to hurt ourselves. As we look back, years of deteriorating conditions reveal we have helplessly and hopelessly drifted in the wrong direction as a society. Undoubtedly, each of us as individuals share in the responsibility. However, facing this fact can be quite beneficial for better understanding ourselves and others. It can also stimulate our vision for a more satisfying and happy life.

The knowledge of how we got into our present predicament can give us valuable insight into what will not be acceptable in tomorrow's game-plan. Maybe our greatest gift as human beings is to be able to learn from our history how to manage our future.

Put another way, it is indispensable for us to want what is better. But what is better... and why? That's not an easy question. As we face the consequences of going down the wrong path... and as we admit overlooking what is important, it becomes easier to figure out the new direction to go... and what it is we do want. Humility, maturity, wisdom and courage are surely important character traits for a chance at change.

When we really want change, we need to figure out what motivation is necessary to make it happen. This needs to be checked out for every person, whether a criminal wants to become a crime fighter or a spender longs to become a saver. We are creatures of habit and usually as stubborn as mules. Sometimes "agonizing pain" propels us to make a switch; and sometimes "great desire" leads us in a new direction; more often than not, both of these need to get us going for what is in our long-term best interests.

What do we need to do to be motivated for change? Quite possibly we need to go through the thoughtful process of how the past has penalized us... as well as of how the future might reward us. Consider again what might go through the mind of a convicted criminal who has the opportunity to be a new kind of person and live a new kind of life. Wouldn't that be powerful motivation for change? Each of us also has an extensive list of positive and negative incentives which can send us off in that new direction, if only we will open our minds and hearts to the possibility. There can be "a new spirit" in living with fantastic opportunities.

What does it take to be motivated for change? Maybe in the most basic sense, it takes something on the order of "falling in love... with that which is very desirable and uplifting." Anyone who has had the joy and excitement of falling in love... knows it means being "fired up" -- stimulated and motivated to a new way of thinking and acting. What exciting days and fun filled times! There's that "can't wait" sort of yearning. A person feels good about complimenting and being complimented. The new lifestyle is extremely desirable, full of adventure, and carries immense benefits. Sometimes there are interesting twists and turns in the new relationship, and often even some ups and downs -- not so very unlike playing a game. But it's all supremely worthwhile, if the object of desire is attractive and brings enduring happiness.

Yes, there can be some excitement in venturing out into healthy, fulfilling change. Learning to fall in love, in a sense, with what we yearn to be and experience in life... can help us put away the destructive habits we face as individuals. We can be powerfully motivated to change.

In reality, we need to look around for the grand inspiration of a new way of life that gives us all the happiness we were meant to experience. When we've found what we've been looking for, we need to go all out for it... and hold on with whatever means are available. This whole experience for better, not worse, should be carefully monitored to insure continued satisfaction and fulfillment. It's almost certain that what we earnestly desire can be won over with the appropriate encouragement, attention and sacrifices.

Romancing what makes us feel satisfied, whole, and happy can provide us with an ongoing boost, encouraging us to go after the greatest goals we could have for our lives. The great exuberance we feel in the process... and the powerful example of faithfulness we have in our dreams -- all this good stuff will ripple out to others in unimaginable ways. Absorbing increasing and exciting goodness... and being ideally *motivated for change*, we will never consider going back to our old, deteriorating, loveless life for anything! Look at the beauty of re-creational change, and go for it!

CHAPTER 5

Inspirations For Desirable Change

"The Success Stories"

BAD LOSER
(Changing behavior and even personality)

In the early 70's I lived in Birchwood -- a little town in Northern Wisconsin. As a High School student in the late 50's I had been a big Green Bay Packer fan. They were big winners in those years, and as the oldest of six children I was usually on (or cheering on) the winning team. One fall Sunday afternoon at home in Birchwood I remember watching the Packers lose. I was angry! In fact, much like many previous Sundays after watching the Packers lose, I was really upset! I didn't want to talk to anyone, and if I did I was bad company. Often my bad mood lasted hours and my unhappiness sometimes lasted for days. On that particular afternoon for some reason I realized that I had a problem and I knew I had to do something about it. I'm not exactly sure how I figured out how to work myself out of being a bad loser, but I do remember that my decision on that day started me on the path to recovery.

The method that I used and found to work exceedingly well over an extended period of time was based on a simple conditioning model: At the next loss (opportunity that I would look for), I would force myself to smile, and no matter how I felt, I would attempt to be nice -- appear to be a good loser! The first time was the most difficult, the second less difficult, the third less, and so on. As time went on, I realized that in fact I could change not only my appearance to others but also my feelings inside. I actually began to look forward to losses so that I could move forward with another step of accomplishment. Now, many years later, I remember where I have been in the past, but I have almost no bad feelings about "the losing experience." Furthermore, I have absolutely no desire to go back to my unhappiness of the past. I feel I am still in the enjoyable process of becoming a "good loser" and I also feel a deep sense of accomplishment at each point of change. A habit of personal growth and happiness has been established in my life. I feel great about it!

BOYS DOING DISHES
(Cultivating unusually good behavior)

Not too many people like washing dishes. Part of the problem is that almost everyone is led to believe that doing the dishes isn't any fun, or that it takes a lot of time, or that it's boring, or that it's a mother's job, or that certain people simply don't do dishes. And what family member doesn't have someplace to go after a meal? That's a lot to overcome. Still, doesn't somebody need to clean up the kitchen?

In our family, we feel that we have a lot going for us and that we should live positive, happy and thankful lives. We hope that we all will learn to be helpful and considerate and kind, etc. Consequently, from the time our boys were very little, we had the understanding that we would not use certain phrases like "I'm bored!", or if a task needed to be done, "I don't want to!" The understanding was that if someone was "bored", apparently that person didn't have enough work to do; or if someone didn't like or want to do something, he hadn't done it enough! In other words, almost anything could be fun or enjoyable if a person would look at the positive side of it.

One's first impression might be that this approach is "heavy handed" or manipulative or just plain stupid! Not so. All human beings are in the process of learning and being influenced in every moment-- for good or for bad. And all human beings are also in the process of establishing habits in every moment-- for good or for bad. In our day and age, many people of influence (parents maybe being the most important) have overlooked this important part of our nature, and we as families and communities are "paying the price!" Few people seem to care what a child thinks or does "in the moment" or about the little things that are done which establish the patterns in every person's life.

We as parents wanted our boys to contribute cheerfully to our family's work and welfare. Very early in their lives, we suggested that we would have an enjoyable time doing the dishes together. And we used various methods to accomplish that goal. If at some point during those "difficult years" we caught some small suggestion that doing the dishes didn't seem to be enjoyable, the thought was raised that maybe the person had been away from it too long and maybe needed to get in on it more often. It didn't take too long to see a change in attitude!

To make a truly long and detailed story a bit shorter, one of our sons (currently in college) wrote a paper about the power of this positive influence and suggestion. He has also seen the same results from the same approach which his Cross Country coach uses to inspire his team to the National Championship almost every year. At age 19 he kiddingly "fights me" for the chance to help with the dishes. But it's not just "in the genes" and a source of only personal pride! Our other son (adopted and a bit older and married) has also impressed his wife and his mother-in-law with his desire to help out with the most common or menial of routine chores-- yes, even offering to do the dishes!

I Needed Help!
(A Female in her 80's: Her courageous struggle to keep on going.)

Early in 1994, I was living a rather rewarding, comfortable and meaningful life with my husband of over 50 years. We have been content, happy and thankful since moving off our farm and into a simple apartment in Altoona,

Wisconsin. As husband and wife, our six children and many grandchildren have continued to be a joy to us during our declining years. We have tried to live our lives thinking about people in need -- especially the poor, hungry, minorities, etc. -- those "little ones" that the Bible talks about. I have considered my time "well spent" when I have had opportunity to speak up for others, whether verbally, by letters to congress or through the news media. However, having had an overriding focus on our family responsibilities and social concerns, I was not ready for what lie just ahead of me.

It was during the cold months that I began to experience a sudden onslaught of physical problems -- a recurring inner ear problem made me dizzy... and tired... and wore me out; I was losing my eyesight and my legs seemed to be giving out on me; somehow I had gotten a stomach ulcer, even though I continued good eating habits, took vitamin supplements and even had a medical technologist's training. Everything seemed to be beyond the doctor's help. Even my medication wasn't working!

Most of all, under all this strain and stress on my body, I felt unable to handle my thinking and emotions -- something I normally controlled under more pleasant circumstances. Just coping was getting harder and harder... and I began to get "tremors" -- uncontrollable shaking. My normal focus outward was almost entirely lost for my physical suffering and consequent inward focus. Physical tests seemed to turn up negative. "I think I'd better go to the hospital," I told my husband and son.

I went into emergency and got check over; but again, believe it or not, there was no solution -- no help for me! Only I understood the feeling of panic I held inside. I could hardly sleep.

I had long been an advocate of positive thinking and relaxation. But I could find nothing positive to think about; nor could I find the power to relax. Suffering remained. "I've got to go to the hospital", I said to my son. He knew my early power of positive thinking and had worked in recent years on the power to control beneficial change. Change -- yes, that was the answer! What could I lose? "I need help!" I said to myself. He had time to help me and I was ready to try anything!

Both my son and I knew that my emotions were getting the best of me. Wasn't it possible to get back some control of my feelings of panic and fear and hopelessness? Both he and I knew that my thinking was still clear, when I could find the inspiration to focus. So that's what we tried -- mind over matter -- I would moment by moment, bit by bit find ways to carry out actions that would relegate my "feelings" to less prominence. I would try to focus my attention on the simple pleasures I still treasured. I would recognize and speak of good things that happened each day. I would tell myself that I was "on the mend" physically. And I would try to smile -- "put on a sunny face" -- and convey to others some positive thinking about myself, even though I might not genuinely feel that way inside. I knew the theory of how this approach might work, but would it work with me?

At first this change seemed impossible. I was reassured that such thoughts were normal and that consistency and practice, if even in "baby steps", would make things easier as time went on. I had a deep desire to be well again, an openness to ask for help when I needed it and plenty of encouragement. Slowly but surely I began to recognize change within me. A habit had begun. What I was trying to do became easier and felt a bit more normal and natural. I soon recognized that my thinking and emotions became better controlled. And soon others began to see the results of this process of change. My ulcer was not gone, but I was off most of my medication and my physical condition was noticeably improved.

During this process of improvement, a simple idea came to me that I thought might help me "escape" from my inner turmoil. The idea was to play TRI OMINOS with my husband. This is a game with many triangular pieces which have numbers on them. Drawing pieces and matching numbers is the challenge of the game... with the winner being the one with the highest point total when all possible pieces have been played.

The enjoyment of this easy game has given me numerous and unexpected benefits during difficult days. In the beginning, I needed some distraction from my inner feelings of concern and panic. Whenever I felt my emotions start to take control of me, I asked my husband if he would like to play Tri Ominos; soon my concentration and enjoyment of the game took over and I felt better. But surprisingly, it wasn't long before I felt my eyesight was improving too. I was concentrating on seeing clearly and doing easy, playful workouts with my eyes. As Tri Ominos became a part of our daily lives, I must admit that there were times I felt like not playing anymore. It seemed like I was always losing... and that didn't make me feel very good! Also, my husband has a nervous habit of toying with the pieces to be drawn; sometimes I wondered if he might be taking a peek; sometimes I wondered if he had the feeling I was taking too much time as I looked for matching numbers. Was I feeling my temper rising? Maybe I should just quit playing! No, I knew that if I quit... I would be "the loser" in many ways.

Momentarily, I had lost sight of all the goodness of this "simple game"... through which I was finding healthy change taking place in my life. Here was an opportunity for me to relax and enjoy being away from my troubles. Here was a game I was using to strengthen my eyesight. And last but not least, I was practicing tolerance; I was even learning a little more each time about how to better communicate with my husband. How could I consider giving up a part of my life that was fun and so good for me at the same time? No I would not quit! I was determined to stay on my course of healing and healthy change.

Slowly but surely I was able to do things I never expected to do again. I went back to using the computer for my writing, and enjoyed my baking and cooking again -- like making pie and chicken noodle soup. So it went, moment by moment, day by day. Negative thinking and emotional set-backs became less and less frequent. Even though some of my physical problems are still with me, I am confident my body has the necessary strength to carry me through each day with stability and hope. I am proud and happy to say that my physical and emotional weaknesses no longer control my mind and spirit as they have in the past. Yes, I've been in the process of change... and I continue... each day.... I'm on the mend. Thanks for the help!

The Computer? No Way!
(A senior citizen -- amazing results!)

In my late 70's -- a mother to six grown children and a "Nana" to many grandchildren -- I've been an avid reader for many years. Beyond my reading, my hobby (if I've had one) has been to do some writing, when I could free up time from normal daily activities. My old manual typewriter was an ancient but familiar friend. Together we got out a booklet or two, articles to magazines and many letters to congress. But we were both beginning to slow down and making a few more errors than in earlier years. Were we coming to an end? I wasn't sure I was ready to give up what I felt was such a rewarding and enjoyable part of my life.

Then there was that day when I felt a hint of change in the air. I remember so well how it came about. Having just left Rochester, Minnesota, where my grandson and his wife lived, we were on our way to the Twin Cities. My oldest son who was driving mentioned that since I still enjoyed writing so much, maybe I should learn to use a computer with a simple "word processing" software package. I needed a new typewriter ribbon and had to admit that the old manual typewriter was outdated and malfunctioning. But when I heard the word "computer" I responded immediately and without hesitation, "No way; not at my age!" We chatted for awhile about the advantages of new technology and about people never being too old to learn. I had to agree; but I remained firm in my conviction that I was far beyond starting out on a computer.

One day back in Altoona, Wisconsin, the doorbell rang, and there stood my son with a real computer! I could tell it was heavy, so obviously there was nothing I could do but let him come into our apartment with it. At that moment, I vowed to let him take over. He did just that, explaining how this used, but fine piece of equipment could become a new friend to me and provide unending pleasure. What choice did I have but to listen? In any event, I felt it was his problem now -- he would soon see for himself what a foolish idea it was to try to teach someone my age how to use a computer. Why the very thought of it!

Soon the computer was on a small table near the kitchen. I was a bit curious... so he just casually showed me some of the different parts of this "high tech" machine. And then he left, saying he would be back the next day. True to his word, the next day he was back, renewing my curiosity and showing me the keyboard. I was surprised to see how much it was like my old typewriter keyboard. So now I expected "the training session". But no! He said all we would do... would be to learn how to turn the computer on and off. He encouraged me to "turn on" and "turn off" the switch. I did it a few times... and then he left... saying he would be back again another day. To tell the truth, I was a little sad that I didn't get to try a little more, considering the way he perked up my curiosity.

My son continued to come over and spend a little time with me almost every day, reviewing what we had done before, showing me just a little bit more, and teaching me only the amount that I seemed anxious to try each time. It wasn't long before I no longer feared learning this computer stuff; in fact, it was quite interesting -- it was fun! I was learning to use a computer, one step at a time. And one easy step after another at that! Looking back, it wasn't that long before I saw my first completed article on the screen. What a thrill! With my daughter-in-law's expertise, I would soon have it "printed out" from my floppy disk. When my article came back, expertly laid out on different sheets with different personalized logos, I could hardly believe my eyes! I could even choose my own logo. Was I surprised and pleased!

In a matter of weeks, the word was out to my other children that I was writing with a computer. Next, my youngest son showed up at the door with a small printer, which wasn't being used by his company. Could I learn to operate this? You bet I could -- slow but sure! Learning to use it made it possible for me to have a complete, versatile writing system, which I could use... to send out my articles and letters without help and... to print copies with almost no effort. What a joy to see the results of my writings!

I know that many people face roadblocks in trying to bring about change in their lives, and I am no exception. Not long ago, I was pretty sick for quite a while. For weeks I couldn't use the computer. In fact, I was hurting for such a long period of time that I thought my computer days might be ended. However, when I was well enough, I couldn't resist getting back in touch with my new "friend." It was good to get back to the computer and find out that I could still remember how to use it. What I had put into practice came back to me quickly. To this day -- I'm over 81 years now -- I am amazed that I learned to use a computer and have so much fun doing it!

THE LONG 1... TO THE FUN 18
(A teenager looks back at a significant change in his life.)

It's 8:15 a.m. -- time to start on the long one mile walk. It's 3:35 p.m. -- time to start on the long one mile walk. That was my daily weekday ritual during the school year. You may think that walking two miles a day doesn't sound too hard. It isn't for most people; but when I was an eight year old... that walk seemed to take an eternity. It wasn't much fun!

My elementary school, Sam Davey, was just under one mile away from our house. As luck had it, children living over a one mile radius from school got to ride the bus. So I was one of those kids that watched my friends ride by in the school bus, while I walked to and from school every day. It didn't seem right, since some friends lived only a block or two away from me.

On those rainy spring mornings or on those cold wintery afternoons, I thought I would never make it. I was just wishing that someone who knew me would drive by and offer me a ride. Rarely did that happen. It wasn't that it was such a long way, or that it tired me out. I just didn't like the fact that it seemed to take so long to take that 20-30 minute walk. Either I missed out on some recess time before school, or my friends were home and playing by the time I finally made it home after school.

At age eight or nine, I got a bright idea about how I could have more time to play after school -- I would run home! One of my friends that lived just a short distance away rode his bike back and forth to school. One day I asked him if he would carry my bag home, while I ran beside him. Before this I had never run any real distance, so my objective was to run as far as I could without stopping. Well, I didn't cover the distance in any record time, but I remember gasping for breath as I touched my garage door. I made it one mile without stopping! Not only did I get home faster, which gave me more time to play, but I felt good about reaching this "goal" I had set for myself.

Of course it wasn't all of a sudden that I started to run

regularly; rather, I did this one mile run home only now and then. After a while, the run seemed to get easier... and I figured I might as well get into my school's one mile "jogathon". After all, I had more experience running a mile than some of my friends! It wasn't long before I became a seasonal runner -- running primarily during the Spring and Fall, when each jogathon was held. Later, in high school, my cross country training was done in the Summer and Fall.

Finally, ten years later, I have just incorporated running into my daily lifestyle. I now have a personal training habit that makes me feel good, gives me a sense of accomplishment and rewards my efforts. The rewards far exceed the costs, and I don't want to see my success come to an end.

It becomes clear what a slow process all this was -- from that first step of wanting to get home faster... on to more recent steps, which have given me much confidence and many rewards. Yet it was that first little idea -- about getting home early -- that got me started on a radical change. Today I decided to run for two hours -- to take a 10 mile run... before joining two high school cross country coaches for a fun 8 mile run.

So I look back... and think about the change -- from the long one... to the fun 18! My present college cross country coach, who inspired us to first and second place at "Nationals" the last two years... tells us that we should "Run for fun and personal bests!" I want to tell you -- I think that's the saying that really got me started.

LOOKING IN THE MIRROR
(Liking what you see... A study of self-image.)

I was fortunate to grow up in a secure and loving family. It must be said at the beginning that this good fortune has given me an enjoyable, satisfying life... with few exceptions. I think it must have been that I was a teenager before I cared much about what I looked like in the mirror. But what kids in their teens don't have real concerns about the way they look? Lots of changes are taking place so rapidly that adjustments to puberty are hard. I guess I wasn't much different -- noticing flaws and things I didn't like about my body. But for me, my most annoying "fault" was what I saw from my neck to my belt line.

I played basketball and football and ran a little track; but I wasn't very big, and I never was an exceptional athlete. Nor did I do much dating. Maybe it was partly because I was late in maturing. Anyway, the bottom line was -- I didn't like the way I looked in the mirror. I remember being embarrassed that I was so "under developed" my ribs were showing.

In college I didn't go out for sports; then it was on to the seminary; finally, I was out working in churches as a minister. Since I didn't get in on much physical activity during those years, my appearance didn't change, even though I had finally become an adult. Standing in front of a mirror was just bothersome. It was reassuring and nice to be married before I left the seminary. Yet even that positive influence didn't do much to boost the physical image I had of myself. I just stayed sort of skinny... in my upper body anyway!

Through the first 10 years of starting my own family, my physical characteristics changed very little. I had married a light weight wife and my eating habits were pretty good. I couldn't complain about my looks, but I sure didn't have anything to brag about either. Well, maybe I bragged a little -- I hadn't gotten very fat, and I felt I could do almost anything I wanted to do physically.

As time marched on, my young body didn't feel quite so young anymore. Any real exercise had gotten to be almost non-existent. I was doing more sitting and snacking. And you guessed it. I started to add a few pounds. I took after my dad I said to myself -- I had that little extra extension on "my lower chest". But I had to admit it still pained me to look up a bit and see those unattractive, unsightly ribs.

The aches and pains were gaining on me by now. In my late 30's, I was definitely beginning to see deterioration of my excellent overall condition. What had happened to my body? Should I be hurting... even before midlife!? The real shock was yet to come. I will never forget the day after we moved. I was down in the basement unpacking some boxes. Our dehumidifier needed to be unpacked, so I decided to just pull it up out of the box. I had prided myself on the fact that I could still do almost everything I had always done. So I have it a yank... and immediately... and dreadfully... and depressingly... I felt a very sharp pain in my back! I almost lost my breath… and I could hardly move! The experience almost caused me to panic. I wondered if I would ever be the same again.

Then there was another day equally as bad. After my shock in the basement I had slowly and quietly recovered -- "nursed that back to health" one might say. It must have just been one of those rare occurrences; I would be just fine! Not! The following crisis was almost worse than the first. I'm not sure what caused it, but I remember lying on our living room floor… and not being able to move because of the pain in my back. What could I do? My wife quickly telephoned a football coach I knew who immediately came over and found me helpless… on the floor. What an embarrassment and what a terrible feeling! I soon understood that I would "live" and that rest and therapy would help me recover. It did… and soon I could walk again. But I often had a sore back… and sometimes a twinge of pain would hit me.

It was about 1989, I was about 47, and we had moved again. I had more time at home, and so that mirror confronted me a bit more often. Having gained about 15 pounds (from my college weight), I really disliked what I saw in the mirror. Yes, I had gotten fat in the middle! True, I wasn't exercising much! Sadly, my cholesterol reading was in the warning zone! And what made it all even worse was that I knew better! There was an answer for all my physical problems and misery. I simply had to change! Yet not so surprising, change came as a friend.

Fortunately, I understood something about "change"

because I had used the idea before -- when I really knew something was wrong... and that it could be right! So the time had come once again. My motivation came from two directions. I felt I desperately wanted to put some things behind me -- that image in the mirror, my bad back and extra weight, the poor cholesterol reading and the feelings of frustration that I knew I was not the person I wanted to be. The other angle was my strong desire to achieve some life-long goals -- like good health, the physical fitness to do all I wanted to do and a more disciplined lifestyle. Simply some satisfaction in front of the mirror wouldn't hurt either. I recognized I could achieve it all with just a little properly directed effort. Yes, and I would watch my progress. It felt good, finally, to get inspired!

There was a plan. I had done research over the past years about some of my problems. For example, there were exercises from the YMCA that people used to get rid of their back pain. Since I didn't have any weights, push-ups would do just fine for building muscle in my arms and chest area. Cutting down on fat was the primary answer to getting down to a better cholesterol reading. So I just decided one day to get started -- some skim milk instead of 1%... my evening ice cream would need to be given up for something lighter... I would do a few push-ups one day for strengthening my upper body... and a little biking the next day for aerobic activity. It was obvious that I didn't need to do much right away... only enough to know I was on my way and having an enjoyable challenge! Clearly, even "the first day" I would be better off than I was the day before. Plus, I wanted to have "a good time" doing what I knew I wanted to continue to do.

At the age of 52, and looking back to that period of time about five or six years ago, I smile to myself thinking about my overall condition. Presently at 145 pounds… with a flat, hard stomach, well developed muscles in my chest and arms, a good cholesterol report, no back pain… and being in the best physical condition of my entire life, I am indeed pleased! But even today I haven't completely succeeded in reaching my goals. I don't remember exactly, but I would imagine I didn't do more than about 10-15 push-ups in a row that first day or week. Now my record is 320. Still, I can't reach that on a regular basis, so I'm still going after more. My other moderate life-style changes are moving along well too. I don't want to give up any of them.

Maybe the whole strategy of finally accomplishing real change is a bit like hitting a few basketball free throws in a row. Why would a person want to stop with such a great feeling of success? Consider the man who has done thousands in a row over many hours. When a person finally gets started on whatever he or she wants to accomplish, and when even one or two successes can develop into a satisfying series and then into a successful habit, and when there is the recognition that every day one can be in the process of moving on to a new level of attainment, and when so much bad is left behind and so much good lies just ahead, why would anyone want call a halt to all those victories and rewards!? I know for sure that I haven't wanted to quit.

In the beginning, the very idea of change can be hard to deal with personally. First of all, what we ultimately want seems so unattainable. Half my life was testimony to the fact that I was dissatisfied with at least one part of me. And my situation had gotten significantly worse over many years. Usually by the time we recognize we want something changed, it seems so powerful and controlling that there doesn't seem to be any other way. I remember that for many years I was simply overwhelmed.

Second, we normally like to have quick solutions to our problems, and if we can't accomplish them immediately, we are tempted to give up. Surely I could have started push-ups at any time over several decades. But I didn't, partly because I figured it might be hard or take too long. We must remember, however, that many things we would like to see changed (such as habits or apparently unresolved problems) in fact, are harder to comprehend or grasp in their small components than they are for us to actually start changing in any particular moment. Maybe for "change" we could say --"its bark is louder than its bite." Putting it in another way, we really have more of a mental or emotional barrier than any significant physical restrictions to most of the things we want to turn around in our lives.

A third barrier is our narrow way of thinking and our unbridled pride. It isn't hard for me to remember my pride and my defense of my activities, while at the very same time I could see I was headed down hill -- deteriorating! Still, it's true that much of the change we have encountered in our lives has been hard for us to bear; so we tend to resist change, no matter what! We tell ourselves that we have done just fine, we are good enough as we are, and we don't need to change. In a sense, the momentum of our lives also tends to push us in the same direction we have always traveled. Most of us have perfected "our way of life", and no matter how detrimental it is to us in the long run, we want to defend our own turf. This isn't so strange, since this "self-preservation" comes out of our basic instinct for survival.

One last reason we hold back from changing our ways is that we are naturally uneasy with anything that is new. Since our infancy, we have always felt the most comfortable with what has been familiar to us. So I might ask myself: Can I start new eating habits, take time out of my day for exercise, and above all, admit that I want to head off in a direction I have never traveled? How will other people react to my change? Will I be really happy with the newness in my life? I can imagine heading down this new path and feeling lost, uneasy, even out of control. So maybe I should just forget it and play it safe. Maybe it all will end in failure.... Yes, there are many reasons that change is not successful. And the "newness" aspect is surely a powerful drawback for most of us. We've had our fill of it!

Considering all of these reasons that we resist change

(which for most of us means getting a new, healthy start in our lives), how can this "study of self image" turn out to be a success story? Well, the truth is that all the above barriers or hindrances to change are rather like "ghosts in the closet" or "monsters under the bed". They certainly are things to be confronted in our heads and our hearts, but even more surely, they are invented visions to be chased away.

Consider once again the above four hurdles we have trouble getting over. Couldn't an overpowering situation also be a great opportunity for success? Isn't our desire for the "quick fix" or our desire to have instant gratification in our lives just an excess of immaturity? Shouldn't we be willing to give up our narrow way of thinking and our excess pride in order to find true satisfaction, fulfillment and happiness in our lives? And finally, can't we think about taking on some "newness" as exciting and fun rather than something that is to be avoided? Yes, with a little courage or a little help from our friends, we can do away with the "monsters" that threaten the change we want and need for healthy, meaningful lives.

I can say with confidence... that acting on my best instincts and taking on needed change in my life is one of the best decisions I ever made for myself. True, some things we do for ourselves can be pretty egocentric and selfish. But when one can see that the goodness and benefits of concrete change enhance all of life -- from the immediate personal impact... and reaching out in unending circles further than one can see -- then one can be in touch with real accomplishment, self-esteem, meaning and hope. I have had fun contemplating "my past" relative to "my future". I feel great satisfaction in my present attainment. And I am enjoying the process of moving toward being the person I want to be. So my success story is unfinished. My self-image is more than just a good look in the mirror. And my hope for you is this -- start any change you want to accomplish. Just do it!

CHAPTER 6

In The Spirit For Christian Survival

"To Choose To Change"

The Holy Bible has been the central standard and resource for the Christian Church... as the Church has laid out its theology down through the ages. Followers of Jesus Christ have also considered the Bible to be the primary inspiration and guide with respect to all matters of faith and life, even as we come closer to the end of the twentieth century. With this in mind, I have chosen a variety of passages from both the Old and New Testaments as touchstones for "a Christian perspective" on the subject of "change." I believe God never changes; yet, we as his creatures are born to change. In Revelation our Lord says from the throne, "I make all things new!" Thankfully, we can enjoy the blessing of recreative change!

It is my conviction that the concept of change is as fundamental to both Testaments... as guilt and sacrifice is to the Old... and as Christ's cross and His Love is to the New. To "repent" means to change -- to admit disobedience and then carry out God's will -- to in a sense "offer sacrifice" and then keep the covenant. And to "follow Jesus" means to change -- to leave the old and go after the new -- in a sense, to be emersed in a kind of "daily baptism" and then live as a "little Christ". No matter when or where we live, change is our "survival kit" on life's difficult and dangerous journey. Through Holy Scripture, God has made known his adequate provisions... that we might go with confidence into the future.

A serious problem arises when we as "God's creatures" feel that we do not need to change. We want to be like God. We lose sight of God's authority and direction. We believe that "we can run our own show" and that we don't need to do things differently. In our day, this becomes evident as right and wrong are made relative to personal perspectives and social fads. Fundamental moral codes are discarded as outdated. And Christian faith is treated casually as intellectual agreement or emotional experience. Sadly, our faith seems no longer understood as confidence in a higher calling or as surrender to servanthood in the power of The Spirit. "Cheap grace" comes to mind as comfortable worship is popularized with empty words rather than valuable actions. This worship is at best "superficial" and maybe at worst "poor entertainment", especially when we consider that God wants us to work out our reverence for him with acts of justice, self-giving love and humble service. So in an age of hate and violence and injustice and fear and self-centeredness and materialism and superficial religion, where do we see change... or even the desire to change?

The time has come for a new re-formation of the fellowship of the faithful -- the Christian Church. And significant change is necessary for every person to carry out that re-formation. The evidence shows that our church-led-society is acting out nearly the opposite life-style that Jesus came to reveal... as The Way, The Truth and The Life. Changeable, committed Christians will understand that in Jesus, God intended that his life-giving Word be put into action... into flesh... into doing self-giving love for Christ's sake. So God's Word in Christ is meant to be made flesh in us here and now! When that happens, mere words of worship will give way to deeds of discipleship. Change through the power of The Holy Spirit will reveal acts of love and peace and concern and courage and self-giving and service... as well as true respect and reverence for our creator, redeemer and comforter.

It is my hope that through our study of the scriptures, we as individuals and as communities of the faithful will not only see the importance and urgency of change in our daily lives, but also will take specific steps to make that change concrete. We will do it to benefit ourselves and our neighbors, as well as our relationship to Almighty God. When we get back to change as a daily essential in our living, we will find the true freedom, meaning and eternal happiness that our creator intended for us from the beginning. We will experience "daily baptism"... and find that what we have messed up, Christ will wash away. What has deteriorated in our lives, Christ will make new. What we face as a hopeless problem, Christ will provide the power and wisdom to solve. Change is a beautiful thing to behold! For as Paul put it to the Philippians...

"He will change our weak mortal bodies and make them like his own glorious body, using that power by which he is able to bring all things under his rule."

In the Beginning (Genesis 1:1-3:24)

God's action within the history of the human race begins with **an unspoken yet explosive dynamic -- change!** The concept of "change" is a fundamental factor that underlies the entire account of the creator God's interaction with mankind. In the beginning, God chooses to change that which is formless, desolate and dark into "the universe" bathed in light. And God was pleased; and it was good! In the creation of people, God passed on **the ability to choose and to change**. It is not long before these special people make the choice to "expand their appetite". They decide to go on their own... to ease off on the rules... to satisfy their unlimited desires. But in so doing, they separate themselves from God's life-giving will and purpose. As a result of their choice, they changed what God intended and hurt themselves; and they experienced arrogance, fear, struggle, pain and death. We note that **choice has its consequences**... and not always good ones.

The Straight and Narrow (Genesis 12:1-24:60)

There are those individuals who seem to want to see things from "the divine perspective". **Abraham** was one of those people. He seemed to understand what God wanted and he tried to do it. **He was open to new direction**. There were no arguments or excuses. There was no worry that he would lose too much by following God's command. Yet it wasn't clear sailing. The Lord said to Abraham, "Leave your native land, your relatives, and your father's home, and go to a country that I am going to show you." How's that for a challenging change?

Sometimes it's not easy to go ahead with change. **Many people today don't want to give up** their comforts, friends, security, etc., for anything or anyone. However, Abraham was willing, and he chose to change the direction of his life, apparently based on faith alone. He is one of the best examples of one who "takes that leap into the unknown" simply out of a deep sense of loyalty, commitment and faithfulness. His God had given him promises and had kept them. His God had calmed him and taken away his fear. His God had led him through inner struggle to make wise decisions. Putting it simply, **he was empowered for change**. Yes, Abraham knew and trusted the source of his hope and well-being. He weathered upheaval and struggle -- ultimately for his own benefit and God's glory. And Abraham was richly blessed to be a blessing. What an example!

From Slavery to Freedom (Exodus 1:1-40:38)

Many years after Abraham, the People of Israel were slaves in Egypt doing hard labor. They suffered under severe taskmasters, who made their lives increasingly difficult. The Israelites were a people crushed physically and spiritually. In their sufferings they cried out to be rescued from their oppressors. From deep within they **yearned for a change**. God heard their cry and called Moses to be instrumental in bringing about their escape. As a self proclaimed "nobody", Moses was not confident about his role in their release from bondage under the Egyptians. But God reassured Moses and **provided a helper to aid him** in carrying out the plan of liberation. "The departure" was finally accomplished and the Israelites crossed the Red Sea to freedom. They entered the desert to find struggle, turmoil and testing as God's chosen people, before finally entering The Promised Land.

The Exodus -- **"The Departure"** -- has tremendous depth of meaning for The People of Israel and Christians because it focuses on **freedom, hope and salvation**. These are some of the most basic elements of "the faith" for those who give testimony to the Creator, Redeemer and Comforter. And they point to "change" as the creative center for "new life". To choose... to change! We too in a moment of revelation cry out from our misery and seek help from on high to find freedom **from that which tears us down**. We too have been crushed physically and spiritually; and Our Lord has heard our cry! Change can arise through those called and chosen by God to work out the details of setting the impulse in motion. (And even chosen ones need their assistants.)

We are weak and our God is strong to bring about the newness we desire so desperately. On the move toward the goal, **it's natural to want "The Promised Land"** of freedom and blessing **immediately**. Yet, it is not unusual that in our process of change we need to go through the desert of struggle, turmoil and testing. We are not perfect. There are those slip-ups. There is also fear of the unknown ahead and fear of the change we want. We may even give up seeking the goal of our desires. Being **tested and tried, we are** reminded of who we are... and whose we are... and what it takes to be **strengthened for goodness**. Through it all, still we can choose. To change or not to change... that is the question. But **venturing back** to the source of our hope -- to Him that has provided our release -- **and keeping in touch** with those who throw us the "life-preservers", **we can finally achieve our goals.**

The Choice and The Witness (Joshua 1:1-24:28)

The book of Joshua is a thrilling story about the Israelite conquest of Canaan -- the Promised Land -- the land flowing with milk and honey. The Children of Israel had finally arrived, and **Joshua was** the man of the moment -- the successor of Moses, who was in charge of **leading them to their promised destiny.** Yet their troubles were not over. Maybe **their struggles were** in fact **multiplied** with all the pleasures and luxuries that confronted them and that they began to enjoy!

After the tribes of Israel had secured the land and before Joshua's death, their great leader **put into perspective all that had been accomplished and what the future might hold.** He spoke about all the Lord God had done for them and how he had kept all his promises. They had come a long way -- from Egypt as slaves all the way to controlling a land of plenty. Finally, he put it to them straight: "Now, honor the Lord and serve him sincerely and faithfully. **Get rid of the gods** which your ancestors used to worship in Mesopotamia and in Egypt, and serve only the Lord. If you are not willing to serve him, **decide today whom you will serve**... As for my family and me, we will serve the Lord."

Joshua's speech had been made and his loyalties were clear; but the question he asked the people was crucial. They replied that they would never leave the Lord to serve other gods. But Joshua reminded them that **they might not be able to serve the Lord...** and that he wouldn't tolerate any rivals. Again the people said that they would serve the Lord. Joshua was persistent: "**You are your own witnesses to the fact that you have chosen to serve the Lord**." They responded, "Yes, we are witnesses." "Then get rid of those foreign gods that you have... and pledge your loyalty," he demanded. And the people said, "We will serve the Lord our God. We will obey his commands." Finally **Joshua** made a covenant for the people that day... and **gave them laws and rules**

to follow. And he wrote these commands in the book of the Law of God. Then he took a large stone and set it up...and said to all the people, **"This stone will be our witness**.... So it will be a witness against you, to keep you from rebelling against your God." The deciding had been done. The choice was clear.

This account can easily bring to mind Peter's three-time denial of Jesus before he was crucified. Peter -- the one who drew his sword to protect Jesus -- was so quickly and easily led to disloyalty. So Joshua must have had some hint as to how easily the peoples' **vows of loyalty could be forgotten -- how transitory it often is to choose and to change**. Consequently, **he wrote down their words** to be remembered forever, **and he set up a visual testimony** or witness to the choice they had made. All this was to benefit them... that they might be kept from rebelling.

The idea of change is often initially quite attractive to people who are made aware of benefits that might be gained. Like the Israelites who willingly decided to go "the new way", many in our society jump at the chance to do the right thing for their present and future welfare. **Words and promises and testimonies come easily.** People are excited and hopeful. And then the realities of real everyday living set in.

Changing direction and **leaving behind the bad choices made in the past isn't easy** for people of any time or place. There are many distractions and temptations to stray from the straight and narrow -- the new commitment.

Joshua knew that the Lord's Chosen Ones would have difficulty "serving the Lord". And so he pressed them for their real intentions... in order to try to help them understand the significance of their choice and verify their convictions. In the end, even **their repeated vows** of loyalty **were** apparently **not good enough** to make sure they carried out their decision for the future. Joshua felt **a concrete visual documentation was necessary** to remind the people of their intended plans and course of action. Beyond that, he even laid out a kind of game plan for them to follow.

Likewise, **today, our willing choice to change is often found fleeting** over the long term. In the final analysis, that fickle part of **our human nature demands** that we repeatedly confirm our intentions to change... and even document those convictions concretely. Only then will we have the **encouragement and support** necessary to finally find the rewards of change we so urgently want and need.

Amos: The Call to Change (Amos 1:1-6:7)

Perhaps no Old Testament prophet saw **the urgent necessity** for change more clearly than Amos. As the "Good News Bible" puts it, the eighth century B.C. "... was a time of great prosperity, notable religious piety, and apparent security. But Amos saw that prosperity was limited to the wealthy, and that it fed on injustice and on oppression of the poor. Religious observance was insincere, and security more apparent than real.

With passion and courage he preached that God would punish the nation."

Amos spoke the word of the Lord and issued **a call to repentance** ...a call to turn around... **a call to change!** The positive and negative consequences were laid out in no uncertain terms. To change would mean life, mercy and restoration; not to change would mean sorrow, disaster and exile. **The alternatives were radical and overwhelming:**

"**Go to the Lord**, and you will live. **If you do not go**, he will sweep down like fire... **You are doomed**, you that twist justice and cheat people out of their rights! You people hate anyone who challenges injustice and speaks the whole truth in court. You have oppressed the poor... **Make it your aim to do what is right**, not what is evil, **so that you may live**.... Perhaps the Lord will be merciful to the people of this nation who are still left alive.

The Lord says, "I hate your religious festivals; I cannot stand them! When you bring me burnt offerings and grain offerings, I will not accept them... **Stop** your noisy songs; I do not want to listen to your harps. Instead, **let justice flow like a stream**, and righteousness like a river that never goes dry.... How terrible it will be for you that have such an easy life... you do not mourn over the ruin of Israel. So you will be the first to go into exile.

Does this prophetic word come **close to home** for those of us who live in the United States in the twentieth century? If so, we urgently need change. Do those of us who live in luxury and apparent security need to repent of our lack of serious concern over **the plight of the poor**? If God knows this is our sin, we should be thinking about change. Do we who live **the easy life with more than enough** food and drink and material wealth have the insight and courage to redirect our priorities into carrying out actions more pleasing to our Lord? If we have gained such insight, then change is the answer. Do we have sincere worship of the Lord of Love and self-giving and sacrifice when we continue to proudly sing our noisy songs of praise... and sink more and more into **the idols we have made of our expensive church buildings**? At the same time, we mouth our narrow minded scriptural doctrines and complain to one another how unhappy we are with the people who live off welfare. **Our Lord** knows what is in our hearts... and he **calls us to change**. So how is justice and righteousness doing these days? Is it flowing like a river?

Change, in Christian terms, cuts to the roots of sin and self-centeredness. Basically, it **means to "plead guilty"** to the undesirable in our lives -- **to turn around** and go in the opposite direction. If we are not open to change we are not in fact open to "the faith of Abraham" and "the discipleship of Christ." Not being able to see **the need to lose ourselves and our selfish egos** in the Lord of love and life, we will be forever doomed to sorrow, deterioration and a tragic ending. We are created and reborn for bringing a fresh, life-giving perspective to the world... for newness and renewal and liberation. In truth, **we as Christians are "in our element"** when we are **in the process of change**, for we are led by our Lord! Ages ago, "the Word made flesh" spoke through the prophet Amos.

Winning the Battle (Daniel 1:1-6:28)

There is probably no Old Testament story more interesting to both young and old alike than the story of **"Daniel in the lion's den."** Not only does the story of Daniel have intrigue, excitement, a moving message and a wonderful ending, but it also shows people of all times and places **a panoramic overview of the dynamics of change.** From very early in history, people have wrestled within themselves as well as with external circumstances to get a grasp on **when and how to choose** as well as **when and what to change**. The Biblical account of Daniel gives us many illustrations and insights in dealing with this struggle.

Daniel lived during **a time** when the Jews endured great suffering because **of persecution and oppression**. Around 580 BC, the Babylonians attacked Jerusalem and captured the King of Judah. Daniel and some of his friends were picked out from among the exiles to serve in the royal court and then taken to Babylon. There Daniel made up his mind that **he was not going to be conformed to the new culture around him.** Meanwhile, God gave Daniel impressive leadership skills as well as the ability to interpret visions and dreams. In fact, Daniel was so successful in explaining the Babylonian King's dreams that he was rewarded and promoted to supervise and look after the King's interests. That's when Daniel's personal troubles began. A number of other leaders in high office were jealous and tried to find a way to destroy him. They nearly succeeded.

In Babylon it was not difficult for Daniel's enemies to get the king to sign a binding law that only the king, "Your Majesty", should be worshipped. Anyone found violating the law would be thrown into a pit filled with lions. Since **Daniel remained faithful** to the God of his fathers and gave regular witness to that fact in prayer, Daniel was soon seen praying and the king was notified. Even though **the king** was upset and tried to find a way for Daniel to escape, he finally was forced to comply with the law. He **ordered Daniel thrown to the lions**... but also voiced his hope that Daniel's God whom he served so faithfully would save him. The king then sealed the pit and spent a sleepless night in worry and turmoil.

The next day the king hurried to the pit and found that **Daniel was not hurt**. The lions' mouths were closed. He was overjoyed and ordered Daniel pulled out of the pit. He then gave orders that Daniel's accusers be arrested and thrown to the lions. They did not survive. Finally, **the king wrote** to the people of all nations, "I command that throughout my empire **everyone should fear and respect Daniel's God**. He is a living God, and he will rule forever... **He saves and rescues**; he performs wonders and miracles..." And Daniel prospered during the reign of the king.

Quite a story indeed -- filled with unusual twists and

turns, good and bad choices, and changes... from concealed tricks and mood swings to international decrees! **We can identify with Daniel's world.** Maybe we are not as much in the public eye nor as popular as Daniel. And maybe it seems like we don't have so much to win or lose by our decisions and opportunities. But we do recognize the fundamental influences and challenges of life.

At times we feel **as though we are in a foreign land: pressures** to live in a new way; **temptations** to conform to that which hurts and destroys us; **conflicts** with traditional values; **difficulties** of loneliness with feelings of abandonment; and the list goes on. Yet we know that we are nurtured and sustained by a faithful community. **Shall we change or shall we reaffirm** that which is good and right and true? And then what will we do with those new challenges of learning, which hit us "flat in the face."

Obviously we have no choice but to face them. But how? Next there is the challenge to our security which seems to turn our world upside down. **Do we give up? Do we "sell out"** our convictions to stay on top? Then "the worst" happens and we feel doomed. Our self esteem or our closest companion or our own physical well-being may be threatened. **Change**... the kind that is **uncontrollable** and takes place **without warning**... this is hard. **But choice remains**.

There is **another kind of change** we see in the story of Daniel. This is the kind that **we can control** and that we can use to make a solid impact on the future, hopefully for good! Daniel was in the process of being "changed" or "renewed" or "modified" by persisting in prayer in his faithfulness to God, rather than be turned around to a false way of life. So **in our positive assertions**, under pressure to do the opposite, we too can be **strengthened and positioned for future victory**, freedom and abundant living. We too can know what is right, choose what is right and do what is right. In the process we can be made new.

This same determination comes into play as we persist against all odds... thrown into the so called "pit of lions." Relying on our faith, strengthened over the years, **our negative emotions can be held in check** and we can remain cool and calm and in control of that which could destroy us. We are in the process of steadily strengthening the good and changing for the better what is inside us and around us. **Knowing freedom from fear of "beasts and men"** there is great security and self confidence in facing all of life's adversities. We can go up against "the worst" and know in our hearts that **with God's help** -- the God who works wonders, saves and rescues -- **we can turn the tide... little by little.** Yes, we are **in the process of change. We are victorious!** We are free! We are hopeful! We are happy!

Receiving "Good News!" (Matthew 1:18-5:48)

The New Testament begins with **the birth of Jesus Christ** -- the Lord of all creation -- "the change agent" above all others! This foreordained birth **brings good**

news to the whole world... and unheard of change! The promised Savior comes to save the world from sin: "For God so loved the world that he gave his only son, that whoever believes in him should not perish, but have everlasting life."

In essence, the birth of "Immanuel" -- God is with us -- brought **forgiveness, hope, abundant life and salvation to all those willing to change allegiance**. And so John the Baptist prepared the way for Jesus, preaching: "Turn away from your sins, because the Kingdom of Heaven is near!" He told everyone who would listen that there was **no way they could escape** the punishment of their hurtful and destructive actions, **unless they repented** and acted differently. Then Jesus was baptized... and the Spirit of God came down on him... and he began his ministry. He offered a changed life and a new way of living to all who followed him.

As Jesus began calling his disciples, he went all over preaching the **Good News about the Kingdom... and healing people** who had all kinds of disease and sickness. Large crowds followed him and he began to teach them:

"Happy are those who mourn; God will comfort them! Happy are those who are humble; they will receive what God has promised!... Happy are those who are merciful to others; God will be merciful to them! Happy are the pure in heart; they will see God! Happy are those who work for peace; God will call them his children!

Jesus announced that **true happiness and blessing is**

found under his Father's reign and authority. So all of Jesus' uplifting words were passed on with the urgent necessity that his followers come **to know and do the Father's will**. He proclaimed a message which called for **"a divine revolution"** -- the truths of the Kingdom of Heaven replacing all earthly rules and traditions. He spoke with authority and made himself explicitly clear in telling his hearers that they must... turn away... **change** their ways!

"...whoever disobeys even the least important of the commandments... will be the least in the Kingdom. On the other hand, **whoever obeys** the Law **and teaches** others to do the same, **will be great...**You have heard that people were told... Do not commit murder... But now I tell you: whoever is angry.... You have heard that it was said, 'An eye for an eye, and a tooth for a tooth.' But now I tell you: **do not take revenge** on someone who wrongs you.... You have heard that it was said, 'Love your friends, hate your enemies.' But now I tell you: **love your enemies** and pray for those who persecute you, so that you may become the sons of your Father in heaven."

It couldn't have been put any more clearly. Jesus told the people in no uncertain terms that they needed to leave one thing... and go for another, if they wanted to inherit abundant and eternal life. They would have to be willing to **change** the **direction** of their lives, in order **to reap the rewards** the Father had in store for them.

In essence, God's Son -- **Jesus** -- began and ended his existence on earth as **the greatest agent of change** the world has ever seen. As "the Word made flesh", his whole life was given to help people change their loyalty and priorities -- to act and live out a new way of life. This would be done under **the influence of love, forgiveness and a creative spirit**, rather than under the control of the law, guilt and the penalty of deterioration and death. Jesus **encouraged and nurtured change in people** by... 1) calling for repentance, clearly pointing out the consequences of their present actions, 2) showing and teaching about the happiness and blessings of the new way, and finally, 3) through his own goodness and love, giving them the power to enter the process of knowing full and abundant living. In his inspiration, forgiveness and healing, Jesus brought faith, hope and love to anyone who was in need. **He was like the mother's womb for the father's love**. And he persisted with planning and insight to the end, seeking to save and liberate the whole world.

Getting to the Goal (Mark 10:17-31)

Jesus' encounter with **"the rich man"** gives us insight into the costs and benefits of change. A certain man who apparently had plenty of wealth came to the "Good Teacher" **looking for something else** -- something a bit different than what he already possessed. **All that he had... didn't seem like quite enough**. So he asked, "What must I do to receive eternal life?" By his question, we can infer that the rich man knew **something would be asked of him**. In fact, Jesus pointed out the requirements of the commandments, which he claimed to have obeyed.

So far, so good! But then Jesus got straight to the point... with love... and said, "**You need only one thing**. Go and sell all you have and give the money to the poor, and you will have riches in heaven; then come and **follow me**." We are told that when the man heard this, gloom spread over his face, and he went away sad, because he was very rich.

One of the necessities of achieving change is to count the cost of the goal desired. The man who came up to Jesus had a good idea of what **he was lacking -- eternal life** -- that which is much more durable than fleeting wealth. But he certainly didn't understand what was necessary to attain it. This was a high goal indeed! Even Jesus' disciples didn't quite grasp what was needed. After the disappointed man left, Jesus said to his followers, "**How hard it will be for rich people** to enter the Kingdom of God! It is much harder for a rich person to enter the Kingdom of God than for a camel to go through the eye of a needle." The disciples were shocked and amazed.

Jesus made clear to his listeners that anything -- **any change -- is possible with God's power**. Then Peter spoke up, "Look, we have left everything and followed you." And Jesus responded, "Yes, and I tell you that **anyone who leaves** home or brothers or sisters or mother or **father or children or fields for me** and for the gospel, will receive much more in this present age. He will receive a hundred times more... and persecutions as well; and in the age to come he **will receive eternal life**."

There it was.. all laid out clearly: The change necessary for this goal was radical enough to send most of us packing! On the other hand, in touch with God's power, everything is possible.

Often when we look directly into the face of radical change, **we are overwhelmed and shocked by noting where we are... and** then getting a glimpse of **where we want to go**. The rich man undoubtedly had lived his whole life accumulating possessions. Who knows where it began. Probably as a boy he started out on that path of **piling up more and more... until** he had "a lot" by most standards. But when had he really become wealthy? Little by little, bit by bit, it had increased on him until it was his center -- he worshipped it! That change happened so slowly, he maybe never was aware of when **it had finally controlled him**... and when he could never leave it. Finally, somehow it hit him that **there was something more eternal!** That would be nice too. **But by then it was too late**, for Jesus enabled him to see the power that had captivated him. He left a sad and gloomy man.

Looking at **what we need to do** in order to make a desired turn-around often **fills us with fear**. The wealthy man was fearful of **letting loose** of his identity **of wealth and** his power of **control**. After all, his whole life was tied up in this. Surely he felt uneasy and disoriented. He was comfortable in his greedy habits. **This new thing was foreign to him** and he resisted it. Beyond that, who would be in charge here? He could not imagine giving up all that he had worked so hard to attain... in order to follow another. **The rich man was different from the disciples, who** had left everything to follow Jesus. Apparently they had not passed "the point of no return" with their accumulations, priorities and loyalties. Where those who answered Jesus' call **were open to the** great possibilities and promises of the **change Jesus asked for**, in the case of the rich man, **we witness his final rejection of** the glimpse he had of the eternal. He also lost a multiplication of the happiness that might have been in store for him had he shifted his loyalty to **the Kingdom of God**.

We live today in a materialistic land, where wealth and riches are glorified by the masses. It is important we realize that **the rich man represents a failed opportunity for eternal and abundant living** in every time and place. On the other hand, Jesus and his disciples give us insight into everything that is ultimately in our best interests as we go about our daily lives. **Every person in every moment is called** to be a citizen of the Kingdom of God --to live on earth as though in transition to an eternal destiny --to focus on divine truth and not settle in too deeply with all that the world values --to stay a safe distance from that which has power to captivate us and tear us down --to live in service and self-giving --to live out a life of faith, hope, and love --yes, and **to be open to ongoing change... following** the upward call of **Christ Jesus our Lord!**

Change that Heals (Luke 5:17-32 & 6:27-36)

The Gospel of **Luke presents** Jesus as the promised Savior of all mankind. An angel joyfully announces the birth of the holy child, "I bring you **good news of great joy that** will be for all the people." This good news **reaches people with all kinds of needs**. Luke, the physician, shows deep interest in how the Son of **God heals and rebuilds the lives of those who come to him**. With concern for the sick, lost and troubled, Luke focuses on important relationships in his classic accounts of the Good Samaritan, the Lost Son, and the Rich Man and Lazarus. The healing, redemptive power of forgiveness, love and concern is made evident over and over again. The Savior's gifts come to all **who are open to changed lives** -- to those who desire to know the secrets of the Kingdom of God and let His power reign within them.

Maybe no one in Luke's Gospel was more radically changed by Jesus' healing power than **the man who was paralyzed**. He truly experienced new life in both body and soul. Within moments, he **was moved from grief to joy** -- from sadness to praise!

This man on his bed had been brought to Jesus during a time when Jesus was teaching and healing many people. The day that he arrived, the crowds were so great that his friends had to lower him down through a roof in order for Jesus to see him. When **Jesus saw their faith**, he said to the man, "Your sins are forgiven, my friend." But there were those who felt Jesus had committed blasphemy, for only God can forgive sins. Jesus knew their thoughts and asked, "Is it easier to say, **'Your sins are forgiven'** or to say, **'Get up and walk'**? I will prove to you that **the Son of Man has authority** on earth to forgive sins." So he said to the paralyzed man, "I tell you, get up, pick up your bed, and go home!" At once the man got up in front of them all, took the bed he had been lying on, and went home, praising God. They were all completely amazed!

Here is a detailed account about how The Savior -- **The Change Agent** above all others -- completely turned around a man's life. We can only imagine **how passionately the paralyzed man desired to get in touch with that power** he hoped would change and heal him. Apparently even his friends thought there was hope, for they got him as far as they could -- in front of Jesus. In the presence of the Promised One, who had been called to "bring good news to the poor... proclaim liberty to the captives and recovery of sight to the blind," he had no doubts. Jesus saw their faith and knew that **the man's most pressing need was to be** forgiven and **raised up spiritually**. So almost immediately his sins were wiped away and he was free to go into the future as a new person. Yet he also soon found himself with even more reason for rejoicing. Get up from your bed and go home! What a spiritual and **physical transformation** that was -- no more bondage! Changed and healed **almost beyond belief!** A new way of life -- all coming from Jesus' power and authority. What an inspiration to praise God!

This is truly exciting testimony concerning the Savior, who brings change and healing into the lives of those who want his help. We recognize that the power of **The Holy Spirit even today can bring similar life-fulfilling blessings to people** -- people who are open to the change that goes with faithful and abundant living under His power and authority. True freedom of body and soul is as close as a person's earnest desire for help; for Jesus and **his power is always on the side of the captive and needy**. In touch with the Savior, we must understand that the liberation of our inner bondage is the most important and enduring gift he can give us. **Getting over the past is what steadies us and** gets us started with hope for the future. Then with our inner peace and freedom assured, we experience change that **can affect healing** in all of the rest of our life's struggles. Being reborn, the "inner child" can look for the creative response and rejoice in the fresh new perspective. Life can be fun and exciting again!

Think how the self-esteem of **the healed man** was improved... just in knowing that his persistence had paid off, say nothing of being raised up for new opportunities. Yet in the beginning, he **had to let go of pride and acknowledge that he needed help.** Only then could Jesus have an impact on his life. This was made even more clear when a bit later **Jesus called** a tax collector named Levi (Matthew) to follow him. He left everything and followed. But the not so needy, proud and independent curiosity seekers of that locale complained that Jesus shouldn't be associating with the lower class and outcasts

-- people like Levi. So Jesus answered them, "People who are well do not need a doctor, but only those who are sick. I have not come to call the righteous but **sinners to repentance.**"

Yes, we remember that Jesus is the kind of Savior who leaves the ninety-nine sheep to go and look for the one that gets lost. He is so happy when he finds it and carries it home... that he calls his friends together to **celebrate**! He concludes, "There is more joy in heaven over **one sinner who repents** than over ninety-nine respectable people who do not need to repent."

There are **people of every time and place** who do not want to acknowledge need or helplessness or suffering. There are those who **don't want to admit guilt or to accept a higher authority.** There are even those who don't want to try out that new idea or strike out in a different direction... even to find newness. They are uneasy and disoriented by anything that seems unfamiliar or challenging. **Such people have no need of a Savior, because they are unwilling to be open to change.** But for those who seek out... and cry out... and act out... there is power and authority to initiate change that heals.

The power behind healed, refreshed and recreated lives... is as special, radical and divine as the new birth announced by angels. **Jesus** announces his Father's Kingdom and **offers unheard of strategies for new ways of living**... on earth as in heaven. He speaks candidly to those open for change:

"**Love your enemies**, do good to those who hate you, bless those who curse you, and **pray for those who mistreat you**. If anyone hits you on one cheek, let him hit the other one too; if someone takes your coat, let him have your shirt as well... If you love only the people who love you, why should you receive a blessing? Even sinners love those who love them! And if you do good only to those who do good to you, why should you receive a blessing? Even sinners do that!... No! Love your enemies and do good to them; lend and expect nothing back. **You will then have a great reward**, and you will be sons of the Most High God."

The world has never heard such a prescription for change. **These words affect our lives so deeply** that we are nearly repulsed at the suggestion. Yet can anyone deny the value of these divine guidelines for living? The question is, "**Are we open to** this new approach to relationships... as well as to the power and blessings that follow?" "Do we want to welcome **this unique approach** to life... and carry the name "Christian" **as children of the Most High God?**" The healing we truly need will only be ours if we listen to our Savior's voice and act on his advice to get up and begin a new way of life. **The rewards certainly will come** as we are caught up **in the process of change...** and get into the joyful celebration of thanking and praising God!

Being Born Again (John 3:1-21)

Jesus was the eternal Word of God -- "the source of life" which **brought light to mankind**. He became a human being and lived among us, full of grace and truth... **giving us one blessing after another**. So it was that a leader named Nicodemus went to Jesus one night and acknowledged that he knew that Jesus was sent from God... considering the miracles he performed. Jesus answered, "No on can **see the Kingdom of God** unless he is born again." "How can a grown man be **born again**?" Nicodemus asked. "He certainly cannot enter his mother's womb and be born a second time!" "I am telling you the truth," replied Jesus, "that no one can enter the Kingdom of God unless he is born **of water and the Spirit**..." "How can this be?" asked Nicodemus.

Many of us are mystified how and why Jesus expects us to go through such **a radical change in order to see and know** the **wonderful blessings** the Father has in store for us. The truth is that Jesus knows that we, like Nicodemus, have become conformed to the world's ways -- those dark, evil deeds that can't stand the light. They eventually lead us to deterioration, sadness and destruction. **We slowly slide into the ways of the world** that put our minds, bodies and souls in chains and that are unproductive of true love and joy and thankfulness. We find ourselves falling **asleep in darkness**... and living in weakness... **and hurting to death**... and not ready for real, satisfying celebration. Only by looking at life through a new perspective will we be able to enter

His divine Kingdom. **So Jesus has come to show us the way to abundant life**, if we would only yield to his insight.

"For **God loved the world so much** that he gave his only Son, so that everyone who believes in him may not die but have eternal life. For God did not send his Son into the world to be its judge, but to be its Savior."

Consequently, Jesus indicated to this Jewish leader and to those of us who hear him... that **we need to be reborn** --to get a new life, as it were --**to receive "eternal life"** through being cleansed and separated from our rebellion --**to share "family blessings"** which the power of God intended for us from the beginning --**to rejoice in "a new viewpoint and a new start"** which seeks the light and truth and love of God the Father, Son and Holy Spirit. Jesus tells us that he has come as **"The Savior"** for the purpose of liberating us from our destructive past. Yes, and he **has come to inspire us to a changed life** that leads us to all that we were meant to be in God's sight.

The Son of God knows how to free us to be at our best. As our Lord he takes the lead to reveal and share **re-creational love. Receiving that love...** and being born again... is like the "bolt out of the blue" that **purifies and empowers us to enter the Kingdom.** We are **forever being changed and made new!** And the miracles and blessings continue...

Catching The Spirit of Change (Acts 2:1-47)

When the day of Pentecost came, all **the believers** were gathered together in one place. Suddenly there was a noise from the sky which sounded like a strong wind blowing, and it filled the whole house where they were sitting. Then they saw what looked like tongues of fire which spread out and touched each person there. They **were all filled with the Holy Spirit** and began to talk in other languages, as the Spirit enabled them to speak.

These first four verses from the second chapter of Acts give witness to an event that Christians recognize as "the birthday of the Christian Church." **This "birth event" gave testimony** to people who had come from all corners of the world **that a big change was beginning to be celebrated**. The followers of Jesus Christ were inspired to "come out" of their confines and speak about the new spirit that had come upon them -- the Holy Spirit of the risen Christ. Much like witnesses to the birth of a new baby, **the observers were excited and amazed** by what they saw. The meaning of it all was conveyed by Peter with the other eleven apostles as they spoke to the crowd concerning the consequences of this pouring out of the Holy Spirit: Because Jesus had been raised to the right side of God, his Father, many miraculous **gifts would be given** to His people... just **as He had promised.** With repentance, baptism in the name of Jesus Christ and forgiveness of sin, the transforming Spirit of the risen Lord would be available. Many people responded... and the fellowship of believers was born.

At Pentecost, **"those who believed" were seen catching the Spirit of change**. This was prominent change -- celebrated change -- and that change is still applauded -- yes, celebrated! Those people who were caught up in Christ's spirit... proclaiming his message and performing miracles and wonders... were certainly pleased to be so moved. **This kind of change came** to them as Jesus had greeted them in the flesh -- **as a confidant and friend.** Their lives were not the same. They spent their time in learning from the apostles, taking part in the fellowship, and sharing in the meals and the prayers. All the believers continued in close fellowship and shared their belongings with one another. They would sell their property and possessions, and distribute the money among all, according to what each one needed. It was recorded that they met as a group daily, eating together in their homes with glad and humble hearts, praising God and enjoying the good will of all the people. And **every day more were added**.

Today we look back at the beginning of this "religious movement" and realize that it was inspired by The Lord, who centuries later is still praised as **The Way, The Truth and The Life**. Jesus' loving presence among his people **brings recreative** and yes, miraculous **powers to those who are open** to being led in a heavenly direction. All who are a part of His Body the Christian Church are committed by baptism to his authority -- his proposals for revolutionary change in their lives. **Being moved to ongoing change** in the power of the Spirit **is essentially what it means to be a disciple of Christ.**

Those early believers were **meant to enjoy a new way of life...** and so are Christ's followers today. **On Pentecost, Peter** spoke in a loud voice about the rebellion of the people and how they had crucified Jesus. He **laid out what they had done... and the consequences** of their self-centered sin. Apparently many of **his listeners "saw the light"** so to speak, because they were deeply troubled **and asked, "What shall we do?"** And Peter had an answer for them... the same answer he has for those who would be saved from bondage in the here and now, "You must turn away...!" Yes, **"You must change!" There's no way around it.** And when you are committed to this process of renewal... there will be miracles and wonders, salvation and security, fellowship and good will.

The miracle and wonder of **the gift of the Spirit** is spread out as the fellowship of the faithful **is blessed with "the ripple effect".** As believers share with one another the goodness of their Lord, many **other people take notice... and desire to catch the spirit of change.** What moves one person to realize **"a new way of living" radiates out** to touch and influence others in glorious ways, multiplying joy and good will! Nurturing and encouraging that change which reduces guilt, suffering and deterioration, while at the same time enhances meaningful and abundant new life -- **this is addictive to thankfulness** and praise! **It's fun!** The rain drops fall one by one... and together they offer the possibility of "great change" and "many rewards" in a land thirsty for healing and wholeness!

Chosen to be Winners (I Cor. 1:26-30; 9:24-27)

The Apostle Paul -- possibly the most **radically changed** follower of Jesus Christ -- **was chosen to be a winner!** He had his life almost instantly turned around as "a light from the sky flashed around him" on his journey to Damascus. Earlier, as a young man named Saul, **he had persecuted the followers of Jesus**, trying to destroy the church. After being filled with the Holy Spirit, Paul's powerful preaching had the impact of establishing many churches... on several missionary journeys. One such church was in the city of Corinth. This servant of The Lord wrote his first letter to the Corinthian **Christians** in order to deal with problems of faith and life that had arisen among them. He wanted them to know that they **had been chosen to be winners too.**

"**Now remember what you were**, my brothers, when God called you. From the human point of view few of you were wise or powerful or of high social standing. God purposely chose what the world considers nonsense in order to shame the wise, and **he chose what the world considers weak** in order to shame the powerful. He chose what the world looks down on and despises and thinks is nothing, in order to destroy what the world thinks is important. This means that **no one can boast** in God's presence. But God has brought you into union with Christ Jesus, and God has made Christ to be our wisdom. By him we are put right with God; **we become God's holy people and are set free.**"

This short paragraph in Paul's letter to the church in

Corinth relates directly to **the identity** of his friends in Christ Jesus. Remember what you were when you were called into the Kingdom, Paul more or less says to them; face it -- **you were in bondage,** weak, foolish, **and in need of help**; but that's exactly where you needed to be for God to work his miracle. In fact, no one can boast before God. **"God's way" is to chose precisely those who are looking for freedom from the past... and for change** in their lives. So you were in the right spot at the right time, in a sense, just as I was when I was chosen and raised up for union with Christ Jesus.

Paul says that essentially, **Jesus does it all!** First of all, as our Savior, **He takes care of the past mess-ups we give him...** and is our perfect stand-in before God. **He gives us a new heart for change.** Then He assures us of our status as a holy people, becoming our wisdom... and showing us "the best way" in our daily living. **We choose to change.** And finally, we are set free for the future! As Christ's obedient servants, his death and resurrection has set us free for glorious new opportunities and enduring happiness. **The process of change is inspired by the cross of Christ.**

Paul knew that his message about Christ's death on the cross was offensive to the Jews and nonsense to the Gentiles. On the other hand, for those being saved, this message made clear the power of God and the wisdom of God. The bottom line revealed that what human insight considered foolish and weak, Jesus had turned into God's wisdom and power. **Paul understood turnaround...**

change... new life... **and so he understood this energy of the Holy Spirit.** In God's Kingdom, death brings about life. Humility turns into exaltation. Love overpowers hate. For sure! And believe it or not, the first will be last... while **the last will be first**. Now for those on "the lower end of living" that kind of award system makes it **worth getting into the chase**... or as Paul put it latter to the Philippians -- **running the race.** "The pearl of great price" was to get the prize of the better life above.

"I do not claim that I have already succeeded or have already become perfect. **I keep striving to win the prize** for which Christ Jesus has already won me to himself. Of course, my brothers, I really do not think that I have already won it; the one thing I do, however, is to **forget what is behind me and do my best to reach** what is ahead. So I run straight toward the goal in order to win the prize, which is **God's call through Christ Jesus to the life above."**

Paul believed that **being a disciple of Christ was a continual** process... of striving... of **changing...** of **perfecting...** of being conformed to the image of Christ. That image was always out in front of him. Leaving the past behind and trying his best to reach the goal, he ran straight for the prize -- eternal and abundant life... through "The Lord" Jesus Christ.

Paul was convinced by his conversion that he had been chosen to be a winner. Christ had given his life on the cross to rescue him... and assure him of final victory. But **Paul** also knew that as **"a chosen one"** privileged to preach the Good News, he had been given the training, technique and power to be a champion life-saver. He would try to win as many as he could for Christ, in whatever way possible. Therefore, **being freed up to "go for it"** in the here and now, **he wanted to be in "strict training"... and "discipline himself"** for this important race. He wanted no distractions or wasted efforts. **There was no looking back**. He felt that every move should count for the cause of Christ's Kingdom; and he hoped that a firm, strong resolve would keep him "in the chase" to the end. **Reaching the goal** and receiving the prize **would be more than worth the effort.** And so it would be the same for others... called to this great contest.

Today, we who claim the name Christian take our cues from this servant of our Lord. **We too are called and chosen** to be winners. It is essential that we too look at daily life as a process of change and as a striving to attain the image of Christ. We are not perfect. **We need to apply a certain amount of strategy to go for the goal in our lives**, be successful in change for Christ's sake and attain the prize He has in store for us. Our Lord has called us to the life above and assures us, "I make all things new!" There is much that might be gained. There is also much to lose.

So let's choose to change... for God's Son we'll run!
To the cross our sin. Get The Spirit to win!
Chase the prize... and the promise!

CHAPTER 7

"Your Money And Your Mouth"

"Put your money where your mouth is!" That's a statement many of us have heard at one time or another. It bounced around in my head one afternoon during a discussion, and then the instigator asked, "If you could take charge of a church, what would you do?" (I had to think for a moment...) "I'd call the congregation together, and we would tear down "the worship center" board by board... and brick by brick."

The above challenge was issued by my mother after she had listened to me talk about the need for a new reformation in today's church. Not long before, I had resigned from the parish ministry and was thinking about my future... apart from leadership in the structured church. My response was my reaction to years of frustration.

The Church in our society today is in desperate need of a new reformation! Just as in Martin Luther's day, when The Roman Catholic Church had radically departed from her roots in the first century, in our day the church has little resemblance to the early Christian fellowship of Peter and Paul. Listen to a few words from "The Acts" of the Apostles. Peter was just finishing his message (after the coming of the Holy Spirit), and he put it this way:

"All the people of Israel, then, are to know for sure that this Jesus whom you crucified, is the one that God has made Lord and Messiah!"

When the people heard this, they were deeply troubled and said to Peter and the other apostles, "What shall we do, brothers?"

Peter said to them, "Each one of you must turn away from his sins and be baptized in the name of Jesus Christ, so that your sins will be forgiven; and you will receive God's gift, the Holy Spirit. For God's promise was made to you and your children, and to all who are far away -- all whom the Lord our God calls to himself."

Peter made this appeal to them and with many other words he urged them, saying, "Save yourselves from the punishment coming on this wicked people!" Many of them believed his message and were baptized, and about three thousand people were added to the group that day. They spent their time in learning from the apostles, taking part in the fellowship, and sharing in the fellowship meals and the prayers.

Listening to this account of the birth of the Christian Church, we can be certain that the simple, transforming life of Jesus played a critical role in the lives of his new followers. Jesus raised up the people around him. They came to him with a multitude of problems and hang-ups -- looking to their savior to straighten out their lives. So the early church was mostly a gathering of "the scum of the earth" -- people who were willing to put their sordid past behind them and live out a new life... of loving and caring and sharing!

It doesn't help us much to point out how the Christian Church slowly turned away from its early beginnings and became a gigantic structure in desperate need of reform. Certainly that first reformation not only changed the Church in countless ways but it played a vital role in changing the world! It does have usefulness, however, to point out how the Church of this new millennium has lost her way as she has accommodated herself to maybe the most materialistic, immoral and selfish culture in all of history.

Have we no sense of shame? Shouldn't there be some sense of uneasiness within our ranks as we are made to feel more and more comfortable, dress up our platitudes, desensitize our leaders with high salaries, gifts and praise as well as build monuments honoring and augmenting our words of worship and entertainment centers? The typical response is to point out all "the good" that the church is doing. There is some truth in that reminder, but it calls to mind a couple of cautions from the Lord Jesus, himself. "Don't even the criminals take care of their friends?" And then there is the story of the rich man... as well as the rich man and Lazarus.

The illustrations Jesus gave were meant to impact the lives of the people he met. One man ran up and asked: "Good Teacher, what must I do to receive eternal life?" Jesus answered, "You know the commandments...." "Teacher," the man said, "ever since I was young, I have obeyed all the commandments." Jesus looked straight at him with love and said, "You need only one thing. Go and sell all you have and give the money to the poor, and you will have riches in heaven; then come and follow me." When the man heard this, gloom spread over his face, and he went away sad, because he was very rich. Jesus looked around at his disciples and said to them, "How hard it will be for rich people to enter the Kingdom of God!" Believe it or not, that was Christ's way of putting it gently.

Then there was a story about a poor man named Lazarus. He lived near a rich man and had a chance to eat the bits of food that fell from the rich man's table. They both died and ended up in different places. The rich man was tormented, so he complained. The answer came, "Remember, my son, that in your lifetime you were given all the good things, while Lazarus got all the bad things. But now he is enjoying himself here, while you are in pain." As the story ends, the rich man gets some perspective and wants this terrible turn of events explained to the living members of his family. He knows from experience that religious warnings often fall on deaf ears. The bad news comes to him that even a messenger from the dead wouldn't be able to convince his brothers to turn from their wicked ways. So, have times changed? It's no wonder we aren't very disturbed. And it's no wonder we aren't listening!

Yes, today's Church is doing "some good." A few crumbs are getting to the poor... even though not much falls outside our circle of friends. We take stabs at getting people "saved" through the message, "Jesus loves you!" We even want to be seen as religious and in prayer throughout the community. Obviously, we are "the good people" and we want "the bad" put away for a long time. After all, they often take away "the nice stuff" we have amassed for ourselves. How wonderful it would be if we could tidy up a bit and make sure the whole country could see our righteous path to salvation. Hopefully, if we work hard enough, we might even get the political power to defend ourselves (and Jesus) with our guns and mighty, military machine! If only we just had a little more of everything!

I'm not sure Jesus ever got queasy, but this demonstration of so-called Christianity must be almost enough to make him want to "throw up", even from his heavenly perspective! The whole kit and caboodle is close to worthless! For we are very rich. We are very religious. We are very pious. We are very arrogant. We are very selfish. We are very obstinate. How far is that from the poor, humble, self-giving servant, who went to the cross silently, begging from heaven, pleading for his killers, and then pardoning the criminal beside him? Could it be that we are in need of a new reformation of the Church

-- the Body of Christ -- as we enter this new century and millennium? Duh!?

An illustration comes to mind that seems to parallel the present condition of the Church. It's recorded in the Old Testament, as the Israelites journeyed toward their Promised Land. Moses was at Mount Sinai where God gave him the two stone tablets on which He had written the commandments. We read in Exodus 32: "When the people saw that Moses had not come down from the mountain but was staying there a long time, they gathered around Aaron and said to him, 'We do not know what has happened to this man Moses, who led us out of Egypt; so make us a god to lead us.' Aaron said to them, 'Take off the gold earrings which wives, your sons, and your daughters are wearing, and bring them to me.' So all the people took off their gold earrings and brought them to Aaron. He took the earrings, melted them, poured the gold into a mold, and made a gold bull."

We are told that the people worshipped the gold bull with a festival, sacrifices, fellowship offerings and a feast. Moses found out what had happened and that they had left the way that the Lord had commanded them to follow. "I know how stubborn these people are," the Lord told Moses. "Now, don't try to stop me. I am angry with them, and I am going to destroy them." Nevertheless, Moses pleaded with the Lord his God, "Stop being angry; change your mind and do not bring this disaster on your people...." So we hear that the

Lord changed his mind and did not bring his people disaster. When Moses went back down the mountain and came close enough to the camp to see the bull and the dancing, he became furious. He threw down the tablets he was carrying and broke them. He then took the bull, which they had made, melted it, ground it into fine powder, and mixed it with water. Then he made the people of Israel drink it. As Exodus 32 concludes, there were excuses and consequences.

The focus of our idol worship today is (not so surprisingly) the glorious church building. In this country at least, we raise lots of money for never ending building programs. These facilities have become our "gold bulls", and we adore them! Church leaders convince members that giving to a building project is giving to the Lord's work. So what "good Christian" doesn't give up some of his personal accumulation to raise the walls of these objects of our affection? We all feel that our churches should be beautiful, and functional for our needs and a testimony to our faith. And they are testimonials... to the fact that we have turned away from our living Lord... giving renewed attention and lavish praise to our materialistic worship centers -- the gold bulls -- our idols!

Today's "worship and education center" is representative of all that is wrong with the structured church in our time and place. And it probably should be ground into pieces -- torn down -- because of all it stands for in our minds. There probably isn't much the Church does that shouldn't be changed radically. Worship, education, missions, ministry, fellowship, confession, forgiveness, sacrifice -- you name it -- all should be re-formed for Christian sanctity in a new age. Yes, change! We need radical change!

Worship is a good place to begin. From the beginning, worship of the Triune God was meant to be a personal sacrifice, an act of dedication encompassing the will of the Almighty, a humble experience seeking guidance, a confession of guilt, plea for forgiveness and desire for change, a work of faithful obedience in the spirit of the Lord… and the like. Notice the personal action involved and self-giving commitment to The Holy One. Worship in the church today consists of music, reading, praying, confessing, preaching, baptizing sometimes, receiving communion, greeting one-another, etc. This almost always is done impersonally, attractively and conveniently within the big worship center. Music is often done "professionally" by the choir, or weakly sung by the congregation. Expensive instruments are used to lead the people in "praise." Preaching is done by the "salaried one", explaining away the radical words of Scripture, making certain no one in the congregation is offended, adding folksy humor, cute illustrations and current affairs, "pleading" for a little more commitment, always speaking in ways to be more popular and desiring to be successful in the eyes of the "faithful fellowship" -- those who pay the bills. That's to say nothing about heresy, preaching political propaganda, yielding to the lowest common denominator for creative leadership and catering to the pride and arrogance of the congregation and/or denomination. And where does the average minister take a stand to go against the grain of an immoral society? Worship in today's church is mainstream American -- flaunting wealth, creature comforts, pretty symbols, competition for attendance, demanding nearly nothing yet always begging for a little more, flowers, air conditioning... well, you get the point. What shouldn't be changed in our contemporary worship?!

Education programs are an attractive part of congregational life in this country. Most "good churches" have classes for the smallest children to the elderly adult. Who can argue against education? On the other hand, the question should be asked, "What should be the purpose Christian education? Jesus surely "educated" people with his stories and comments, and the early church certainly had some educating to do as new members were baptized. Yet Jesus Christ -- the Lord who Christians follow -- would certainly say that his disciples were intended to learn a "way of life" rather than learn "Christian theology" or Christian truths. In fact, early Christians were known as followers of "The Way."

Today we send people to church to be educated. We do education in our culturally accepted way, but we teach Christianity all wrong! Rather than parents raising their children in a "way of life... of following Jesus", parents send their children off to Sunday school... for about one hour a week, for learning facts, for impersonal training by usually a play-time teacher, for undisciplined and sectarian training, in a special classroom, in a formal atmosphere, in a non-controversial setting, with nice materials, with a popular agenda and with arm twisting encouragement. And when it comes to the end of childhood education, we wonder why the young people aren't more committed… even to the church! Could there be something wrong? Or how about more Bible studies for adults? Maybe what we really need in our society is more exclusivity or more information or more personal ways of looking at things or more pride enhancing social activities. To bad that Bible studies in our country have focused more on words than deeds, stayed within a Pharisaical setting, blinded us to the real world and made us more spineless, sloppy, sentimental and self-centered! Should the education unit be salvaged in our time and place? For what? Is seems to be more a hindrance than a help!

"Missions" is the pride and joy of the structured Church in today's world. If the Church truly is The Body of Christ on earth, then certainly that Body should be doing what He would be doing. It can be safely said that in as much as the Church is The Holy Spirit of Jesus, currently carrying out His ministry, Christ's work is being accomplished among the multitudes. But what about the Church we claim as our own in these United States? What happens when missions gets the crumbs and the prayers? What happens when missions is essentially for our own kind of people and churches walk by on the other side? What happens to the mission of the Church when our contributions are primarily meant to promote our western culture and tally up for ourselves "the souls saved for Jesus?" And what happens to our claims for mission outreach when "a Christian nation" can justify consuming more than 50% of the world's wealth, trashing the environment and controlling food supplies, while a high portion of the world's population goes hungry? Could it be that we really need our military industrial complex? What does that say about the mission of Christ or the mission of the Church? Could it be the Church is so weak that it doesn't have much to say about what happens in this country!? What would happen if the Christian Church in this country had a mission for which the Church would give its life? Right now, who would lead with this kind of love? Could change be an important word in this context?

What about ministry? Isn't that what ministers do? One would think that shouldn't need much overhaul these days. Since they have good training in the best schools and seminaries, shouldn't they be doing their job in a proper Christian manner? If only Christ's ministry could be so easily contained. All the way from Peter and Paul, through all the priests and the popes, from the reformers to today's congregational pastors -- hardly any have been really good at ministry. Ministry in word and deed -- like Jesus carried out -- has been rarely seen, except maybe among the early Christians. It's not that people can't be loving, and sensitive, and humble, and poor, and selfless, and insightful, and awesomely committed; it's just that all these things are so unusual to find in one person. Probably today's ministers are about as far away as one could get from good ministry. Think about the popes and the pastors you know. No place to lay their heads? Penniless? Dependent on others for their next meal? Willing to "wash feet"? Willing to go into fancy "holy places" and overturn tables? Willing to stand up to the authorities? Willing to take the side of convicts and open up the jails? Live close to the ugly and dirty ones in city slums? Tell off the rich, pious, pretty, know it all church people? Get real! Maybe the closest we have come to that in our age is Mother Teresa. Truth be told, Christian ministry is one tough cookie! One person cannot possibly encompass Christ's ministry. Consequently, His ministry was meant to be accomplished by all of His followers -- together! That's called "the fellowship of all believers!" With that kind of fellowship, a group of His followers would find today's worship / education building a real hindrance.

Speaking of fellowship -- there's a word with a lot of baggage! We've heard about all kinds of "fellowships" -- all kinds of companionships, brotherhoods and mutual sharing of interests and activities. Today's congregation is also a certain kind of fellowship. Maybe it's a religious clique, a social club, a comfortable grouping of similar families or a mutual service society. It could be that almost every church could be a little different kind of fellowship in our mobile, shifting society. But listen to a description of "a special kind of fellowship." Here's another comment on the early Christian Church: "Life among the Believers" --

"Many miracles and wonders were being done through the apostles, and everyone was filled with awe. All the believers continued together in close fellowship and shared their belongings with one another. They would sell their possessions, and distribute the money among all, according to what each one needed."

Consider the roots of such a fellowship. The apostles must have had considerable influence in bringing together this gathering of people, and we know from other sources that Jesus' chosen ones had some serious commitment. "Save yourselves from the punishment coming on this wicked people!" -- that's no "ride the fence" exhortation. The "awe part" might be fairly common to close fellowships of all kinds. However, the fact that thousands were continuing together in close fellowship and sharing their belongings with one another indicates that there's a good chance these early Christians had picked up some ideas about radical lifestyle from their Lord. Imagine sharing everything with people of all kinds as each one needed. That's a pretty heavy duty fellowship!

What kind of fellowship do we find in the contemporary Church around us? It's true that there are all kind of examples, but few are anywhere close to what was asked for by those early followers of Jesus. To become a member of most congregations, a person needs to study the church's principles, be baptized and promise to participate and contribute. That's about it. And you can be sure that you won't be dropped off the membership list for hardly any reason, for the saying goes, "Who's to judge?!" No one should be offended, we should try to keep in touch with everyone, membership roles shouldn't decline and we shouldn't be too rigid with our requirements! That's the kind of arguments that yield the result of working with "the least common denominator." What an example to the world of what it means to be a Christian. Could there be any need for a new reformation of the Church in our society or culture?

"Confession" was where it all started in Jesus' day. Remember John the Baptist who prepared the way for Jesus? There was a man who saw the need for confession -- "Turn away from your sins, because the Kingdom of heaven is near!" He even lived the part: John's clothes were made of camel's hear; he wore a leather belt around his waist, and his food was locusts and wild honey. We hear that people came to him... "They confessed their sins, and he baptized them in the Jordan." The religious people wanted in, and he said to them, "You snakes -- who told you that you could escape from the punishment God is about to send? Do those things that will show that you have turned from your sins. And don't think you can escape punishment by saying that Abraham is your ancestor... The ax is ready to cut down the trees at the roots; every tree that does not bear good fruit will be cut down and thrown in the fire. I baptize you with water to show that you have repented, but the one who will come after me will baptize you with the Holy Spirit and fire. He is much greater than I am.... He has his winnowing shovel with him to thresh out all the grain. He will gather his wheat into his barn, but he will burn the chaff in a fire that never goes out." Now there was one who made clear the urgent need for change… and it began with the urgent and critical need for confession. The flip side is… if there is no acknowledgement of personal or corporate sin there is no need for personal or corporate confession.

In this modern, sophisticated age, the concept of real "sin" has all but evaporated. And so naturally, the need for confession has also evaporated. Now to be sure, confession can't be totally eliminated from the Bible, so we do go through the motions of confession in our "worship services." "I have sinned… I have grieviously sinned…" we mouth the words. But how? Even the Roman Catholic confessional seems to have gone the way of the horse and buggy. Show me "the confession of sin" after which the wealth is sold, the enemy is helped, the terrible words are forgotten, a radical change of lifestyle is made or the ego is put away. On the contrary, in our time and place we speak up for our rights, we want to dictate our religious values to others, we build up each other's egos, we fight for wealth and security and we hold out for our own religious perspective. That's a long way from humble confession and servanthood in submission to the Lordship of Christ! What direction is the Church headed in this "enlightened age?"

Of course, <u>forgiveness</u> follows on the heals of real confession. We even hear that the Almighty God "changed his mind" after his people yielded to his will. Isn't forgiveness beautiful? "Forgive us our trespasses, as we forgive those who trespass against us." What a wonderful environment for change. But of course, forgiveness is one of those things that needs to come from the heart. And hardened hearts are not forgiving hearts. Sad to say, we teach "hardness of heart" -- we just wouldn't want to call it by such a callous name. It goes along with "the winning mentality", rights issues, aggressiveness in the workplace, military superiority, racism, capitalism, consumerism and the like. To put it simply, we are taught how to beat our enemies not forgive our enemies. Furthermore, if we do not acknowledge our sin or our need to change -- to go a different direction -- then what is to be forgiven? Maybe the most obvious reason that we can't receive or give away forgiveness is that we feel very little humility in our day and age. And we don't feel humility because we don't teach it. You can be sure that we are not born with it. Can you imagine this powerful, wealthy, materialistic, capitalistic, religious nation getting humble? Not without a serious turn-about, reevaluation -- change!

The last word we will highlight, which urges us toward a new re-formation of the Church... is sacrifice. Now war veterans know a lot about what sacrifice is all about. Laying it all on the line -- sacrificing your life, for example -- is a good demonstration of giving up something of great value for something even greater. Yet we also know that people can sacrifice a lot for really shabby things. That's the tragedy of many people in our country and many church people as we move into the 21st century. If there is one overwhelming, glaring fault of the church in our day and age, with consideration to the Lord of the Church, it's that the Church has not taught its members sacrifice.

It is true that we have an intellectual concept of what sacrifice is all about… as members of the structured church in the United States. After all, most of us have been taught a "theology of the cross," which points to Christ's action on our behalf. He submitted himself to human form and gave all he had -- even his own life -- that we might have life and have it abundantly! What a travesty that we have interpreted living life abundantly as living with a lot of "stuff". On the contrary, Jesus living as a "street person" -- without knowing where his next meal was coming from and without home and family -- this certainly made clear his intention to live humbly and sacrificially as the "lamb of God"! How many times have we heard all this? True, we have sent missionaries out to the far corners of the world telling about our sacrificial savior and encouraging them to live their lives patterned after His life. That's "the good news" message about becoming a Christian, a Christ-follower or a disciple. In following "Our Lord", "Our Commander", "Our King", we are not only united with him in his sufferings, but we are also united with him in his victory over sin, death and the power of the devil! What a message of liberation to the heathen, the hungry, the powerless, the victimized, the homeless and the hopeless. Maybe that's why "The Gospel" has taken some root in poor and desperate places around the globe. But where does all that leave us? Is it in "our theology" to come across to all these "lost souls" as God's great "messenger"? What are our credentials? Where is our foot-washing? How are we doing in setting the prisoners free? How are we loving our enemies? What is happening to our bigger barns... or the loaves and fishes we seem to have left over? Remember, even the criminals take care of their friends. And then there are those "golden calves"...

Sacrifice. What does sacrifice mean as it is portrayed to us in the Bible? Certainly it was no little thing for Abraham to be willing to offer up his son. And certainly our Heavenly Father's sacrifice of His only son was not given so that we might latch onto His "coat-tails", grab as much as we can get, sit down to "worship" in comfortable pews and then have the guts to sing pious songs. Has the church in our time taught us anything about what it means to live a life of sacrifice, say nothing of humility? It is most certainly true that the church (of the comfortable pew in "our Christian nation") is ripe for a re-formation -- a radical change -- if it has any hope for divine mercy and blessing. Maybe the most critical question is this (here is the one question that we do have the ability to answer): Can I see within myself any ray of hope or speck of interest in the possibility of change? Can I dare to... not only try to see things differently, but to take even the first step toward newness in my own life? Can I sacrifice anything "that I have been" to become more like my Lord, my Master and my Savior?

Can I change and see things in a new, divine light? It is important that we understand that we cannot change others; we can only change ourselves. After all is said and done, sacrifice gets personal… at least any that suits Christ's Body in our time and place. Jesus quickly got to the heart of the matter with the rich man. Leave it all and follow me. Someone has put it crudely, "Put up or shut up"! Speaking in words that may suit the growing gap between the rich and poor in the new millennium it's, "Your Money and Your Mouth"!

CHAPTER 8

"The Fight For Freedom"

Honestly, I've about had my fill of "fighting" in our day and age. We see kids fight, parents fight, gangs fight and countries fight; we see fighting in video games, in the movies, on T-V and on the street corner. Fighting is everywhere... almost... except in church! At least <u>there</u> is one place where we can count on experiencing quiet and peace and acceptance.

Wait a minute. Something isn't quite right here. Jesus didn't seem to bring much peace and quiet along with him on his journey through life. In fact, he suggested that instead of peace, he brought a sword! And then he talked about even families being divided up over what he brought to the table. The truth is that the religious establishment correctly considered Jesus a trouble-maker. He disrupted the good things they had going for themselves -- the status quo and their convenient, man-made, profitable religious activities.

The above confusion which seems apparent is not really so confusing after all, when you start to think about it. The fighting meant to selfishly grab what others need, subdue and control others, pile up wealth, power and prestige, walk over the weak and wounded and destroy the other side is clearly the evidence of "evil" in our midst. There's no other way to put it. Now if the "Body of Christ" simply watches in the midst of such turmoil with quiet and acceptance, that church is not related to the Lord Jesus. We live in evil times, so being passive in the midst of deterioration, destruction and death is a total cop-out... especially if we are intended to represent God's life-giving Word made flesh!

Today, we certainly need some peace and acceptance in the places where we are seeing a lot of fighting and turmoil. And maybe equally as much, we need some courageous, powerful resistance... to fight (yes, to battle) business as usual in our religious, political and economic systems. A large majority of the world's population is held captive by man's inhumanity to man. Poverty, political subjugation, military expansion, religious, racial and moral persecution, economic injustice and debilitating incarceration are just some of the serious forms of bondage intolerable to loving and caring people raised up for the divine mission of agape love. Christians have always said that the Spirit of the risen Christ is Lord of the whole creation. He speaks and acts to liberate every creature from the forces of evil and destruction. So Christ's disciples and followers are his living and breathing "freedom fighters" in the present struggle. They are not meant to be passive pawns transfixed by the idols of this present age.

It seems like we would certainly be prepared to rise up against the personal forms of bondage that most of us are knowingly and unknowingly caught in, but apparently one form of bondage just leads to another. The webs of our own making are taking a serious toll on even our physical and mental health today, say nothing of on our spiritual well-being. If we don't learn to "fight" the forces of destruction within us and around us, we and our children will be finally subdued to reap the consequences of our own ignorance and rebelliousness. Consider the "weight" pulling us down in just the luxuries and wealth which surrounds us. There is no better way to "do in" a fighting force than continue to feed it fattening foods, pamper it with excesses and lure it into sleepy contentment. So it's no wonder that the ways of the world have gotten to us and we hardly recognize what we are to do anymore. In a telling way, we have become the cause of a large part of the world's deterioration and injustices.

Again, it must be said that facing up to the truth -- even if it's hard to take, depressing and upsetting -- is not the worst thing in the world for our ultimate health and happiness. The truth (even as we understand Jesus to be The Way, The Truth and The Life) puts us into a hopeful position, if we take seriously the words of scripture and the inspired mission of God's people. Our God and Father only wants the best for each of us (and all of us together) and that means he is interested in more than our temporary pleasure. From the beginning, he has only desired that we stay in a healthy relationship with Him, our fellow human beings and His creation. It's only when we start putting ourselves ahead of others and causing trouble that he wants us to stop, turn around and get headed down a more beneficial path for all parties concerned.

The people who are still reading this "sermon" about change are probably those who are open to new considerations about a better way of life for people on this planet. Looking back at history can help define our erroneous ways and sometimes point us in the right direction. We know that down through history, Christians have studied the Bible to get inspiration and insight into what is appropriate response to God's voice in each new age. Continuing in that tradition, we become aware that both the Old and New Testaments give testimony to God's action in directing "earth shaking change"... in order to advance His life-giving purposes on earth. In the Old Testament the central story is about The Exodus -- the freeing of the Israelites from slavery in Egypt. The central story in the New Testament concerns the life of Jesus, as he made clear God's redeeming love for His whole creation. Much testimony has been given to how "God's Chosen One" laid his whole life on the line to show all the earth's inhabitants "The Way" to God's blessing.

Our current chapter title is "The Fight For Freedom". Putting my uneasiness about fighting aside, the situation the people of Israel faced as they were confined in slavery was a problem "worth getting up in arms about." They groaned under their taskmasters, they had lost almost everything that made life worth living, and as for their spirit -- "they were not happy campers." The Bible relates how dependent they were on inspirational leadership, how terribly time consuming it was for them to get free, how persistent they needed to be with their new agenda, how committed they needed to be to one another and how overwhelming their goals often appeared. Yet they became convinced that their "fight for freedom" was the only game in town -- their only opportunity for a bright and blessed future. Hard? Yes! Meaningful? Definitely! Their only hope? Absolutely! So the Israelites persisted through thick and thin to the Promised Land. History tells us about the value of their journey for all the world's inhabitants.

Jesus arrived on the scene in the midst of a little different kind of captivity. Yet just as certainly as slavery in Egypt, weighty circumstances were subjugating and overwhelming the masses. The political scene was dictatorial and suffocating while the economic picture was bleak. Moreover, true spirituality had been lost... with the religious leadership serving the status quo, making arrogant demands and flaunting their power and prestige. Jesus called for newness all around -- freedom from hunger and disease, newness of spirit and mission, a change of commitment and loyalty, as well as no less than divine insights into all vertical and horizontal relationships. He not only talked the talk but He also walked the walk. His was a different kind of "fight to the finish" where love was presented to overcome hate, repentance was an option to conquer bad behavior, humility was revealed to show greatness and submission was offered to do away with violence. This was a new power for all ages and pointed to liberation on all levels of human interaction. But again, in all Jesus announced, the requirements for freedom were anything but common sense and status quo. His followers were called out to give up all that was near and dear to them, act out self-giving love and trust in divine mercy and blessing. An eternal "promised land" would be theirs as the gift of His Spirit. What a revival, revolution and re-formation! And what a "fight for freedom" leading to the cross!

What does the Bible say to those who identify with The Exodus and/or The Savior while moving into the next thousand years? Basic to both accounts is the urgency for a new outlook and commitment in carrying forward a new challenge. Now naturally, people who have merely short-term goals will act in a certain way while people with long-term or eternal goals will act in another. Naturally, what people want to have to satisfy their immediate desires will not take a lot of leadership, insight or commitment. Frankly, all that stuff can come rather naturally to many of us -- born nearsighted as we are in "the jungle." But not so naturally, what is needed for people with real concern for the future... is truly divine inspiration and a willingness to fight for the changes needed to win the battle. Business as usual just won't do the job when even one person is in bondage and losing to the forces of evil. On the other hand, with real committed resistance to evil by an empowered and disciplined fellowship, the hope is that everyone can reach "the promised land" -- a land flowing with love and peace and blessing.

Today, we as citizens of the most dominating and wealthy nation to ever exist on the face of the earth have unconsciously drifted into a life-threatening disaster. And those of us who would claim the name "Christian" (with all that entails) are essentially in bondage... captivated by sin and evil... going through the motions in "a foreign land." It hurts to acknowledge our predicament, say nothing of face the cause of our pointless labors and fruitless sufferings. What is it like to live in slavery in the great U.S. of A... and hardly remember where you have come from or where you are going? We can't expect people who do not claim any "Inspiration" to have any reference point for what is truly good or right or perfect. So certainly they can't be counted on to understand a divine perspective or a sense of long-term mission. That leaves merely "a remnant" of God's chosen ones to truly listen to the message, confess, come clean and ask how to head off in a new direction. For many who have even casually listened to "The Word", even in our time and place, it is not beyond our "gut feelings" or at least "our better self" to sense that a lot is not right with the world. It should bother us that future generations will note our hopeless quest for more of "nothing"... and how we slid into meaningless routines within the prisons or confines of our own making. Still, truth be told, we are not unlike other peoples in other times. Today possibly, the "signs" of our captivity are just a bit more subtle; and we are in too deep to feel there is much of any way out.

How do we get out? Do we dare to pose the question, and if so, does anyone care? Let's go with it for argument's sake. For many people who get in trouble, "the way out" only becomes evident when "the hurting" gets serious enough. We all know about the alcoholic, who only will seek help after he or she has hit bottom. On the other hand, church people are usually the ones hearing society's seductive music -- "let the good times roll!" Generally that tune is not conducive to urgent reformation or change. Maybe the real key is in figuring out who to listen to and who to trust... in connection with an eternal set of standards. At least that's the ticket for the historical account found in the Bible. Thank goodness this testimony to God's work in history can still be found and taken seriously by some. It seems there has always been that "remnant." Could it be there is among us a remnant of inspired ones, even in these good times? Could it be "a chosen people" might see a new light of purpose and hope, even in the midst of a seductive era? Yes, there just might be Biblical precedent for such an occurrence.

Again, how do we get out of captivity? The first step is to acknowledge our problem or sin or vulnerability. Only when we honestly desire a better road to travel will we be willing to turn around and ask directions. Remember the question that those first Christians came up with, "What shall we do bothers?" They had clearly understood the message of that first Christian church and it's leaders. They were clearly prepared to leave their old, overpowering taskmasters and fight for their freedom. You can be sure that their old ways were put behind them as they prepared themselves to move forward under new leadership.

We have no less a challenge within the context of contemporary Christian religion and the new millennium. It is in the nature of our "Christian calling" to "fight for freedom" over all the forces of evil in our culture and materialistic system. That does not mean everything surrounding us needs to be rejected or abolished, but it does mean that a new "measuring stick" is needed to determine what is healthy and beneficial for all people… as well as for the rest of the creation.

Christianity has always been about following the leader – Jesus Christ "The Lord!" Consider how church people have gotten "off the track" down through the centuries. What a shame that so much "stuff" has been erected between the way Jesus lived out his life and the way His Body, The Church, orchestrated the movement which was intended to follow after Him. While the "imperfect" Bible stories written about His life and love and faithfulness to His Heavenly Father are the most treasured words ever written, still they are only human words pointing to the life and love of Jesus. His whole being and mission was designed to "make disciples" (followers)… not to develop theology, monuments and a praise network. But the latter is exactly what we have done! Consider Christ's challenge to feed the hungry, heal the sick, free the prisoners, love your enemies, do the servant's chores, love the unlovable, upset the money changers and stand up for the truth! Compare that to the convenient and comfortable path we have taken in proclaiming, studying and debating theological precepts, arguing over denominational differences, building glamorous cathedrals, temples and churches, "praying and agonizing" over our over-fed, fearful, addicted, hospitalized friends, sitting in worship centers listening to accomplished music and "religiously correct" words of wisdom, "sacrificing" contributions for our friends and families and even trying to force religious morality on our neighbors. Imagine Christians having no shame in padding luxurious living standards, salaries, security forces, insurance policies and pension benefits! Do we see these things as our rewards for getting "saved"? Sadly, the list of our "false advertising schemes" done in His memory goes on and on. Certainly there is plenty of room for reformation of the church in the 21st century, that is, if we truly want to follow our leader in liberating all people from the powers that defeat and destroy them.

Church people should be aware that Jesus made very clear early on what his mission or ministry of liberation was all about. He even stood up among the religious leaders of his day and said in effect, "Here's what I want to accomplish!"

As the prophet Isaiah put it, "The Spirit of the Lord is upon me, because he has chosen me to bring good news to the poor. He has sent me to proclaim liberty to the captives and recovery of sight to the blind, to set free the oppressed and announce that the time has come when the Lord will save his people."

> What a program of upside down politics! Here was "The Chosen One," sent from God to change life for people in the city… and even in the countryside. Still, He would have to win a contentious war for the hearts and minds of those who would see him and hear him. The people He saw in bondage to all kinds of terrible tragedies would not be freed without a fight. Surprisingly, however, His power would not be dictatorial (although He had the ultimate authority). It would find fulfillment in the dedication and commitment of his followers, especially among the various members of His Spirit-led body after His death and resurrection. Can you imagine? All this was based on "follow the leader."

What does it mean to follow the leader? Don't even children do this with some understanding? This isn't something that's deeply mysterious. Put simply, Jesus speaks His revolutionary message, and his followers vocalize the same convictions. Jesus ministers to needy ones, and Christians are committed to an identical mission. Jesus trusts His Heavenly Father for his security and needs, and those within the fellowship of the faithful are with Him in perspective and life-style. What's so hard to understand about that? Nothing – nothing at all. However, we do know it takes some guts and commitment to join forces with a revolutionary. We can accept the glory and the rewards; but action on the front lines can be a bit risky. Going against "the ways of the world" can take its toll on who we are and what we have laid up for ourselves. Oh how natural it is to look out for our own interests. So how much difference can we see between our outlook and the public's perception of that first Palm Sunday and Good Friday? We enjoy the pageantry and the parties but not the call for change and giving ourselves up for others.

The best place to start as a truly Christian "freedom fighter" is to identify our inspired leader and what his crusade is all about. That's what 1st century people had to do when they ran into John the Baptist and Jesus. If we are not comfortable with the true "mission" of Christ's Risen Body (The Spirit-led Christian Church) then there's no point in joining the resurrection forces for change... or pretending we are something that we are not. In other words, if our intention is just to be "saved," get together with friends, find some "moral standards" we like, be a productive U.S. citizen and sing His praises, then we certainly shouldn't be signing up as a disciple of Christ with the intention of taking on the forces of evil! And so the Bible has told us that Jesus put people on the spot – those who saw him and listened to him. This wasn't just some play-time activity Jesus was calling people to share with him, even though 2000 years later we might think so. Come and join us in our beautiful house of worship. We have such a nice pastor, a wonderful choir and a great youth program!

We forget to say, "And it won't cost you a cent!" How far removed we are in this technological, pleasure seeking society. In fact, are we so far removed that we can no longer identify the leader – our Lord – or His mission!?

"Prepare the way of the Lord!" – that's the way John the Baptist put it as he ushered in the new, unique revolution. Almost nothing would ever be seen in the same way again. The Baptist set the tone and the requirements by calling for repentance. Depart from your sins! Change your ways! Turn around! There was no mincing words and no concessions for softies. He even went further to say that his baptism (his cleansing) was of water while Jesus' baptism was of fire. Now here was some serious business; and they didn't argue with John much because of where he lived and the way he was dressed! Yet surprisingly enough, the people didn't flee – they didn't run away... even from this wild man out of the desert. Something must have really hit home, because they came to hear him from all over country. And they submitted themselves to his suggestions and demands. Obviously, they were in desperate need of something radically new!

Jesus was baptized by John in the Jordan and the crowds were not disappointed. Not only did they hear, "Turn away from your sins!" but also, "The Kingdom of heaven is near!" Power. Hope. Security. Meaning. Fellowship. Love. Caring. And even happiness!

"Happy are those who know they are spiritually poor..."

"Happy are those who mourn..."

"Happy are those who are humble..."

"Happy are those whose great desire is to do what God requires..."

"Happy are those who are merciful to others..."

"Happy are those who are pure in heart..."

"Happy are those who work for peace..."

"Happy are those who are persecuted because they do what God requires..."

"Happy are you when people insult you and persecute you and tell all kinds of evil lies against you because you are my followers...." To one and all, Jesus proclaimed that they would have their needs met. Be sure about this – you will be greatly rewarded. Just step up to get the Spirit... and be changed by fire!

Convicts – every one! Now that is different! We know that convicts are people who are proven guilty. A "convict" by definition is one who is guilty of an offense as charged... or one serving a sentence of confinement, as in a penitentiary. In other words, very precisely, a convict is one who is found guilty of a crime. As we have come to know Christians -- those called out to face up to their guilt, repent and follow Christ in His mission of liberation -- we are faced with the fact that all human beings start out at ground zero. No one is perfect, no not one. As we measure ourselves in the light of Christ, we have to admit that we all fall far short of the ideals of the Kingdom of Heaven, where agape love, self-less sacrifice, passionate servant-hood, enduring faith, inner peace and unending hope abound. We understand what John and Jesus are saying about the need for confession. So before our Lord and one-another, we need to humbly acknowledge our rebellious ways. Before our Creator, Redeemer God, we simply throw ourselves on His mercy. Guilty. Convicted. Convicts. It's true that every person baptized with the Holy Spirit is raised up to fight for freedom alongside his or her Master. Every foot-soldier for the Kingdom of Heaven is thrown into this struggle for personal accomplishment and newness as well as to see liberation accomplished for all others. But get it straight -- we're all convicts who are continually in need of being made new. That's downright helpful to acknowledge in the eternal scheme of things.

It's interesting that Christians are convicts in more than one sense. We have noted that a convict is also one "serving a sentence of confinement, as in a penitentiary." In a sense, the real uplifting and yet scary aspect of living as though the Kingdom of Heaven is at hand… is that we acknowledge that we are presently making our living in "a foreign land." We know that our ultimate residence is our Heavenly home, just as the Israelites in the desert understood that they were ultimately headed for the promised land of Israel. Consequently, Christ's fighting force for freedom is really doing its serving within a place of confinement… as in a penitentiary. Certainly none of us are ever fully free within our environment. We know the battle is never fully won. Even though we have been liberated, in another sense, we are still captive within our environment.

It's interesting that word "penitentiary" comes in part from the word "penance," which involves the confession of sin, repentance and submission to penalties imposed. In a very real and earth-shaking sense, we as Christ's disciples and followers are to identify ourselves as convicts radically in need of change on a daily basis. The humility required of our foot-washing position next to our Lord and Master drives us to identify with other convicted ones, who not only recognize our need to be more and more conformed to the image of Christ but also heed the warning that we should not put down our roots too deeply in this present place. Maybe even more to the point, this is a world which requires our penance as convicts before the Judge!

Christians are convicts in need of change. That's certainly a sobering thought. Yet it's also a liberating one, because it's only in changing and being more conformed to the image of Christ that we can be truly free. We also can help others in their struggle for freedom as we are in the process of becoming free ourselves. There's nothing like being helped by someone who has been there, and so we can console and understand one-another in our struggles through life.

Consider the position of convicts. Convicts are people who have been stopped, thank the Lord. Most of us know what happens when any individual gets away with an act of disobedience or lawlessness. Rarely is there any slowing up to consider the consequences. In fact, successful lawlessness simply promotes more experienced and advanced lawlessness. Tragically enough, not many of us get caught in that first act of disobedience, rebellion or ignorance. So we advance further and further toward more serious consequences for committing our crimes... not really fearing we will be stopped, because that is not our experience. Obviously, no criminals of any kind are exceptions to such behavior. It's often even hard for most of us to differentiate between the seriousness of human errors, blunders, violations and crimes. So, impulsive people that we are, we do most of what we want to do and figure out what the consequences are later – if they ever confront us. Admittedly, some of us may be a bit more fortunate than others in getting stopped early in our rebellious activity. Whatever the case, all of this puts us as individual human beings on pretty much the same level, exactly as our Lord suggests. The bottom line is that there is no serving with Jesus Christ without deep humility. Together we fight for freedom; and we fight as convicts in need of change.

CHAPTER 9

"Christian Basic Training"

Has anyone ever really wanted to go to "basic training?" The basic training which comes to my mind has to do with entrance into the U.S. military -- the group of fighting forces which has been organized to defend our country. Every branch of the military takes itself very seriously, and rightfully so. A recruit learns pretty quickly that life and death issues are at the heart of the military's mission. Most of us are acquainted with what happens in those first weeks and months of military service. There's regimentation, rigorous physical training, "brainwashing" for survival, social conformity, life-saving instruction, general education and all kinds of testing. A person has to be pretty committed to the mission and benefits of the armed forces to want to go through all the required life-style changes. In fact, some parents and youth leaders believe that "military training" is a good place to get a wayward young man or woman straightened out. There aren't many young people who don't come out of basic training looking quite a bit different than they appeared going in. We'd be surprised to have it otherwise.

Basic training, then, quite literally speaks for itself –

it's basic (fundamental, essential, crucial and critical) and it's training (exercise, preparation, guidance and instruction). For example, Jesus called his disciples into a kind of basic training. They had to leave home… take on a new mission… look into some new training… and in solidarity with others, conform themselves to new leadership. There wasn't room on his team for "fence straddlers" or people who wanted what "the world" had to offer. Jesus reminded his followers, as he carried out some foot washing, that no one was above his master. He was in the process of molding an "opposing force" that would turn conventional wisdom upside down. His reference point was the Kingdom of Heaven. Paul put it on target when he wrote to the church in Corinth:

"Now remember what you were, my brothers, when God called you. From the human point of view few of you were wise or powerful or of high social standing. God purposely chose what the world considers nonsense in order to shame the wise, and he chose what the world considers weak in order to shame the powerful. He chose what world looks down on and despises and thinks is nothing, in order to destroy what the world thinks is important. This means that no one can boast in God's presence. But God has brought you into union with Christ Jesus, and God has made Christ to be our wisdom. By him we are put right with God; we become God's holy people and are set free. So then, as the scripture says, "Whoever wants to boast must boast of what the Lord has done."

With this kind of training and with a Lord who had given his life for others, how could followers of "The Way" see themselves in any other terms than as an inspired, disciplined force... picked out to provide creative alternatives to the world? The early church was prepared to implement the revolutionary life-style and purposes they had been taught. Here too was a force that represented life and death issues. No one could join this close knit fellowship without being "humbled" – without admitting their selfish, sin or wayward ways. Yet no one, whatever their former position in life, was turned away. On the contrary, all were conformed to the "Spirit of Christ" and set free to be "holy people" in the business of uplifting those fallen by the wayside. We hear historical testimony that a great number of the "down and out" became dedicated to the fellowship of the faithful and gave it their complete loyalty.

As we think of how the early Christians endured sufferings and persecutions for their faith, we might wonder how they could endure. How could common folk stand up for their convictions of love and sacrifice and faith as they were being thrown to the lions? Some young men and women in past wars have also endured unspeakable torture and persecution as a result of their commitments to fighting for their country. However, could they have lasted in the enemy's torture chambers if it wasn't for going through their "basic training?" Maybe that's a bit like asking if a "couch potato" could run a marathon? No way! None of us can expect to be successful with challenges we are not in any sense prepared to handle. Obviously then, those early Christians learned what was involved in being committed to Christ-like love, fighting for freedom and preparing for a Heavenly home! It seems like people of every time and place who dedicate themselves to a great venture need to "count the cost" before going full steam ahead.

So let's get to the question of "Christian basic training" today. First of all, the aspect of "counting the cost" is something that most of us understand pretty well. We should be able to figure out quite easily whether we as church people are equipped to meet the challenges of our world or not. If it's our feeling we live in a Christian nation, sin is pretty much a thing of the past, almost everyone is headed for heaven, and just about everything is right with the world, then I would have to admit that today's basic training in most Christian churches is close to adequate. What's to prepare for… or worry about… or resist… or challenge? Jesus has done the work, he's still doing it, and he has the job practically accomplished. We've got it made in the shade, and about all we've got to do is cheer him on, celebrate his accomplishments and satisfy ourselves we are saved. That's one way to look at what's going on in today's churches. On the other hand, if it's our conviction we live in tempting and dangerous times, the world's addicting and incarcerating forces are powerful enemies, materialism has become the god of choice, our environment is heading downhill, misplaced people are fearful, confused and overwhelmed, and most of the world's nations are in desperate conditions with regard to basic needs, then we desperately should come to understand that our structured churches today are offering us almost nothing appropriate to insure our spiritual survival say nothing of success. What kind of preparation are we getting to rescue our fellow human beings who have almost lost hope? I am of the opinion that this last sad state of affairs is the one we find ourselves facing these days, and that the Christian basic training we all desperately need is nearly non-existent.

What are churches providing for their members these days? Not much of anything valuable for an age when the challenge to Christ's work and perspective is maybe the greatest it's ever been. Obviously, worship in the traditional sense is at the center of what most churches offer. It usually includes greetings, Bible reading, traditional ritual, singing, prayer and a sermon. Prayer for people who are physically sick or hurting has usually been a more personal part of that hour when the congregation gathers for inspiration and remembering. A recent addition has been a "passing of the peace," or probably more accurately, handshakes all around. Unfortunately, most of what happens can be classified as a kind of entertainment – passive and pleasing for the most part. "Providing a good show" is usually for the purpose of keeping the membership growing and money flowing. The minister (the professional) does most of the praying and speaking while "the practicing people" lead with the reading and singing. It must be acknowledged that ministers (priests / pastors) do try to make their message or sermon applicable to daily life; and it probably is relevant to many lives, at least intellectually. Yet like poor education in the classroom, it's in one ear and out the other. For the most part, people in our society today are habitually unable to act on what is said within the walls of the church. It's take it... and leave it... with maybe a comment at the door. In the end, the worshippers who come together, if they remember anything, move back into the real world of hard knocks with pious phrases, cute stories, and theological concepts – nowhere enough preparation to even begin to do battle with the world.

Outside the worship service, many Christian congregations schedule Bible studies, specialized groups for those who have difficulties, Sunday School classes, youth programs and outings, fund raising projects, fellowship meals, home visitations and other similar activities. In some cases, a congregation may even prepare individuals for an outreach to the un-churched, homeless or the needy in a foreign land. Most of the above is not detrimental in itself and in some cases is quite important for healthy functioning of Christ's Body, the Church. Yet it must be said that most of this turns out to be simply a distraction from the Church's essential calling to do battle with the world, fight to free the captives, and win the war for The Kingdom of Heaven.

An illustration may be appropriate at this critical point, for there is no doubt that most church people are very much defensive people, status quo people and pious people. They treasure their church (or religious faith) and they do not like to be told they are headed down the wrong road. However, most intellectually honest people will agree that youth education is quite important for laying down the fundamentals or the basics of anything worth learning. It's especially important for one's entire "Christian life" to understand one's roots, one's name, one's loyalty and one's inspiration. That's why most churches have Sunday Schools or their equivalent... along with maybe a "confirmation program." But consider for a moment not only <u>what</u> is being taught by the church during a child's growing up years but <u>how</u> it is being taught. A little supplemental training added to serious home instruction probably was somewhat beneficial, back when Mom and Dad were home with the kids most of the time. Think about what is happening these days in the home. What family is taking time for quality Christian education, say nothing about quantity. We certainly are educating our children for a trip to the mall, but how are we educating for "basic spiritual survival," when almost all of us are living or trying to survive in the most terrifying and seductive "materialistic jungle" the world has ever seen?

Look at the "spiritual journey" most youngsters take: First, for many, there's baptism or some early ritual that occurs in the presence of the congregation. Certainly we shouldn't consider much mindful or purposeful education in that event. Maybe a summer "Vacation Bible School" is part of a parent's plan for pre-school children. The best that could be hoped for during these special days would be some Bible stories along with fun and games. Covering the elementary school years, parents sending their children to an hour of "study" on Sunday morning is about as much as they can accomplish… especially if they offer some help with the Sunday school lessons. Remember that the volunteer teacher is usually without training or experience. Would such a teacher even bring discipline into the classroom during this one hour weekly? Minimally in the home, quite naturally, there should be Bible stories, prayers before meals and bedtime moments with God. Going to church with Mom and Dad would certainly be the instructional centerpiece of the week. It's rare indeed for parents to schedule "daily devotions" with the whole family present. Not so surprisingly then, it's clear that without much time, parents generally turn over the Christian education of their children to the "professionals" in the church.

Up to the teen-age years, children raised in the church probably sense that church life is important for Christian families and that it's important to parents that Christian education classes are attended. Consequently, they accept what is offered and follow their parents' instructions. What do they really receive during these formative years? The answer is – Bible stories, prayers, fun and games, organized worship, maybe some retreat and / or devotional experience, almost imperceptible "offering experience" and some church rituals. Yes, the answer focuses nearly completely on words and rituals… that turn out to signify almost nothing in daily life. Even as important as prayer appears to be for the congregation, how much of even that spiritual exercise is transferred to the student? Ask yourself this question. Is personal prayer commonly used in a student's weekday school… or even before a meal within that school? Could there be a more weak "Christian witness?" Before being too hard on children, however, we must be clear that the church and parents are to blame.

The junior high, high school and college years can show us what our Christian education programs are worth. Before saying that young people will always be "free spirits" and without convictions, look to the "basic training camps" of hurting, third world people; look to the desperate "fighting peoples" of the world with nothing to lose; look to cultures where there's some serious business to get accomplished either religiously, politically or economically. As we look at young men and women in such settings, it's certainly easy to see awesome commitments and loyalty. We have heard by the grape-vine how even young children are found "fighting for their country" – willing to give their lives for the mission they are trained to accomplish. Our young people are committed too – to shopping mall trips and expensive clothes, to nice cars and fast food, to beach parties and beer parties, to national sporting and racing events, to Christmas and party spending, to winning teams and prestige schools, to big-time music events and short-lived relationships, to international travel and credit-card purchasing. Of course, we know of exceptions. A few of today's young people are committed to goals other than selfish ones. Yet for the most part our children are good followers – they know what living examples look like in the flesh. Words can be pretty meaningless.

Our children who are ready to leave home are not prepared to take on the battles that Jesus fought. Most of them have become increasingly troublesome in confirmation class or church school. They have dropped out of church attendance and have become worldly, selfish and addicted to all kinds of momentary desires. Still, the church in our culture carries on its pious, near-sighted convictions and activities, while the world as we know it goes to hell… or more graciously put, drifts more and more deeply into deterioration and death. Where was the church in Hitler's Germany? Did the church recognize the non-Christian role it played? Might there have been, in fact, any role for reformation in that time and place? Our role in the U.S. at this time in history is no less serious, but only maybe a little more subtle: Millions of lives are going down the tubes – hungry, homeless, addicted, incarcerated, trampled upon, fenced out, fenced in, war torn, persecuted, forgotten, judged and victimized human beings. Meanwhile, we talk about our love for Jesus, we sing his praises, we build him churches, and we live out our materialistic lives… leading our children and others toward a wordy, powerless, egocentric Christianity.

As this youth education illustration points out, the contemporary church is failing in its basic mission. Some leaders would maintain that a focus on adult education would help to revitalize essential ministry. However, poor education for adults would not do much more for revitalizing Christianity than it has done for children and youth. As long as our pious words and egocentric worship are the dominant modes of testifying to Jesus and his love, we will be like church people in Nazi Germany – doing Peter impersonations of denial… while Jesus is ridiculed, persecuted and killed by the dominant culture. The tragic truth is that we either know the truth about what Jesus represents in life and what he wants us to do… and we knowingly run in the opposite direction, or we do not understand the true significance of the arrival of Jesus as God's Son and Messiah. Jesus did not come in order to get more enthusiastic worship for Himself and His Heavenly Father. He did not come to inspire people to dedicate more church buildings for the convenience of the self-righteous. The Old Testament makes clear that the Israelite creator God, the God of Abraham, Isaac and Jacob, the Yahweh of the Exodus was downright sick of all the religious noise and materialistic monuments. Jesus Christ was promised and sent for one purpose – to make God's Word "flesh" – a human being -- and to call everyone to the mission and ministry of making God's Word take on human form at all times and in all places. For this single purpose Jesus wanted his followers to make disciples of all nations.

The "Good News according to John" spoke about the Word of Life.

"Before the world was created, the Word already existed; he was with God, and he was the same as

God.... The Word was the source of life, and this life brought light to mankind.... The Word was in the world, and though God made the world through him, yet the world did not recognize him.... The Word became a human being and, full of grace and truth, lived among us. We saw his glory, the glory which he received as the Father's only Son.

In this modern, technological age, the Christian Church (The Risen Body of Christ) is called out as a "remnant" to put the living, eternal Word of God into action and on display. That's intended for the whole world's life, health and eternal welfare. The ever-present Spirit of Christ is available to infiltrate the minds and bodies of all people, everywhere. Since Jesus came to liberate all of humanity from evil, destructive forces in the world, so his followers go about the same business. What a challenge in an age when nearly all God's children are caught in some kind of bullying, bondage, devastating behavior or destructive goals. A concerned and caring person doesn't just say to a starving person, "Jesus loves you, this I know, for the Bible tells me so." No, food is handed out with a loving spirit. Even a child know how words coming from a parent can be ignored and almost unheard. Children learn easily and quickly how to tune out mere repetitions and insincere lectures. But wait until a parent takes action and watch how a child takes notice. Taking the lead in carrying out what needs to be done is powerful stuff for teaching anyone how to follow. Try this -- illustrate with decisive movement, put your life on the line, get down a dirty – Jesus got down on his knees and started washing feet! That really got the attention of his disciples.

We have noted that Jesus was interested in freeing people from all kinds of problems. He announced his mission was one of liberation. He fed people. He healed the sick. He corrected bad habits. He led people away from mere religious customs. He defended those who were persecuted. He showed wealthy people the way to enduring happiness and proud people the place to find humility. That wasn't all of it, by any means. Yet what he had to say about the power his followers would have after his death seemed almost more outrageous than his actions. It was his suggestion that his followers would do even greater things than he had done… through the power of His Spirit. Since His Church has been led to believe his words, we know that even today Christians can follow their leader and carry out the task of liberating all kinds of captives. This is the work of "The Body of Christ," in order that those who witness The Spirit's work will be won over to The Kingdom of Heaven.

As we have heard testimony to the work of Christ, it is not hard for us to understand that the church is not meant to be an entertainment center, but more a "basic training center" for carrying forward our Lord's work. If the church building is to survive in our age as a facility to be used for His purposes, then it must be transformed into a place of serious, "basic training" for the purpose of liberating the captives! Nothing less will be adequate, if we are to successfully face the contemporary world's barriers to full, rich, abundant living for everyone. Now certainly that might mean that our churches won't be so full of spectators or curiosity seekers. Can you imagine a "worship service" where dedicated "Christ followers" gather to immediately hit the streets for the sake of humble service to all the disadvantaged and oppressed? That indeed would be what worship basically means – that we work out our loyal dedication to God "giving Him glory" by carrying out his commands as his foot soldiers. What could be better basic training for… bearing fruit of The Spirit, giving witness to His Holy Name and working out our own salvation with fear and trembling?

It's typical of "basic training" that the ego of the recruit is left behind… for the benefit of the regiment and it's goals and mission. Christians must acknowledge that the challenge of following Jesus is not an easy or casual calling. More demanding than even military service, the call of Christ is to lay oneself before one's God in total surrender, in order to be "reborn" for divine purposes. Think of what revolutionary changes that should bring about among today's disciples. Consider what real life activities might go on within the walls of today's churches (if in fact those buildings would be needed at all)! Recall that down through the ages, the theology of "the fellowship of the faithful" always contended that the church is not a building but people. And even more fundamental is the fact that The Body of Christ is instituted to have unlimited members, many with different functions, but all <u>conformed</u> to the head, who is The Risen Lord. So how are we to be conformed? What is meant to replace the ego or our old nature? The New Testament is full of documentation as to "the mind and spirit," which is to fill the void within each person liberated by our Lord.

Maybe the most basic belief of Christian people for the last 2000 years has been formulated in a simple sentence even small children have uttered – God is love. "For God so loved the world, that He gave His only Son…" Jesus came into the world as a baby to show in a personal way God's love for all people. Now certainly that love of God is not just any, old, run of the mill kind of love. It's called "agape love." More than simply a feeling, it's love, desire or affection for even the unlovable or worthless. To seek to understand Christ's love for us is to try to understand what he meant when he told us, "Love your enemies." Love those who have tried to do you harm. The Savior's example is that while we were yet sinners (repulsive, rebellious, worldly, idol worshippers) Christ died for us. In other words, we as egocentric, selfish, judgmental, pious human beings were not a pretty sight, yet Jesus went into enemy territory to rescue us from the power of evil. That's a different kind of love than "the world" explains to us or shows us. It's natural for most of us to love the attractive, desirable, worthy, valuable and useful. It's not so natural, without inspiration from our liberating God, to be drawn to do good things for those who have caused us trouble or misery. Getting right down to the Christian core of the coming of Jesus Christ, our religious "faith" in Him is the certainty that

God's intervention into our world with His kind of love turns the tide of the battle. Whether The Kingdom of God wins or loses in our time and place depends upon whether we believe in and are willing to follow God's divine love. This "faith in the trenches" is where the real battle between good and evil takes place. What will happen in the world of our new millennium? Only the Spirit of Christ, who survives in his followers, will determine the direction of His liberation movement behind enemy lines.

True Christians (not the false advertisers) can and will follow their leader and fight for freedom among our world's helpless people. The Bible testifies that Christ came to enable change to take place in hearts and minds and churches and communities. What is available... where the living Spirit is actively affecting hearers of The Word... is a whole host of regretful, contrite people, washed in purifying blessings and inspired to take on marching orders from The One Above All Others. Our Lord is our Savior, our front lines leader and the one who will bring certain victory our way, when all is said and done. Essentially, we are called out to follow in his pattern, to do things his way, to lighten the burdens of all needy ones and to be "little Christs" wherever we live. Granted Christ's followers do not have an easy task, especially in the world as we know it. It also must be said that doing Christ-like work is not for everyone. The Bible suggests that few people will desire to resist those forces that like to make us feel so good, often at least temporarily. We are all continually being seduced by "the enemy." We are made to feel that we can have whatever the world would like to offer us – not so far different from Jesus' temptations in the desert. Take your ease. Do what you want. The pleasure is yours. You deserve it. It's your life. That's an easy sell these days in our country. No wonder that so many of our contemporaries are in trouble – they are those seemingly on top of the heap, on the bottom and even in the middle. So by what power can we stay on the straight and narrow? Only the reassuring voice of Our Lord letting us know that "he will be with us" and that "we can accomplish his goals" will give us the power to get us through these difficult times.

The difficulty of our God-given mission really does require that we get "Christian basic training," as unromantic or as rigorous as that process might seem to us. We must remember that there are <u>some recruits</u> called into battle who enter the service with excitement and wonder at what lies ahead. Similarly, learning to be a "little Christ" can be the most exiting, meaningful and productive experience a human being could ever encounter. For example, first consider the opportunity of "getting into shape" physically, mentally and spiritually, maybe for the first time in your life. One could take a lot of humble "pride" in learning how to discipline oneself for the immediate and long-term future of serving in Christ's special forces. Look at the stature of one of our country's military recruits following "basic training"… and you will get a limited idea of what glorious radiance a disciple of Christ might take on after Christian basic training. The image of Mother Theresa comes to my mind as being in that mold. Then what's involved in the real world challenge of getting prepared to take on the opposing forces? Be certain that this would be hands-on training under "close simulation" if not real life circumstances. Would that mean sitting down to eat with a homeless person, housing a family without shelter, speaking up for a convicted felon, protesting the sale of military hardware or re-inventing a church building? Whatever the task, there would be some new experiences and serious challenges.

Imagine for a moment what would happen with no more entertainment sessions in church buildings. Would the name "Christian" be heard with curses on the streets? Would politicians proclaim, "God bless America" to get votes? Would the millionaire sports heroes continue to give their Christian testimonials? Imagine children learning how to resist the luxurious temptations of the world (from the mall and television screen), in order to make it easier for families to share with others and use less of the world's finite resources. Imagine young people from the slums and the suburbs meeting to help one-another battle their own particular demons. Imagine adult members of Christ's Body gathering in a home to figure out how to encourage our politicians to lead our country to less consumption and more life-enhancing foreign aid or to figure out how to help set their fellow Americans free from addictions to overeating, alcohol and other drugs, shopping, gambling, promiscuousness, competitiveness, selfish, extravagant spending and the like. Imagine religious leaders gathering in a community to share and learn how to live by choice with decreasing salaries, pension plans, health insurance, etc. or laying themselves on the line for a prisoner release program. Yes, imagine what churches would be like with "little Christs" infiltrating communities all across America... revealing self-giving love that asks for no reward in return... begging that captives be rehabilitated and released... and proclaiming that The Kingdom of Heaven is at hand! What a fantastic vision. The promise is given that it all can happen. We must start with Christian basic training.

CHAPTER 10

"A Liberating Reformation"

The time is right for the Christian Church to identify itself with it's Savior and Lord through its actions of liberation. What does freedom mean to us as we enter the third millennium? What is it worth to us? Having been in contact with The Risen Christ of the New Testament all our lives, what is our conviction about who He truly is and what He represents in today's world? Up to this point, a good share of the Christian church in our society has been tagging along... behind this Holy Man from a bygone era... with a spectator's mentality. We have heard his words, watched his miracles, prayed with him at appropriate times and cheered him on, when he has made a difference in the lives of our kind of people. Not unlike the crowd who rallied to his side as he entered Jerusalem on Palm Sunday, we have done our cheering for him too. In fact, we have carried out our public display for centuries. Jesus is a good guy God. He saves us from our sins. He has done miracles for us. He challenges those in authority over us. He even feeds us and comforts us. What's not to like? But then one day he gets personal with us. He suggests that we have to figure out what we want in our lives... other than to be taken care of and have someone in power meet all of our needs and wants. "Who do you say that I am?" he asks. In other words, am I just another excuse for you to go about your religious rituals and feel pious in celebrating your worldly life-style? Am I your God merely as long as you can feel saved, secure and superior to others? Am I simply a matter of convenience, so that you can fight for your "Christian culture" and feel justified in holding off the neglected multitudes in my name? Do we "turn away" when he tells us the cost, or are we ready to "sign up" and sacrifice our old life-style for a new beginning? The time has come for the Christian church in the western world to choose.

We know that true freedom is a wonderful thing. Underneath our pushy exterior, which gets us into all kinds of trouble, we know in our tender, humble moments that Jesus Christ has what everyone needs – love, freedom and security. All our racing around to find the things we think we want doesn't do a lot of good for ourselves or for the world we live in. Usually we have thought of people in prison as the ones who have lost their liberty and are forced to live in chains. But we have come to know better. We too are convicts in need of change and as church members we need not only Christ's vision of what life should be like in The Kingdom; we also need His dedication as a humble servant... to live truly abundant lives sharing his love. This conviction demands a change in priorities for those of us who want to get in on Christ's mission to the world. As we have said before, today's entertaining, spectator church is desperately in need of a new reformation – basically a re-formulation of what the church is and what it is commissioned to accomplish.

Educated people who have some knowledge of history know what a reformation is all about. In Martin Luther's day the reform movement certainly shook up the status quo wherever one looked. All the way from the powerful pope to the small child, it seemed like more and more people got stimulated to figure out how to go about significant life events with a different perspective. They found that they needed to get in step with the program or get out of the way. As history tells us, not very many church members got committed immediately. Luther didn't command a great following a he posted his 95 theses, but then again, neither did Jesus when he cleansed the temple. Most reform movements don't turn the world upside down immediately. The majority of us need to take a new look, try out a new experience, get put together with some like-minded people and be inspired to committed activities that carry out any new mission. It doesn't happen over night. Even destructive change takes some time to do its dirty work. Basically, we need to know in our minds and hearts that the primary thing is to just get started… on almost any little thing! Martin Luther had to have it in him to find a hammer and pound in the nail that posted the principles he believed should be debated about the church in his day. Be certain, however, that each and every person can have a part in "getting the ball rolling" on the road to a liberating reformation. In being set free, each of Christ's followers begins to contribute a useful gift to the new life of others.

"You are the salt of the earth!" Jesus proclaimed. Did Jesus really mean that Christians are meant to be the salary (salt) or "paycheck of the world?" Could Christians be "the uplift" or "the full paycheck" the world needs to be a wonderful place to live in the third millennium? As these words flow onto my "Word" computer screen, outside my window the snow falls… making for slippery conditions on all our roads. It won't be long before the city trucks spread their thin layer of salt… in order to melt the snow and ice… for the safety of many people on the move. Common salt can make nature more manageable for all of us this time of year. But salt also serves a much more important purpose for all of us. It enhances the flavor of food and provides an essential physical element for good life and health. Through God's eternal purpose and Christ's coming, Christians were not only meant to provide the basic element for healthy life on this earth but also give the world some good flavor. That means that just as Jesus laid himself out for the security and healthy living of all who follow him, so we who follow in his footsteps are meant to be "used up" or "laid out" for the safe passage of others.

Christians are called to move out as "foot soldiers" on a new mission. As our venture begins, we take our "marching orders" standing at the base of the cross. That is where every person must start; and that is where we are united with Him. We too must die to our old life in the world. Commissioned as we move out into the battlefield, it is our mission to reveal the power and new life of the resurrection. All that we as Christ's followers stand for and fight for requires we make our moves for life-enhancing change. The objective is that through death to one's old, captive nature new life can spring forth. Having been liberated, we are called to be liberators.

During the many centuries after Christ's death and resurrection, the Christian church split and headed off in two different directions with regard to the Biblical witness of His short life. The eastern church focused on the resurrection of Our Lord, while the western church focused on the cross. These two emphases have shaped not only each church's basic theology but also the way all members have conducted themselves on their personal journeys through life. Obviously the cross has been at the center of our Roman Catholic roots and worship traditions. Sadly however, for the most part, these two emphases have remained separated – each of these church traditions having lost part of its proper understanding of God's action in history through Jesus Christ. Today's reformation in the church must bring these two important parts of Christ's action into union with one-another. In a very real sense, living in the spirit of our Lord was always intended to be living in the light and recreation of both the cross and the resurrection. How good that was meant to be!

As a reformed church, the Christian Church in action

can bring resurrection to all of life. That's what Jesus meant, in part, when he suggested that we are the salt of the earth, for example. The resurrection signifies "new life," "new perspective," "new opportunities," "new purpose and mission," "new joy," "new contentment," and "new peace" – in a special sense, really all of these! Instead of being caught in an old, demoralizing, degrading, frustrating, fruitless and useless way of living life, people living in the footsteps of Jesus can provide all of the world's people with great goodness and lift. That doesn't mean that the cross (or doing away with the old) is forgotten. It merely means that the resurrected life is immediately provided as the exciting, vibrant and meaningful alternative to the old way. The present, living, Body of Christ, acting out its spirit-filled life is meant to be the earth-born Creator God -- God's life-giving Word in the flesh or in person. Today, members of His Body are called to effectively multiply by millions His resurrected power. Consider what being "little Christs" could mean to not only our own richly blessed land but also to people in all places! What "Good News" might be passed on to everyone! And what a liberating crusade to launch!

Take a glimpse into the new world of a liberating reformation. As church buildings are torn down (or used up for the liberation movement), think of the resources that would be released for mission… or for the work of the liberating forces! Most of us know about the basic costs involved in building, remodeling, beautifying and repairing, say nothing about the captivating interest payments. There's not only the money but also the time, energies and emotions involved. We may have wondered how the Israelites could have gotten sucked into throwing their precious metals into that worthless gold bull. But consider how our Creator God or our Lord of the Cross must react to the ostentatious show-places we have put up with such pride. Do we really think that the creator of neutrons and protons and the infinite universe would be stirred or impressed with our places of worship? Not when he speaks through his prophets words like --

"You people hate anyone who challenges injustice and speaks the whole truth in court. You have oppressed the poor and robbed them of their grain. And so you will not live in the fine stone houses you build or drink wine from the beautiful vineyards you plant…. Hate what is evil, love what is right, and see that justice prevails in the courts…. I hate your religious festivals; I cannot stand them!… Stop your noisy songs; I do not want to listen to your harps. Instead, let justice flow like a stream, and righteousness like a river that never goes dry."

The God of the Old and New Testaments is obviously a Father who cares about the relationships of all his children. He is not impressed with the things we build in his name. Jesus came with His dynamic, new perspective on the meaning and mission of life to make that message concrete in our minds. So idols are to be ground up and thrown away; the focus of our spirits, then, will be on the serious issues of the day. Both the Father and

Son have made clear that people who cry out for help are the ones who should get help. We are to follow our Lord's lead. If there is any doubt about the work that we should do, we learn from the scriptures that God is on the side of the "under-dogs." On the other hand, we can see from our daily experiences that the world is on the side of the rich and powerful – the winners! Countless stories from "the lost sheep" to "the beaten man beside the road" point to how God cares... and how his children should live their lives in that same spirit. Since resources are always limited, they should be used wisely to feed the hungry, house the homeless, do what can be done for the stranger and love all God's children, just as Jesus has loved us.

Worship surely would seem to be in jeopardy with church buildings on their way out. Yet there has never been any theological mandate that worship needs to be accomplished with big numbers of people. If we understand that God-pleasing worship consists of doing the work of "little Christs" throughout His creation... in thankful remembrance of Him, then that blessed experience is probably best carried out in small groups in many different places. Worship like this might be done best on a street corner, in a home, near a social service building, at a political rally or maybe even within a jail or mental institution. Christians have heard, "Where two or three are gathered in my name, there I am in the midst of them." Those words should certainly supply us with plenty of inspiration for a proper place of worship. However, those people who have merely shown up in the past for nice music, a good moral message and a comfortable feeling inside might be seriously dismayed. The "house of worship" would be gone and Christian entertainment would be only a thing of the past.

There are many other aspects of worship in our age which deserve our consideration. For example, the time many members spend in practicing music, making things for the sanctuary, laying out worship materials as well as preparing messages, prayers, liturgy, Bible readings, etc. -- all this is just so much busy-work in God's eyes. Think of the preparation done for the benefit of the many whose purpose is merely to "go to church, be comforted and feel reassured they are going to heaven." Do today's church members really believe that they are somehow doing God a favor by laying out so much of their time and talents in today's corporate worship? Or are these people intentionally "playing church" for all to see? Think of what congregations do to compete for members, church-goers or contributors. Some may feel the need to put together a radio or television program. Obviously, that demands a certain kind of technological expertise and commitment. For the "survival" of other churches, the status quo would require that publicizing should be done, welcoming committees organized, house calls made, and stewardship campaigns carried out. Practically all of this "activity" (sold to the membership as quite spiritual and beneficial to The Kingdom of God) is meant to compete in the marketplace for "lost souls." No less important to the church is the necessity that contributions keep the professional salaries paid, the debts and monthly bills covered, the programs of the church supported and maybe even a mission project funded. What a waste! The old-style worship service of contemporary America has got to go… along with the special building that makes it happen!

Tragically enough, the structured church is not only "flashy" with its showy buildings, but it is also "fat and sloppy" within its hierarchy. It's no secret that desk jobs are rampant throughout the various levels of the contemporary church. While some Christian denominations may parade wealth and power more aggressively than others, churches are few and far between where humble servant life is evident among leaders. Contrast the separation between Mother Theresa and almost any pope of the past. Which noteworthy Christian do you think more clearly follows in the line of Christ's disciples? Obviously if our Lord was thinking clearly when he suggested in the foot-washing display that his true followers and disciples would need to be servants, where does that place most of today's church leaders who have attained their status positions? What kind of example is this for poor souls who look for some kind of liberation and hope? Is the structured church anywhere to be seen?

Yes, in a truly reformed Christian church there wouldn't be much need for "king of the hill" desk jobs. The church's true leadership would be on the front lines of the forces called out to liberate those who acknowledge the burden of their chains. There is no question that today's leaders of the structured church are both talented and experienced with regard to their particular responsibilities. However, as with many privileged people, they need to be liberated from their generally meaningless tasks to use their God-given talents for truly divine goals. Of course, as with any human being, beginning to act in a new way needs to be a choice made by the heart. Jesus himself saw that struggle taking place in the many deeply religious leaders he confronted 2,000 years ago. There may be all kinds of benefits in venturing out to take on self-giving, loving challenges in the name of Jesus, yet as self-sufficient, creatures of habit who have fallen in love with all the world offers, even leaders who "know better" find Christ's calling into servant-hood seemingly too risky and too difficult a challenge to accept.

Many of our top Christian leaders do know the language of "the theology of the cross" and the purpose of the discipleship role of servant-hood. Unfortunately, over time, this tried and true mission of the Christian church has been lost -- like an old book buried in dust back in the archives. It may have been intentionally relegated to "the lost stacks area" because other popular and acceptable promotions have seemed more logical and contemporary, or it may have just drifted out of favor with the public as a result of other more profitable ventures; but in any case, "the sacred Word" on how to lay oneself out to free up the prisoners is not on anyone's reading list these days. The glimmer of hope we may still have before us rests in the fact that a good number of leaders do know where and how to find the answers to "what the world needs now." That's love, sweet love, but not sentimentally or syrupy sweet -- only the beautiful, self-sacrificing kind of love Jesus poured out on his way to the cross and resurrection.

One of the big distractions for the contemporary, structured church has been the issue of disunity and discord within the various denominations. There certainly still is a long list of theological and structural differences between many segments of what is generally considered today's "Christian" church. The real center of the problem lies in the fact that almost all the noted differences are a matter of quite unimportant concerns, considering the divine perspective. Think about how trite the differences in worship really are if what we maintain as entertaining worship is essentially abolished. Is the issue of how one interprets the Scriptures really critical in reference to how a person carries out self-giving love or how a person liberates a certain group of captives? Is even the method of baptism or the interpretation of communion a big deal when people are being called up to follow Christ into battle? What issues of great concern along denominational lines are worth losing any sleep over? Maybe it should be suggested that within the present structure of the church, the weekly agenda is so superficial that about the only things we can think of to "wrestle with" or "get exited about" are the obvious tradition-bound gaps between ourselves and other believers in the community. Here again we could all use some liberation from ego stroking campaigns that are meant to look good to the world.

It can be stated confidently that the ecumenical movement has been highly overrated.

While it is important that The Body of Christ should be united and working harmoniously under the leadership of our Lord, it is not important that church leaders spend time in trying to get the various parts of the body to think or operate in the same way. In fact when we get right down to the fundamentals of the issue, diversity rather than conformity may be more valuable to the overall performance of the church. In some future age, consider how leaders might look back and realize how many years were spent with the rather foolish and pointless drive for unity and conformity. Could a lot of these efforts (along with other similar ones) be rather like spinning our wheels to look good and make us feel as though we can feel a sense of real accomplishment, when there really wasn't much we should have been doing along that line in the first place?

The value of diversity can hardly be overstated. We only need to look at the creation… which proceeded directly from The Word of God… to realize the wonder and infinite benefits of our colorful and varied surroundings. Look at the flowers of the field and the birds of the air, listen to the sounds we hear and the words we speak, taste the delicately different flavors of all kinds of foods, smell the scents of the kitchen as well as the aromas of the wilderness and you begin to realize that our Creator God could not have intended that we be conformed to some uniform standard in expressing our spiritual nature and goals. With as many personalized "hang-ups" as we "fallen creatures" possess, it's surely necessary that the healing approaches and methods be as wide-ranging as possible. That requires the broadest band of perspectives one can possibly imagine for the healthy development and abundant living of all the peoples of the world. As much as we might think our lives would be enhanced and simplified to have a "one size fits all" religion, we would certainly be near the level of extinction if we got our wish. It seems obvious that a properly reformed and liberated church would certainly be a multicolored, free-flowing and diversified illustration of the whole universe.

Considering the important function of each person and group within an active, healthy Christian fellowship, we might marvel at the awesome tasks that could be accomplished in Jesus' name. Since each and every person has a unique history of both great successes and embarrassing defeats, in testimony to the experiences of good and bad, each person would be vitally important in the overall mission of Christ's Body. Just as one plant or animal enhances all living things around it through its living and dying, so similarly every individual would be accounted as exceedingly beneficial to the whole. The only limitation would be that each person would need to minister to others within the limits of his or her own special role and not get caught up in trying to do someone else's job. Implicit within this limitation would be the understanding that no one would need to carry an unmanageable load just as no one would be of more value to the whole than others. A considerable number of benefits would become evident within such a corporate structure: A feeling of tremendous self-worth among all individuals would pervade the church from one end to the other. The interdependence of all members would deepen and enhance security throughout all times and places as well as multiply the power available to all people. A spirit of cooperation, accountability and mutual up-building would replace jealously between different levels of authority and raise the spirit of peace, excitement and joy (just as found within healthy family life). Clarity of mission and the practice of Christ-like daily activities would free members from meaninglessness and the drab life of "running in circles." In understanding the church's vital place within contemporary culture and our environment, the ongoing process of learning our proper role in both would have serious implications for healthy, peaceful life on this planet as well as for healthy, peaceful relationships horizontally and vertically.

It's no wonder that Jesus came to "free the captives." Who is not a potential captive to some kind of detrimental influence at almost every moment of life? We have our addictions to selfish interests, working for our own security, grabbing too much of the good stuff of life, our desires for control and power over others as well as messing ourselves up -- mind, body and spirit. That's to say nothing about how we might find ourselves making mistakes that could literally find us in chains. The Lord came into our world to fight all that. Jesus said he came to give us abundant life. He wanted to redeem us for life as it was meant from the beginning -- before our fall from cooperation to destruction. Just imagine that he calls us to continue that fight for freedom! He also knows that it's going to take the best that each of us has (through his power) to win the battles we face in our place and time. Yet together in the power of his Holy Spirit we will be able to pull off "the upsets" that will enhance living and even dying for all people.

Most of us today are held tightly in bondage with regard to our use of time. As we consider our use of each day, we realize how few choices we really have… to do the kind of things that we should have as our highest priority. Make some mental notations about how much time you feel required to use for guaranteeing your own security, health and happiness, for example. Our 40 plus hours a week jobs have a central place in most of our lives along with the work it takes to exercise, eat, do our household chores, take care of home and transportation maintenance and get in on the amount of education and entertainment we believe we need to survive the rigors of our workday world. No wonder that some "thinking people" in the most envied positions our culture has to offer are taking steps to seek out a much more simple life. Christians have a more important reason to "trust in the Lord" and not get bound up just trying to secure the necessities of life – food, drink, shelter, etc. For the Christ follower, the mission to live in cooperation and balance with all people and things on this planet as well as in reverence and obedience to God takes center stage in consideration of one's use of time. This most certainly directs "little Christs" to be about the business of breaking free of bondage to worldly things and going about the business of helping others to get free also. What we are talking about here is living out a liberated life-style for the benefit of all creatures everywhere.

On of the most serious problems facing the church, especially in our capitalistic western world, is the desire of most people to move up the ladder of success – success as our culture defines it. Most of us do what is required for the materialistic rewards and the helpful "perks" we think we need. Consequently, we are chained into the daily grind as surely as a convicted criminal is attached to his or her leg irons. We even know our destiny – to strive after new job requirements, new things, new addictions, new vacations, new entertainment and new excitement, etc.… But none of it gives us satisfaction for long. As soon as we get to one level, we seem to feel the need to move on to the next level of desire, privilege, prestige or power. We live on a treadmill to nowhere.

Of course the way out this drive for superiority is the flip side of the coin -- contentment with humility. Put in another way, the divine alternative to comparing ourselves with who has more… is checking out who has less. Essentially isn't this what Jesus' birth as a baby should be teaching us? Imagine a world where sports heroes would not be thinking merely about the people above them in salary but primarily about the people who have lower income. Imagine what our world would be like if we Americans began comparing the boundless luxuries we purchase with the meager food supplies of our much poorer travelers on spaceship earth. Imagine Christ's disciples in a reformed church speaking up for an honest sharing of the world's resources, where both the very wealthy and the very poor would greatly benefit in finding the middle ground. At minimum, I would hope we "fat cats" of the world would begin to count our blessings, cut our continual striving for more and begin to consider sharing our abundance with those who have less. Christians should be leading a fresh analysis of the troubling and disastrous economic picture in today's world. Not needing to spend our lives wastefully and endlessly climbing a ladder to nowhere, think about the hours a day we would have getting into the process of freeing up fellow children of God for truly abundant living. There's an awful lot of work to be done "liberating the slaves" in our own back yard, if we can find the time and the wisdom to get ourselves on the right track.

Stepping back from our "upward mobility rat race" would focus some needed attention on the true essentials of life. How much does any one person need to live a full, rich life in God's presence? How much is enough? As technology grows and expands these days, are we headed toward a better life for all people on our planet or are we simply headed down a dead end street? Because we have a large amount of technology entering the third millennium, does that mean we need to use it or develop it… especially if our world isn't enhanced and liberated through the use of that technology? Along a similar more practical line of thinking, should we strive for more income simply because we can figure out a way to get our hands on more? Are we individuals who only react to our immediate desires for more? Considering people around the globe as well as future generations, what are the long range consequences of pulling in more income, doing more consuming or even accepting more than our fair share? These are questions that we as Christians should think about as we consider our responsibility to be sensitive and perceptive caretakers of the world we call home.

Most people who share today's small world are acquainted with family life and how members of each family try to look out for other members of that family. Age, abilities, appearance, gender, maturity, political perspective, religious conviction – none of these cause us to reject or lose concern for our brothers or sisters in a good, healthy family. Isn't this admirable interdependence "a fact of life" which should have far reaching implications for almost everyone's outlook on living in today's world? The truth is that we are all members of one family on this earth and we most certainly should be looking out for one another. This is quite the opposite of "wealthy people" being forced by masses of impoverished people to "give up what they have" for the basic survival of desperate multitudes. The far better alternative would be for Christ's followers to cut back on excessive working hours, higher salaries, luxurious purchasing and the like, realizing that they are opening up opportunities and resources for other "family members" close to home, around the globe and far into the future. With such an intuitive and comfortable perspective on our planet and its inhabitants, divinely inspired liberation could become the norm within our society and between all peoples of the world.

Speaking of some of the ideals of family life, it's important to envision the liberating and revolutionary impact upon today's basic family unit as the Christian church takes on the likeness of Christ. We must acknowledge that within our present religious, political and economic state of affairs there's some trouble brewing within the basic family unit. How could it be otherwise? Individual children and parents head off in different directions practically every day of the week. There's little cohesiveness, little communication, little understanding and little empathy for the difficulties of other family members. If a person had to point to one specific reason why we face broken down families it's this -- there just isn't enough time for parents to accomplish much of anything more enduring. The consequences are disastrous and far-reaching. Children like their parents are shallow spiritually, terribly materialistic, easily addicted to destructive habits, selfish, egocentric and often troubled. But again, how could we expect any other outcome when moral, spiritual, political and economic standards are so much in flux? What do we expect to happen when the computer/television screen, playmates and paid caretakers make most of the contributions to a child's life? It is the responsibility of the Christian church to see that such corruption does not take place. On the contrary, Christian parents who walk in Christ's footsteps are meant to "pass on" the nature of Jesus to their little ones from the time they are infants. No job is meant to be more important than spending a lot of time – from dawn until dusk -- teaching by example what serving in Christ's ministry is all about.

There's no question that parents who are liberated from materialism, upward mobility, competition, spiritual entertainment and cultural addictions could make a major impact upon their children. Almost everyone would agree parents could best spend their time teaching the next generation the fundamentals of morality, spirituality and happiness. Who could better provide perspective on the meaning of life and our final purpose and destiny than parents? Grade school through college teachers have a totally different set of directions for preparing young people to face the challenges of living in our culture today. If Mom's and Dad's had time to think about it, how could they ever imagine it would be satisfactory to endlessly transport children from one sports or entertainment event to another or yield to daily requests from their children to spend time with their friends? Contrast that kind of contemporary pressure to experiencing and practicing what it might mean to teach children how to be "little Christs" around home, at school, with friends, in loving mission to the needy and caring for the environment, etc.

It would indeed be revolutionary for this new generation

to lead us into the future thinking about the overall health policies and sustainable activities human beings should be promoting. A liberating reformation within the Christian church could set us on a path headed in that direction. The Christian mission of liberation was always meant to infiltrate every level of society as well as reach out to the most distant places of the world. All this begins with each person passing on goodness in the form of uplifting and life enhancing actions, even to the point of giving up life for another human being. It should be stated that this is a much more glorious mission than sacrificing life in the midst of today's military battlefield. Rather than learning to kill, the Christian learns to sacrifice self; rather than grabbing what others possess, the Christ follower gives of what one has to benefit others; rather than defending personal rights or one's own country, the "little Christ" points the way through a meaningful present to an eternal destiny of infinite potential. It would be awesome for a parents to know the fantastic potential of leading their offspring into abundant life and eternal happiness.

An overwhelming blessing of revolutionary living is the present enjoyment and satisfaction of The Father's creation. It must be declared off the top -- Christ came that all people might have life and have it abundantly! Since that Biblical statement had no qualifiers, it seems the statement encompasses both the present and the future. Sadly enough, often the church of the past has negated life in the present in order for "the saved" to focus on some future life apart from this world. In some ways that tendency has given church people an easy escape from responsibilities in this world. For a focus on getting saved, they have given up trying to exhibit "the fruits of the Spirit." On the contrary, the Son of God came into this world to save it, preserve it and extend it forever through His followers. The joy of seeing others benefit through receiving a fair share of the world's production should give "in the Spirit" Christians an enduring "high." But there are other "warm fuzzys"… for seeking justice, loving others and avoiding the traps of self-centered living. Watching Jesus walk the paths of righteousness and following him, his followers can't help but relax a bit in the simple life of… smelling the flowers, watching sunsets, visiting with neighbors, cheering for prisoners being set free and extemporaneously praising and thanking God for his goodness!

There is "great beauty" and "fine art" in doing The Master's bidding. In the process of being liberated in our own lives… as reformed church members and actors on the stage of divine intervention, we desire to see even our old enemies up and running free of harmful, destructive and contaminating forces. A world of peace and love is always on the doorstep, although there is no kidding ourselves that we can attain God's ultimate hope for us in the present. Looking into the infinite heavens we come to understand that we are faulty and fallible, yet still called and chosen to do the most precious things that can be done in the universe. There does not seem to be any rigid containment scheme in the stars, as far as we can see. There is only freedom and beauty and simple creativity for us to build our earthly models around. On the bright side – maybe only encompassed in the star of Bethlehem – we can come to understand and practice self-giving love in our Lord's footsteps! What a beautiful, liberated and revolutionary calling from The Master of the universe.

CHAPTER 11

"Criminals Becoming Crime Fighters"

"A miracle" can come down to earth for every human being. Would any one of us deny a miracle to even a person we might perceive as "the scum of the earth?" All people on this planet have their ups and downs, their good days and bad days, their victories and defeats as well as their successes and even their "crimes." In some ways we are all cut from the same cloth – vulnerable, centered on ourselves, susceptible to addictions and somewhat rebellious. There's no question that most of us would like to see ourselves as better than other people or maybe even superior to a majority of people. Yet even if this was true, can any of us claim to have attained such a lofty position on our own? It's only reasonable to admit that each and every one of us is a product of our genes (what we have inherited biologically) and our environment (what has surrounded us since we have entered the world). Essentially then we have been given almost all of who we are and what we possess, obviously with some of us having received more benefits than others. My parents always reminded us as children that "life is not fair." Usually that would be at a time when we felt we had not received our fair share and so felt hurt or mistreated. I seem to remember, however, that my parents almost always tried to even things out a bit if one of us seemed to be doing a lot better than another. It wasn't necessarily that we "deserved it" but more a matter of understanding our hurt or weakness and trying to compensate for the world's harshness. Here was something given to us "out of the ordinary" or beyond the scope of the fairness of the world. In some small way a tiny miracle had occurred and we were uplifted and encouraged to plow ahead through the world's inequity.

Since we live in a world where we all compete to the best of our ability in "a survival of the fittest", almost all creatures on this planet (ourselves included) struggle for some superiority. Children are trained to work hard, compete and even fight for the top. This helps to insure survival, say nothing about advancing our species or our particular biological make-up. So we struggle forward and even try to push others back if it seems to be in our own interest. Nothing is very surprising in all of this – life is not fair! But again, since there is quite a bit of goodness in "family life" where we have people who look over us and compensate for the inequities (also giving us more security), it's rather reassuring that there is some "justice or fairness" distributed from above, maybe even beyond our understanding. Most of us even in our moments of feeling superior understand the value of such living because we never know for sure that we won't need some outside help someday. The real insightful method of finding success in the rough and tumble of life is to... learn everything you can, work hard, do your best and always carry some "insurance for failure." In other words, don't ever figure that you will be above getting some special help or needing "a miracle" somewhere along the line. Outside "intervention" activates the goodness of family life, provides a way to accomplish survival, and gives motivation for balancing up the score. In a way, this all just makes sense in a world such as ours.

To elaborate just a little, most citizens of the world are deeply into advancing their own personal interests; yet truth be told, human beings have always have been broad based survivalists. On the one hand, there aren't very many people who generally consider themselves in the business of leveling out inequities or providing a miracle for someone else. We are just too busy trying to get ahead of those who are running from behind and wanting to take our places. However, in our smarter or more inspired moments, most of us realize that we also have some part in an overall "insurance plan." It's essential that we contribute to the welfare of all, if we ever hope to collect any special benefits ourselves. We know that we need to be smart and not just instinctively selfish. This is the place where we need to face up to the fact that it's also in our long-term interests to look out for the "underdog"… or the one who has gotten "a raw deal" from the jungle out there. Not only is this outlook a valuable spiritual insight, but it is also a family thing and even a matter of survival.

Where the rubber hits the road is where we start looking

over the inequities of life and trying to decide what if anything we should do for the sake of "righting the wrongs." Our instinct is to over-look other people's problems but generally not our own, especially in our younger years. When we are little, we can easily feel the roughness of life's bad breaks. Also there are the problems of receiving insurmountable handicaps, going down the wrong road out of ignorance or limited choices or maybe even getting pushed around by those who don't play by the rules. At certain times in our lives it appears that everyone needs some help to be able to endure life's onslaught. Why is it few families are able to steer clear of endless problems during a child's teen-age years, for example? What about the children that don't seem to get needed help to stay away from dangers in society? When we start thinking about it, the real fortunate ones among us are the ones who get stopped early and often after drifting into trouble spots. Such people learn their lessons at a young age and are able to build on good habits, good training, good resources, good feelings and good environmental factors, etc. We know only too well what happens to young people who experience the opposite – the bad side of living conditions. In fact, most of us know what it means to be "hurting," because in focusing our attention on those who have it better, we feel the sting of those who have it worse. In the final analysis, almost all of us are in the same boat – facing many challenges to our rush for success. The only real difference between the winners and the losers is that some people seem to get a lot more of the advantages. People on the losing end usually just get one setback after another. Surprisingly enough these poor souls might not even recognize how they are hurting or disadvantaged until it's too late.

Let's take a look at the situation of people who have been judged to be in conflict with the law – real "disadvantaged" people -- convicts, for example. Recently a popular and newsworthy National Football League athlete was interviewed and quoted at length. One of the questions he was asked… was about where his troubles got started. Even though he was extremely talented, wealthy, popular and had tremendous advantages, he still found himself in serious conflict with the law and had to serve what amounted to a brief but traumatic time in prison. His short answer as to how he could jeopardize his great advantages and get himself into such trouble was simple and yet very insightful: "I would have to say it started way back in high school!" If he had thought about it a bit longer, he might have indicated that it started soon after he was born. He took a lot of steps, some small and some large, to a place in life he never would have dreamed he would experience. After the whole humbling and tragic event, he took it upon himself to warn his fortunate friends about how seductive the path was to a destination that nearly destroyed him.

Clearly most people born into any particular society have similar temptations. It becomes quickly obvious that in a materialistic culture such as ours there is a tendency to desire what others possess. All forms of advertising encourage such desires. As children are in contact with other children, almost all act as "walking billboards" for others who are without. Such interaction is undoubtedly accentuated in certain pockets of poverty where deprivation is highlighted... even as examples of wealthy accumulation and consumption are not far away. So how does an individual go about securing desirables that one's peers possess? We all are trained to use whatever method works in our particular environment. Using the example of children – some ask their parents for what they want; some receive gifts; some compete; some work; some earn money; some learn to live without; some steal; some become frustrated or angry; some might even kill to have a certain attractive object. Usually our environment dictates the acceptable or necessary methods to use, with any one particular approach virtually impossible to use in different circumstances. Where in one place a gun is available but no money, it's nonsense to suggest money is the answer. We all learn and adapt to our surroundings or we are left behind and become extinct. The whole scene is pretty basic and we learn to survive. Backed against the wall in certain places within our society, crime appears to be and maybe is the only way to catch up, even though it might seem a bit risky to some. Still who ever plans to get caught, especially when no individual ever gets caught in every circumstance? We learn to take our chances... and we sometimes find ourselves living close to crime.

Crime happens. Has anyone ever lived who never broke the law? Maybe there has been someone who has never been caught breaking the law, but who has not found him or herself at least (in a sense) "committing a crime?" This is why we all as special creatures of the earth should be examples to one another – in our temptations, vulnerability, responsibility and adaptability. Consider the similarities of our emotions, intellects and physical functions. To illustrate, think about how the human emotion of anger has carried all of us close to hurting another person and how a slight increase of that anger, in certain circumstances, could have severely hurt or even killed another. None of us are so very far away from that criminal serving a life sentence. It also would be good for us to think about the accidents of life – like being in the wrong place at the wrong time… and being responsible for whatever disastrous event may have occurred, as sad or as tragic as circumstances dictated. Who deserves to have another chance? Who would we want to control whether or not we receive that opportunity?

None of us on this earth honestly knows the future. If we did we might see with the eyes of God… or at least we probably could command almost unlimited wealth. Since we do not know what's ahead of us, we can't easily know the outcome of many of our choices nor the outcome of what our environment offers us. The only wisdom we have that's truly valuable and enlightening is where our steps have taken us in the past. Normally parents are the specialists who can give us some guidance with regard to the usual consequences of certain actions. It's good that children have a chance to learn from experienced people willing to share their personal successes and defeats and who also care about their children's long-term welfare. What could be a better way for a child to be able to avoid a lot of hurts and disasters than by following parental advice with a spirit of happiness and thankfulness? Still, many youngsters feel the need to learn on their own and since they are especially susceptible to following their inexperienced friends, they often stumble from one bad experience to another. It turns out we are all quite vulnerable people... since we do not know the future... and since we often don't want to learn from those who we should trust the most.

How enlightening it would be for us to understand some of the pitfalls, handicaps, environmental hazards, bad choices, bad breaks, seductions and just simple screw-ups that can cause a person to finally get caught and sent to prison. That's usually a fundamental experience only a convicted person knows enough about to pass on. Knowledge of that kind might be enough to set us off in a different direction, so it's extremely valuable information indeed. What might be the small but ongoing steps in a person's life that takes one... from smoking a first cigarette as a child... to killing another person as a young adult? How does a person move from a rather innocent action to a desperate one... in an attempt to steal money for the sake of getting more mind altering drugs? Only "the criminal mind" can know how that progression takes place. Just as doctors can warn their patients about the consequences of taking certain medications or carrying out certain physical activities, so any and all criminals have inside information as to the process involved in drifting into a certain criminal activities. A lot of people could benefit from hearing testimony about critical life events that are shared for the purpose of warning others. For some children at certain stages of vulnerability, a former criminal's insight into dangerous behavior just might be one step above even parental sharing of their experiences. Rehabilitated criminals could be wonderful resources for communities interested in healthy change.

As good as it might be for us to get critical warnings from those who have hurt themselves, criminals prepared to fight crime in vulnerable communities would need to both show ability to succeed at their assigned tasks and avoid drifting back into their old patterns. Neither of these objectives would be easy. Yet they could be accomplished in a relatively short period of time using proven techniques. Aside from intensive analysis of why, when, where and how they broke the law… as well as preparation to help others stay away from crime, these changed specialists could work successfully in twos. In many parts of the world the practicality of such teamwork has been proven in the area of shared economic responsibility – interdependency in small businesses. Applied to rehabilitated convicts, the wisdom and reliability of the approach would be simple: First, each relies on the other for freedom from prison. If one betrays the trust of society or messes up, both are returned to their previous confinement with significantly less chance of a new opportunity. Second, they are paired to help each other resist the temptations of criminal activity. Third, as inter-reliant, they encourage, reinforce and even correct one another in the tasks they are assigned. Fourth, and finally, they climb the ladder of success together – receiving incentives and rewards as a team and sharing economically. We can quickly understand how critical it would be for both to stay on "the straight and narrow" in order to hold onto the rewards, prestige and freedom they have worked hard to attain.

The question arises as to what specifically rehabilitated law-breakers might do to fight crime in society. The first consideration should come from the specific needs of any community. Are teen-agers getting into serious trouble with the law? Is there a major drug problem? Do dangerous gangs roam the streets freely? Could parents use some direction and support in raising their children? What are the discipline problems that schools can't seem to master? Changed people from prison could spend time offering perspectives and warnings that arise from their own experience. They have felt the weaknesses that lead people down the road to bondage and disaster. They know why certain individuals yield to certain pressures and what the final results are likely to be. What are the personal risks that an individual should never take because of the probable outcome? What is the ultimate damage to society as a whole… in lost freedom, costs of incarceration, family disintegration, personal economic setback, limited productivity and other detrimental factors? People who have been there and have overcome their weaknesses could offer critical assistance to many who have little or no previous experience.

Here are a few other insights as to what experts in crime could offer to immature lawbreakers. Meditate on the value of getting "inside information" concerning a gang's plans, a robber's techniques or a killer's mentality. What would it be like for a child to hear a convicted adult talk about temptations experienced at the same age… as well as what could be done to resist? Ideas to prevent crime from getting a foot-hold in a community would serve as extremely helpful for its leaders and planners. Law makers would be well served to learn how to put together better laws to restrain the development of crime and to properly deal with the victims of crime as well as the perpetrators. Imagine what families could learn about how crime is inspired, what both children and adults need to resist corruption, when to say no to social pressures, where bad influences lurk nearby and why everyone needs to feel good about corrective change. The options for dedicated crime fighters are almost endless.

Criminals are the best experts society has on the origins of crime. We may wonder at times about where crime comes from, if we happen to be far removed from the source of a certain type of crime. It's hard for anyone who has never known hunger, for example, to truly empathize with someone who lives in the midst of hunger every day. Contrast the life-styles and life experiences of people who throw away large amounts of food in a wealthy suburb with street people in a run down inner city looking through garbage containers for something to eat. It doesn't take much imagination to figure out that these contrasting individuals and situations don't have much in common. Likewise it seems pretty clear that there isn't usually much understanding of what goes on in any totally unfamiliar place. This is the complex and troublesome situation in most societies where the rich, powerful and relatively lawful people are in charge of dictating what happens to the poor, powerless and relatively unlawful members of a community. Not much works very well. What does become clear is that if leaders in a community want to understand something about the source of any problem that needs to be faced, they had better try to get some answers from where the problem originates. Think about how foolish a doctor would be to jump to the conclusion that an infected hand needs to be amputated rather than try to find out the source of an infection and remove it. Obviously criminals can tell us a lot about crime if we are willing to take the time to listen.

One of the serious problems we have in dealing with crime has to do with our impatience and frustration with something we don't understand very well. Let's use the illustration of "the family unit" to try to figure out our hang-ups, since most of us do know something about how the family in our culture functions for the benefit of everyone. Getting right to the point, children are generally the ones in a family who break the rules established by the parents. Of course, parents are the ones who stop the rule-breakers as well as punish them, if that seems to be the answer. Now no one in a family wants anything but the best for every member, although neither does anyone want to be hurt or set back by any other member of the family. Certainly good parents establish both positive and negative incentives for their children at different stages of their lives. The critical question in all of this has to do with how parents carry out good training and discipline in family life. Think about whether you would agree or disagree with the following principles in raising a good family: All family members are interested in the welfare of all the others. There is no possibility of giving up on any family member. Very rarely does a family member think much about the punishment he or she might get before breaking a rule. Punishment usually doesn't help a law-breaker to live life better. Parents need to motivate their children to good behavior with positive and sometimes negative incentives. Parents need to stop the hitting and hurting at the earliest possible time. At no time should a parent resort to hurting a child. At no time should a parent lock a child away or deprive that child of love, basic needs and a healthy environment. It's desirable that all family members learn from one another and be interested in forgiving one another. All members of a family hold one another responsible for caring and sharing within the household. Everyone understands that the family unit is very important to the survival of individuals within society as well as to their healthy growth and development. I would guess that most people around the world would agree that a majority of these principles are wise and worthwhile to implement in families everywhere. However, most people would also agree that they are somewhat idealistic and not easy to practice. In fact, the problem many people face in today's society, where there seems to be little time for the family unit to share... or even communicate... is that parents as well as children are frustrated, impatient, intolerant and judgmental about their fellow family members. It's no wonder then that considering our difficulty in practicing healthy family principles, it's also extremely hard for us to understand how crime in our society should be handled. We are caught doing many wrong things in raising our children as well as being colossal failures in dealing with criminals.

As many people have shifted with the tide of those who have given up on loving, healthy, family relationships, so society also has given up on our fellow citizens who have gone wrong. Many of us don't have much patience with those who have broken the rules and screwed up their lives. Let them suffer the consequences of their bad decisions, we say to ourselves. If they don't learn from their punishments, then the law-enforcers and judges should just increase the penalties. This is about where we are in the public's general perception of "the justice system" today. To be blunt about it, we are just flat out going the wrong way – a way that will bring us eventually to a total collapse of civilized living. Hate will not remove hate from our society. Mere punishment will not bring thoughtfulness and concern for others. Retribution will never produce peace and newness of life. Terrible prison conditions will not produce renewed minds, bodies and souls. It all seems so obvious when a person thinks about it. Yet we just roll along with letting the lowest common misconceptions inform the decisions we make with regard to how we want to treat others. Should there be public outrage when a child is found literally locked in a cage, feeling anger and deprivation and having almost no chance to grow into a contributing, loving human being? What should be our proper reaction? Now consider how those parents of the caged child should be treated. Are they any less confused, messed up, spiritually starved or needing help than the poor child? As decision-makers in society, should we just give up on all deprived people and throw away the keys!? That would be the only solution if there were no hope for change. We all need to project our best thinking into how healthy change can take place within the mind, body and spirit of every member of our society.

Most of us would acknowledge that children can change, but it's no less important for us to acknowledge that adults, mental patients and even old people can also change. It may well be true that people who have "grown up" could be even better at beneficial change and handling change than young people! We have already seen the helpfulness of looking into the past for inspiring reference points, especially when we are able to gracefully face up to where and how we have gone wrong. It doesn't take too much wisdom to turn the tables on wrong decisions and make some improvements. There are no better people to figure out the best way to go than mature adults because they have a perspective on the past – what hasn't worked and what can be improved upon. Since most criminals generally are by definition adults rather than children there is often some understanding about what has gone wrong. Maybe adults are often unwilling to consider the fact that they may get caught, since that may well be their experience, but they aren't mystified by the idea that certain things are against the law and that there should be payment for crime. Generally people would agree that people who violate the law should be stopped. It's just that we would like to exclude ourselves from the rule because we think that our circumstances are special. Of course we never stop to think that almost everyone has special circumstances. It's a rare individual indeed who wants to get stopped for speeding by the patrol officer. Contemplate the perspective of a person who recognizes the wrong action they have taken immediately after that action takes place and then also feels the need for correction. That's pretty close to penitence. On the other hand, a child might not understand why there are speeding laws in the first place.

It might be interesting to consider how many convicts are actually "penitent people" after they have been judged guilty. Penitent people are those who acknowledge that they have done wrong, are sorry that they committed crimes and are willing to pay for their mistakes. From the perspective of a civilized society, the truly dangerous people – the impenitent, the people who should be "put away" for a time – are those who in fact have carried out serious crimes but are unwilling to acknowledge or understand them. They are the ones who are an ongoing problem to a civilized society because they are high risks to the safety and well being of people in community. There many examples of powerful and influential people who continually deny wrong-doing, as if their lives depended on it. Why has our society made it so trendy to deny guilt or crime? Is it because we can't handle guilt… or will feel worthless forever? Is it that society will take everything away from us? What would happen if admitting guilt and learning how to change were the accepted and rewarded way of coping with breaking the law? Think of the benefits to society as well as to individuals themselves. Obviously penitent people would not need to be punished to change. Obviously society would not be doing itself any favor by spending a large amount of money to incarcerate productive people. Obviously changed convicts might be able to repay part or all the debt they incurred in committing their crime. Obviously rehabilitated convicts could be wonderful examples to others who are tempted to tie themselves up in bondage and deterioration. So how could society go wrong in helping its most unproductive citizens become some of its most productive?

Many law-abiding citizens around the world care about what happens to their fellow human beings. Such concern goes beyond simply the natural caring that would be evident between family members. Where people are starving, others send food. Natural disasters such as hurricanes, floods, fires and droughts usually bring aid from all parts of the planet. Most people feel good about helping others who are hurting. Sick individuals are sent to hospitals or the equivalent in practically every culture. We all want our loved ones to get the help they need and that feeling often spreads beyond families to empathy with very different people in very different cultures. Considering "different" human beings, we can't very easily overlook criminals or people in prison. How strange or out of the ordinary would it be for law-abiding citizens to voice the opinion that criminals need help? In fact, isn't that exactly what law-breakers (those who have done bad things to others) need is help? They need to learn where they got started down the wrong path, why the law should protect everyone, what it feels like to be hurt or treated roughly, what the results are of an addiction, how they have injured a community with their crime, how one bad experience can easily lead to an even worse experience, how they have let down many of their family and friends… and on and on. People who have violated the law, maybe even more than any others, need special help or treatment in order to become trustworthy and productive citizens. Not unlike a person with cancer, heart disease, broken bones or paralysis, a criminal need some serious intervention, insight as to what not to do in the future, a way out of their particular weakness and encouragement from the people with whom they come in contact. Maybe we should even feel "a bit sorry" for those who have experienced "bad breaks," whether they were self-inflicted or not. In the end, for more reasons than one, it's good when we truly care about one another. We are truly interdependent people.

Specialists in an "emergency ward" have to know proper procedures for getting a patient from a crisis situation back to healthy, productive living. So also individuals who have drifted from hopefully "at least good conditions" into "the crisis situation of crime" also need to be led through their desperate state of affairs back into a healthy environment. That's going from health to sickness and from sickness back to health again. With the complexity of the body, the challenge in the hospital's "emergency ward" is not simple. With the criminal and the complexity of the mind, the intervention needed is often considered very difficult to impossible. Drastic problems call for drastic measures and today's prison probably does provide a measure of what is needed. Crime, criminal activity, law-breaking, a hurtful life-style, personal deterioration, mental problems, bad habits, spiritual sickness -- all this and more has to be stopped dead in its tracks. A prison cell and chains are probably needed to "stop the hemorrhaging." It's further instructive to remember that people in crisis are not usually to be counted on for suggestions as to what they might need. The person convicted of a crime probably has more than one personal problem and needs to have a lot of previous activities, habits and desires come to a screeching halt. The "corrections" of the prison as well as the "disciplined" environment can help to bring some stability to a life in desperate straits.

Anyone who is "soft on crime" undoubtedly doesn't fully comprehend the importance of liberating change. Crime is serious business. Society makes laws that are meant to benefit the harmonious functioning of all its members. Everyone is entitled to benefit from good laws and consequently breaking those laws constitutes a break with the welfare of all. Turning around a criminal is of critical importance to the justice system. Considering most criminals will be back on the streets sooner or later, it's critically important that change within the criminal mind takes place early and sincerely. What does it take to get a messed up mind, body and spirit working toward the desired result – humility, penitence, change in perspective and a healthy life-style? For the cocky, aggressive, self-centered and uncontrollable individual, treatment in the beginning might be as radical as putting a drug addict in a straight jacket and padded cell. A "loved one" might prescribe such an approach for getting a deteriorating life under control. Probably a high number of law-breakers are accustomed to doing what they want, when they want, how they want. Some may even think the crime they committed is funny, deserved, justified or insignificant. Obviously such a pattern can't continue, so some form of prison life will hopefully bring a stop to detrimental patterns and hurtful behaviors, open their entire existence to new possibilities, direct their efforts toward a better life and help them change into admirable members of any community. That's what any caring society should hope to accomplish.

Few criminals, if any, have probably ever considered their conviction and prison sentence to be "a miracle from above." It doesn't take much imagination to think about such an "upset" in exactly this way, however. Many if not most people pray for some radical "turn-around" in their fortunes, although they might have in mind "winning the big one," becoming the president of some impressive corporation or maybe even just finding a hide-a-way in some beautiful surroundings to live in peace and comfort. Their prayer is for a radical change when they are confronted with difficult or troublesome living conditions. So consider carefully what it might mean to "an out of control troublemaker" to get problematic, fearful, detrimental and socially unacceptable behavior stopped by an outside force. What might it mean to envision a new, profitable, satisfying and respected life as a very real option for the future? And finally what might mean to find oneself in the process of changing one's life into a beautiful, inspired, creative example of hope to others in need? Criminals can become crime fighters; and such a reversal is quite close to a "miracle sent from above."

CHAPTER 12

"Training Centers For A New Social Order"

Most prisons should be a major embarrassment for civilized people entering the 21st century. Possibly the greatest disaster can be found in the fact that there are probably few significant differences in prisons from one part of the world to another. The "hell holes" of one country are close to the "hell holes" of another. Different generations and races have made great strides to honor and uplift the human race – from unbelievable technological advances to awesome artistic expressions. Yet from one culture or era to another we have accomplished little in our understanding about how to deal with the "the bad person" and bring about mental and spiritual change. When any individual within a particular society has violated established law... that person is "put away" – out of sight and out of mind -- as garbage would be relegated to the dumping grounds. Societies may be unwilling to take the time or make the effort to rehabilitate troublesome citizens or good citizens may want to punish bad citizens for their misdeeds. In any case, troublesome people around the world are continuing to be treated as so much trash.

Our problems with prisons have become much more than just an embarrassment. They cost us the time and resources put into building them as well as the staff to keep them running. Overall costs for each inmate per year are far greater than a student's costs of working for a degree in one of our best private colleges or universities. Prisons are also documented evidence that people on the right side of the law are not willing (or have not been able) to do much to properly care for those on the wrong side. Whether social failures, neglected citizens, punished troublemakers, immature adults, poor decision-makers or even flat out innocent people, in effect, all are thrown into cages of neglect and despair. No one knows all the sick and terrible acts that are committed within prison walls, where bad habits to unspeakable acts are carried out as merely part of the environment. Is this what any person would "wish" for a loved one in trouble? Not only are prisoners corrupted even more deeply within such a detrimental place, but a high percentage of families must also get caught up in resentment, anger, frustration and enduring pain. Without much help to get their messed up lives straightened out, most prisoners are drawn to the "professionals" to perfect their terrifying techniques of paying back "the system" for the horrifying treatment they have received. How could any sane people think that prisoners could do anything different considering their "treatment?" What could possibly give them the wisdom or the strength to counter-act their detrimental surroundings? Finally having served their time, who but a few courageous citizens would want to take a chance on employing these social rejects just out of prison? The last straw is... even law-abiding citizens like criminals would undoubtedly choose to go back to the environment called "home", probably where all the trouble started. It may be surprising that there isn't more recidivism as we contemplate the status quo in prisons today.

Prisons operate as they do in large part because of the "normal reactions" of those who have been "hurt" in many ways by criminals. It's natural for a person to be angry when targeted with any crime, whether that constitutes money being stolen or the murder of one's child. After any crime is committed, a community feels somewhat less secure. The rules of every law-abiding citizen are violated. It's irritating that anyone should feel above the law. The time, effort and cost of stopping a criminal act require that a community pays a price. The legal system also requires much time, patience, persistence and extensive funding. For the individual or group hurt by a criminal act there's personal loss, feelings of frustration about fairness, time loss, why it happened, who committed the crime, slow court proceedings, what (if any) payback there will be, and other such concerns. Undoubtedly, this is just the beginning of the pain and suffering any crime causes respectable citizens. There's a lot of anger to go around, and consequently our justified reaction is to punish the law-breaker. Sometimes a life sentence or the electric chair doesn't seem to be enough. A community spokesman is unapologetic in saying that death is too good for a certain killer. That brings us to the "fairness issue" which also naturally causes a lot of dismay. Why does so-and-so get only a few months in prison while such-and-such gets fifteen years? With all the hurt, anger and frustration about crime, there's no wonder that reactionary punishment is on the minds of many.

As justified as any person or group might feel in prolonged anger and desire for retribution, there are major problems for a society facing such an approach in dealing with criminals. Who wants any crime that is committed carried out a second or third time? Without rehabilitation the likely-hood is quite high. Isn't change and stopping that crime more important? Is anyone more healthy, better off or even truly satisfied in seeking severe punishment for a convicted criminal? Certainly a vengeful attitude hinders health and happiness just as forgiveness promotes them; moreover, citizens who are outside the scope of the crime have very little to gain from retribution. Does one tragic event even the score with a second tragic event? Everyone knows that two wrongs do not make a right. In fact, the hurt, outreach and disaster of the crime is greatly increased. Is it wise for mature and lawful people to carry out questionable practices in the name of justice? It needs to be said that few (if any) intelligent people weigh out the consequences of a crime before committing it. That very thought process would probably keep most crimes from happening. Men, women and children not only do not know the future, but they tend to justify their particular circumstances. Especially "immature minds" minimize the possibilities for getting caught say nothing about overlooking the punishment they might receive. Surely a good justice system would reveal the ability to get beyond "an eye for an eye"... into righting wrongs and helping all those who have been hurt in one way or another. Who is responsible for prison atrocities? None of us should feel good about terrible acts being committed under our community's guidance and support. Should responsible citizens feel good about doing something bad to anyone? Most members of good families are aware that loving and caring go a lot further in correcting bad behavior than "striking back" ever accomplished. Is it proper for payback or punishment to be supported by community funding? Who wants to be the "hit man" for "getting even" with even the worst offenders? Where does a solid moral perspective come into play, say nothing of a spiritual one? Not all religions or moral philosophies would subscribe to such a standard as "love your enemies", but almost all would urge at least civilized treatment for people who admittedly have made big mistakes. Would we like history to show us as reactionary and vengeful people? No culture wants to be relegated to "the dark ages" of history with regard to any serious endeavor. Yes, there are a lot of troubling questions, moral dilemmas and spiritual gaps involved in our prison policies today. But with clear thinking and insightful ideas, we can overcome the detrimental "status quo" of our depressing justice system.

This basic question comes up quickly in any discussion of prisons and their functions: "Why should I or anyone else care what happens in a prison?" The underlying attitude is that "criminals have made their beds, so now let them sleep in them." There is some truth to the idea that people who violate the law probably "deserve" some lawlessness. We think that those who treat others in a shabby manner should find out what it feels like. Furthermore, who hasn't had some warning about the consequences of breaking the law? Yet all these comments are at a level of some immaturity – the child in kindergarten scolding that if you hit me then I'll hit you back. It's the way the world works, but it's pretty infantile -- not much more than a jungle mentality. Human beings, as reasoning, caring, spiritual creatures (some say, created in the image of God), should move on to a bit higher level of insight. Almost everyone should be aware that criminals finally serve their time and come back into society. Consequently, it should be in society's self-interest that those who commit crimes (at minimum) be helped or changed enough in a positive way to insure that crimes are not committed again. A second reason citizens should care what happens in a prison... is that in the event of some "quirk of fate," it's possible any person might find themselves behind bars and want a second chance for a profitable life. Third, everyone should be interested in the most cost-effective way to get a law-breaker's mind straightened out... for selfish reasons if not for the sake of their caretakers, families and any future contacts. Finally, just as interdependent people want their neighbors to get the help they need (such as in receiving medical treatment or encouraging laboratories to find a cure for cancer), similarly all participants in our system of justice should be continually striving to learn what successfully can bring about desired change among those who have violated the law. Prisons are in a great position to do experimentation, gain valuable knowledge and come to the aid of their assigned inhabitants -- people that are in effect "a captive audience." Certainly it's evident there are many good reasons why everyone should care about what happens in prisons today.

It's worth emphasizing that a prison is an excellent facility for distributing good information as well as encouraging change. Not too many residents will miss classes or meetings because of prior commitments or vacation plans. Still, profitable education can't possibly take place if it's not readily available; whether "it is" or "is not" is determined by political and social initiatives, pressures and the general wisdom and progressiveness of any society. It's also obvious that learning can't take place very easily if inmates aren't interested in receiving what is offered. In any community's school system, where money and strong encouragement is granted for a good educational system, teachers know that it's difficult to teach if there isn't inspiration to learn. As much as we might like prisons to change convicts and educate them for productive positions in society, these institutions can't do the job without several pretty important common denominators as well as encouragement from the outside world.

Inspirational educators are essential to prisons, if prisons are to be training centers for accomplishing necessary change with inmates and for gaining expertise in what needs to be done to uplift society. Businesses call in "motivational speakers" who are experts in enhancing business production. Think about what people like this might be able to do for convicts who are wiped out and without almost everything they desire. Furthermore, prisoners would need instruction and inspiration for coping with problems in body, mind and spirit, since we know that each part of our being interacts with the others. Moral training "by the book" and "through practical experience" would likewise be very important to both understanding and practicing change. Spiritual guidance might be of great benefit in coping with years of deterioration and neglect. Essentially, a lot of experts in different fields could be of great usefulness as could educators with broad experience across many fields. What might be the personal rewards for people working in training centers... equipping the most challenging members of our society to become not only non-destructive but a nearby warning to others? Imagine what it would be like to become a personal trainer for an inmate rather than a personal jailer.

On the other side, it must be tough to work in a prison as primarily one who continually needs to assert control, enforce restrictions and distribute punishment. That must be a little bit like trying to live in the same battlefield trench as "the enemy". It may be somewhat helpful for us to understand the mind of the convict who deals daily with the fact that within the prison walls society calls the shots, but outside those same walls the criminal has the opportunity for control. The task or mission of the change agent or educator is to begin to release the chains and ease the punishment within the confines of the prison… so that outside those confines there is little incentive for the convict to reverse the power struggle. It's possible that helpfulness within the walls of the prison (through motivation, training and encouragement) might bring similar helpfulness outside that same environment. In any case, the level of hurt and recrimination is lowered with more understanding and caring treatment. Both patients and care takers are better off.

One part of the goal for getting convicts into contributing roles within the community is to prepare them for positive interaction with other individuals and groups. Only as people interact in healthy ways with other partners within the community can they find meaning and true satisfaction in their work. With such interaction there is the second benefit of positive peer pressure to continue the drive toward responsible and productive citizenship. It seems very probable that the lack of close interaction with parents, family, loved ones, positive role models and law-abiding authority figures may have been a major factor in their slide into criminal behavior. Consequently, it's quite important that serious encouragement should be offered incarcerated individuals to reestablish good, complimentary, healthy ties with a broad range of upstanding citizens. One positive step down this road to interdependence might be taken in involving as many family members as possible in the rehabilitative process. Family members as well as close friends have quite a number of beneficial things to contribute in the process of learning, healing and changing. Such important people in a convict's life know the environment from which he or she departed... whether those surroundings were a help or a hindrance. Such people could undoubtedly be a real plus for providing encouragement and understanding throughout what might be a somewhat difficult process of change. Of course, their interaction with the convicted person would need to be coordinated carefully with prison trainers and other personnel so that all participants would be seeking the same harmonious results.

If significant strides were being made to encourage criminals to become crime fighters... within certain prisons, then it would be advisable to turn at least a certain portion of those prisons into good quality educational facilities. All members of the human race are deeply affected by their surroundings -- mentally, emotionally and perhaps even physically. A drab, dull, tight enclosure certainly will not catch the eye, push the body or inspire the spirit to acknowledge inspiration, hope or newness. Words, deeds and facilities all need to function together and relate to everyone involved that something new, refreshing and wonderful is in the process of happening. It isn't necessary in the short term that education or training facilities or resources be extravagant or "top of the line". However, they should be enough to serve the basic needs of both teachers and students. The example of what public universities are given to train students might be a practical reference point, since relevant expertise and innovative training methods would be greatly beneficial.

A prison functioning as a training center for convicted criminals needs a proper curriculum of education matched with good resources and surroundings. Today's prison population has about as many educational needs as anyone could possibly imagine. Inmates vary within specialized prisons serving different functions, but as a rule inhabitants range all the way from having the most basic needs to having some of the most sophisticated. One could imagine needing to teach a convict how to read and write as well as try to understand how a convict might cope with the most complicated mental disease. That challenge gets a bit frightening when attempting to look at the big picture. A conscientious prison official might become frustrated with the overwhelming challenge of trying to heal everyone, where clearly no one could ever be completely cured. The more reasonable and workable solution for prison workers would be to try to make each person's life just a bit better, moment by moment, step by step and insight by insight. The real uplift for everyone is that lives are nearly always improving in a somewhat controlled, ongoing process. As training moves forward and all the inmates begin to understand their benefits as well as their opportunities, nearly everyone could feel needed and honored playing a part in raising up others for a more liberated, fulfilled and happy life.

Addiction is one of the most common acute problems among residents of a prison. No doubt a good share of the population in our western culture suffers from at least a mild form of this failing. Within a culture that elevates individualism, self-centeredness and hostility, it's easy to overlook the benefits of limitations. From childhood all through adulthood, most people are trained to push for the top spot, win as much as possible, hold out for the best salary and strive for power and prestige. This orientation is inclined toward doing whatever it takes to be number one. When you think about it, undoubtedly any individual is pushed into a form of addiction by even trying to secure "the top spot." Criminals are especially vulnerable to "seductive advertising", so to speak. They do whatever is necessary to get what they want, whether the objects of their desire are material things, money, popularity, power, prestige or drugs. To attain their desires they have to become narrow minded, desensitized to the needs of others, habitual and therefore addicted. It's important to recognize that we all lose some freedom within ourselves and even for our fellow citizens by yielding to addiction.

Prisons are probably ideal places to deal with the problems of the addict. By their very nature, prisons restrict (if they don't terminate) personal desires. Counselors may suggest that it's difficult indeed to stop any addiction "cold turkey". Yet that's exactly the way prisons operate... and probably for the short and long term benefit of those who are addicted. It's interesting that most people find it quite easy to see addiction in other people, yet find it quite difficult to see it in themselves. In any and all cases, its extremely helpful to understand how addiction can get started, the problems addiction causes, the way to freedom from addiction and the proper techniques to help overcome this form of bondage. A caring community of support can go a long way in helping addicts to overcome and resist addiction. With proper guidance, incarcerated people could become understanding and supportive guides as well as inspirations to one another in the struggle for freedom.

Since the problem of addiction is common to not only people in prison but also to most people in society, it would be beneficial to individuals both inside and outside the walls to figure out how to escape this danger to society's well-being. Addiction really means being controlled by a habit, especially a bad habit. Convicted individuals in prison are especially appropriate illustrations of how bad habits can put a person in serious difficulty. However, citizens who have never been convicted of a crime also can be seriously hurt by uncontrolled bad habits. A business executive alcoholic who drinks himself to death, a depressed mother who overdoses on drugs or a popular teen-ager who eats too much or too little -- these people are in nearly as much trouble as the person in the prison cell. All can be helped if they are open to suggestion; yet the prisoner may have the advantage -- in being forced to stop the addiction and in learning how to change the destructive behavior. Moreover, the prisoner who has learned what the consequences are of addiction may be able to help the law-abiding citizen envision the eventual outcome of the personal enslavement.

Prisons in the new millennium should become training centers for reform in society. The broad range of people in our prisons today can show all of us -- common citizens, business executives, political leaders, service workers, young and old, rich and poor, whatever your classification you prefer -- where and how society has lost its ability to raise healthy and productive citizens. Yes, individuals are to be held accountable for their choices, but all individuals are raised within the environment of a society -- a society that can bring about almost any change it desires... in any person's life... at any particular moment. As a corporate body, every community has vast powers to bring about desired results. At the very moment we read these words, members of our society can choose to "throw away" criminals into the garbage heap of waste and deterioration or to "recycle them" in a profitable and renewable way. Responsible members of all communities carry within certain presuppositions about crime and criminals. They end up being part of the influence that creates, structures and modifies whatever happens in our justice system. It's rather tragic that our present attitudes are hindering the opportunities we could have to learn "prevention" from the serious errors being made by individuals as well as by the society that nurtures them.

Every reasonably informed person in our day and age would admit that all societies as well as all individuals within those societies are a good distance away from perfection. Even the very elite -- economically, politically and socially -- would agree that we all have important lessons to learn personally and corporately. So where is society's "classroom" for learning the rationale for (and the benefits of) local, regional, national and international laws? Where is society's classroom for finding out the far-ranging consequences of violating a society's rules and regulations? Where is society's classroom for researching the long and short-term effects of the practices of capitalism or communism or any other "ism" for that matter? Where is society's classroom for debating personal versus corporate responsibility and how that affects the world in which we live? Where is society's classroom for learning when to change, where to change, why to change and how to change? Don't count on today's family unit to pursue such interests. And don't count on the school, the university, the church or even the government to arrange for such appropriate research and studies. They are all occupied with their own specialties, whether those areas of expertise are of any great value or not. What does seem clear is that at the point of error and confusion and violation and frustration there is an appropriate opportunity to offer insight and practical experimentation with a specialized group of people. Prisoners have life experiences relevant to the above issues. Many could be found to have the motivation to offer relevant data as well as to learn the prescribed "studies". Also, a high proportion of inmates could be prepared to help their fellow human beings (at all levels of community life) attain a far more desirable, sustainable and meaningful quality of life. The prison may well be the almost ideal setting for research and development. Furthermore, it may well be the best launching pad for doing things differently -- hopefully in a more healthy, hopeful, sustainable way for everyone on our planet.

Let's look at one of the important principles that would help to implement "a new social order" through prison reform. Put simply, each and every human being is of great value to others and consequently should receive a healthy portion of basic needs (food, shelter and medical care), quality education, meaningful employment, renewal, encouragement and hope. It must be admitted that these words would be difficult to apply specifically and legally to any individual, even though the words might not be far removed from many national ideals and religious beliefs. Such a principle might work best if it was not "set in stone" or adopted in such a way as to be used in a court of law. Think of it as a social guideline for political decisions and for citizens to consider... like "concern for family" or "coming to the aid of a neighbor down the street." The implementation of such a principle nationally or world-wide would necessarily reorder social priorities over some period of time. Nations would be concerned about leveling out resources between nations and about how human beings might live in balance with nature. Communities would be interested in calling attention to groups in need of help and in methods of working harmoniously toward common goals. Individuals would find meaning in rescuing, sustaining and encouraging people with difficulties, inadequacies, addictions or other problems. Eventually there might be the understanding that it would be in everyone's long-term interests to take or accumulate no more than needed for "a good life", which might be defined eventually as comparable to the living standard of other people in other parts of the world. Would this be a radical departure from the way people interact in today's world? Yes, but in reality such change would not be suitable for some time. As caretakers of the world, we may be meant to change or even evolve, but the world is not prepared for earth shaking changes overnight. Just let the most serious bondage, hurting and deterioration stop as soon as possible. And let the beginning of the new social order take root in our prisons as we begin a new era.

Prisons as training centers could start out as perhaps no more than one experiment with a small group of convicts in one prison with almost no cost. Let's envision a volunteer "change agent" entering a prison and making arrangements with prison authorities to counsel volunteer inmates for the purpose of giving them a bit more preparation for life in the outside world after serving out their sentences. Prison officials would need to understand that the "counseling" being done would hopefully make their lives somewhat easier and provide both short-term and long-range benefits to everyone involved. Information would be laid out for all levels of the prison staff as various steps in the process might be implemented. It would be helpful if incentives and rewards could be provided for cooperation and reinforcement from all people in contact with the inmates. To give officials a positive and exciting vision of the future, depending upon the success of the program, their efforts might be highlighted as the beginning point of a great social change for the benefit of society as a whole. "The vision" would be to bring positive change into the lives of everyone even remotely connected with the prison.

Contact with convicts would be handled in groups as well as with individual sessions of research, counseling and training. Informing all the inmates about the overall program in general terms would be of first priority, since the overall hope would be to involve everyone to some degree as soon as possible. Here are a few introductory suggestions that might interest the entire prison population. Every prisoner constitutes a very important person (VIP) for the healthy functioning of our society and therefore could make significant life enhancing contributions to others from within their own personality and experience. A critical goal from the very beginning would be to have every individual within the walls have a better quality of life each day... extending on indefinitely. Just as each and every convict would have valuable contributions and insights, so each and every convict would need to be open to change and constructive training. As a sports team might desire to win a championship, a prison might desire to be the best "model prison/training facility" possible. All convicts should work cooperatively toward the eventual possibility of being rewarded "crime fighters" outside the walls. Everything from a complement (or a smile) to risking life and health for a fellow inmate would count significantly toward benefiting relationships inside and outside prison walls. Personal counseling would seek to set individuals on the road to healing and health, and secondly, to enable them to bring about personal change within their lives as well as in the lives of others. Team-work would be emphasized as critical to reaching desired goals as well as to implement checks and balances on desirable behavior. The ongoing process of training would focus on small steps toward great goals and on compromising ego-centric preferences for over-all quality of life and health. Humility, openness to suggested change along with a flexible mind and moldable personality would be desirable attributes in successful crime fighters. The initial goal of the change agent would be to "sell" the outstanding benefits of healthy living, the joys of losing detrimental addictions, the stimulation of creative change, the satisfaction of being rewarded for playing with a new winning team and the self-esteem of finding happiness and meaning in life. Hopefully these advantages would provide motivation for successful transformation in daily living patterns.

It should be made clear that the full thrust of the

somewhat abbreviated suggestions above would not be pushed at prisoners in one or two sessions. None of us like to learn important things in segments too large to handle comfortably. Since learning takes place best in an atmosphere of excitement and good feelings, predictably, narrow-minded convicts would need special encouragement initially. Starting with praise and small steps, advances in corrections and new perspectives could accelerate as convicts get a feel for new possibilities in their lives. Verbal guidance would be reinforced and balanced where suitable by the written word, visual presentations and task oriented training. Since a prisoner's environment is controlled in many ways, the setting is nearly perfect for maintaining focus and eliminating detrimental influences. Furthermore, the possibility of team-work aiding in the accomplishment of some personal successes could provide significant inspiration. From the beginning, group sessions would only be profitable as long as clearly all participants follow along with attention and careful listening. Inattentive or disruptive members of the group would be at least temporarily excluded from meetings. If problems began to occur while the convicts were assembled in large groups, increasingly smaller group meetings would be arranged to handle appropriate instruction. On the other hand, as participants would start to buy into the program… questions, comments and suggestions would be encouraged.

An appropriate decision to be made by the prison population as a whole might be to figure out how to choose a designated group of "lead crime fighters," who would be appointed to "break ground" for all other inmates. Naturally during an investigation to figure out whether such a program could work among inmates, "a test group" would need to be selected. Not only would voting for such an experimental class give all inmates a voice in making the program work but it might also provide incentive for showing their neighbors appropriate, creative, caring, inter-personal skills. Careful selection of such an experimental group would be extremely important. The success or failure of such "leaders" would reveal to other inmates, prison officials, leaders of the justice system and law-abiding citizens in general, what the possibilities might be for a more compassionate treatment of incarcerated individuals as well as for their leadership potential in society. Hopefully there would be a high degree of motivation among all inmates to see that such a pilot project would succeed. Not only would every convict's future quality of life depend upon the daily atmosphere, activities and training done within the prison walls, but their self-esteem, prestige, wisdom, care-taking ability and earning potential would also be on the line.

Maybe the most comprehensive work by those selected to initiate such a prison program would be in analysis, counseling and training with individual inmates. Undoubtedly the challenges among this deprived, addicted, wasted and judged community would seem to be overwhelming. The counter-balance to envisioning this staggering job would be to understand the nearly unlimited possibilities for improvements... plus the vast human potential for healing within a nurturing, uplifting, inter-dependent community. Furthermore, there would be the realization that healthy change takes place best very slowly, methodically, beneficially and creatively. No prison worker, educator, counselor or official would need to take on too much responsibility or burden. As time went on, team goals should begin to supersede personal goals for the sake of individual security and healthy living standards. Working with incarcerated individuals would need to be done with compassion, sensitivity, reassurance, introspection, creativity and patience. Each person's life-history would be central to not only healing and health but also to a sense of significance and worth. A spirit of friendliness, respect and trust should permeate the relationship between the two cooperating "investigators." The times spent with any particular individual should be dependent upon the quality of the interaction as well as on the amount of healthy progress that could take place. Research and training assignments would probably be advisable in most cases, since that type of work between sessions would probably contribute to more rapid progress in healing and personal development. Time would be spent in giving some perspective on how change has taken place in the past, how it is happening in the present and how it may affect any person in the future. So intense and creative interaction with inmates would provide significant and enduring results. Through enlightenment and initiative society could witness that even convicts can take action to change present circumstances and positively impact the future.

Certainly any prison in the process of becoming a "training center" for social reform should be highly commended. This a gigantic leap forward from "wasted" human productivity, financial resources, court proceedings, prison facilities, crime studies, political analysis and lawsuits. Few people would disagree that human beings should be nurtured carefully from the beginning of life. Yet because of personal mistakes as well as social inadequacies, some people take off down wrong roads and end up in bad and sad circumstances. Many of these people have not received the care, attention, guidance and inspiration they have needed at appropriate times. Some have violated or abandon good training for some unknown reason. Most of us are not divine enough to know why seemingly good people go wrong. However, perceptive leaders can understand that through a process of careful change, mistakes of the past can be admitted, paid for and even corrected by those who have committed crimes. It's not a satisfactory solution that societies in our age discard individuals because they are no good anymore. Only the most hopeless must be restrained and restricted from doing more harm to law-abiding people around them. True, it must be admitted that not all people choose to change the badness and sadness in their lives. An important decision is critical. Convicted criminals serving time must decide whether or not to switch sides.

CHAPTER 13

"Switching Sides To Success"

Many people are very skeptical that criminals can change and begin to walk the straight and narrow. How can those who undoubtedly have spent significant time and effort violating the law and "taking from others" in many ways… just turn-around, obey the law and "give to others?" It's quite apparent that people who are arrested for breaking the law have in all probability broken the law before. It's also true that such people have probably established a habit or pattern of lawless behavior. What most of us do not consider is that the end point of arrest or incarceration was achieved over a long period of time and certainly through a lot of problematic decisions. Another thing to remember is that every criminal is similar to every non-criminal in having many of the very same desires. Whether proper thinking or not, criminals are led to believe that the easiest or maybe only way to satisfying their desires is through illegal methods. Sadly enough, they may be correct in thinking that what they desire will never be theirs lawfully. It may be true that legally they don't have what it takes to get what they want. Imagine people in underdeveloped countries desiring to be rich in the United States or refugees imagining that an opposition government will give their land back. For the most part, such things just don't happen. Consequently, people who have any hope at all are left with difficult or desperate means. The final nail in the coffin of inevitable criminal activity is that very few people living in western civilization learn to limit much of their appetites or desires. Who doesn't grow up to "want it all?" After coming to know all the good things, good experiences, good times, good tastes, sights, sounds and feelings that flash across the screen, what normal person doesn't try to figure out how to attain it? Most criminals are much like law-abiding citizens in striving to go after the life society advertises so well. They may even be raised to be enthusiastic consumers. Tragically, they simply aren't processed though the proper channels of our society. They get caught and put away.

Some sympathetic citizens might suggest that criminal behavior is just a big, bad mistake and that with just a bit of "tweaking" almost everybody would turn out all right. They usually assert that it's all society's fault and nobody's really responsible. Yet such argument does not hold individuals accountable, it doesn't motivate change, and it doesn't establish the high ground of a healthy morality. All human beings can be led toward the highest plateaus of moral behavior. The question is merely "what amount of time and effort" and "what amount and kind of motivation" is appropriate in each case. Certainly there are some criminals and mentally disabled individuals that need a lot more time, help, insight and hopefulness spent on their behalf than others. They may well have been hurt so seriously by their genetic make-up, environment or social conditioning that they will need extraordinary attention. Who will give what it takes to try to correct or heal what has developed in such an individual life? There have been a few examples in human history of sacrificial efforts given to raise up "the depressed," "the destitute" "the degenerate" and even "the dying." Our age is no less able to produce people capable of revealing or acting out such love.

An extremely basic question, then, has to do with whether or not our society wants to spend the time and give the effort to rehabilitate the criminal. The question is not so absurd when consideration is given to the time and effort allotted to raise even our own children. Will we as a people ever feel it's important enough to break into the cycle of poverty, crime or hatred with a "will" to do what is right? How close must we be to going over Niagara Falls? The beauty of criminals becoming crime fighters is that those people who are "locked away" are a good deal more aware of a real crisis in their lives than average law-abiding citizens. They also are aware of how indirectly and unobtrusively a person can travel from goodness to badness and from happiness to sadness... little thought, concern or seriousness involved. Might these convicts in crisis have what it takes to shake up "the status quo" and show us where we are headed? Maybe all we need to do to do to change our restricted vision is to encourage prisoners to show us the way. That would give Christians a whole fresh insight into God using what is weak and of little value in the world to astonish the strong and wealthy. Yet maybe those kinds of sentiments from "the good book" don't have much authority or value to a sophisticated culture… enjoying a cruise down the river of life. Who knows?

We are still left with the problem of whether or not a criminal might turn around and be a credit to society rather than a detriment. First of all, there is the immediate reality of a hurtful situation -- being cut off from almost all that is dearly desired, living close to other undesirables, restricted access to family and friends, the realization of failure and embarrassment, the depressing realities of the future, etc. No wonder that criminals want to break out of this kind of a situation. Next we can't help but acknowledge that no matter how deprived a person might get, basic desires developed and reinforced over a life time remain active. Such desires are generally only properly satisfied outside the walls. Another factor involves the hopes and dreams of getting out and fitting in somehow. We might push this to the point of suggesting even criminals in general have it within themselves to want to help others in some way. One final point has to do with basic self-esteem and the possibility of change. Doesn't almost everyone like to imagine being on top of the mountain, so to speak? These are some of the reasons that a criminal might be receptive to some sort of change in his or her circumstances.

Envision for a moment the circumstance of wanting to

go to jail or prison to enhance one's circumstances of life. As caring citizens, most of us would feel some real sadness that any person would be in such a bad situation. Yet the sad reality of a person who commits a crime is that such a person would be better off in prison -- better to be stopped than to continue to "live life" hurting people as a criminal. A practical goal of counseling convicts is to have them come to the realization that they have more hope for the future as prison inmates than as criminals hurting society. It seems natural then that the prison as "a training center for a new social order" should be a valuable place for getting life's priorities, ideals and addictions straightened out. Maybe that's a bit like going to the hospital to get a number of life-threatening problems all fixed up at once. The whole experience may be a real challenge to go through, but after it's all over there is a feeling of satisfaction, relief and overall good health. Surely a training center is meant to be a good environment for some positive adjustments to life. Where a convict's old life had its detrimental influences, the convict's new environment reveals the advantages of the new exercises and the final results. It's no more than right for those who have slipped through the cracks into dangerous living patterns that eventually bad surroundings are overpowered by good surroundings.

Prisoners should be assured that life "on the other side" is much better and more rewarding for utilizing the talents they possess. The following basketball team analogy might be helpful for trying to understand the inmate's struggle. The first team happened to be the one for whom the inmate was drafted and learned to play the game. This was a place of comfortable experiences and "feeling needed." The rewards were quite good and moving up the ladder of success seemed to be at an acceptable pace. Then one day, after almost breaking into the starting line up, an opposing team stopped the player/inmate cold. There was no more playing time, no more income and no more hope for the future. Feelings of frustration, anger and defeat took center stage. Would there be revenge? Would that be the end of the story?

Presently and somewhat surprisingly, the opposing team envisions this inmate to have special talents to use for long-term, winning purposes. This happens to be "the championship team" after all, and there is apparent honor in being asked to suit up to play. They envision an important role to be played and time for preparation will be forthcoming. In fact, the new team sees a staring role available if the old team is left behind. The new team offers to far exceed the old team's salary over the life of the contract. There is much more prestige and opportunity to play the game. The real honor of being selected however, is tempered with the understanding that there will be a new coach, with a new practice schedule, a new game plan and new teammates with whom to work closely. What will be the decision? Will this player/inmate give his or her consent to switching sides?

There are natural reactions to being asked to "switch

sides:" You've got to be kidding. Why do you think I can play for you? Do I have it in me to make a switch? How can I adapt to your style of play? What's in it for me? What's in it for you? When do you plan on hiring me? Will my new teammates and fans accept me? What do I have to give up? I have some emotional attachments to my old team. What does the new coach expect of me? Obviously such questions and comments are almost never ending when any person is asked to make a big change in life. And as expected, it's not so easy for the convict, as good as the whole offer might sound. Then there's also the attitude of the new team about the possibility of bringing in a player from the opposing side. Might there be skepticism, apathy, down right rejection? We can be sure of it. There's at least one cautionary consideration, however. Remember that this "talent" could be strongly motivated to contend "down to the wire" for the other team... or this skilled player might be working to keep the championship team on top. We all know from experience that championship caliber teams can't afford to make a good chunk of the opposition "fighting mad."

We can be sure that it's in society's interest to encourage convicts to change and become crime fighters. Our communities have almost everything to gain and almost nothing to lose... other than some minimal risk of recidivism. It's worth emphasizing that fighting crime is much better than committing crime (as a repeat offender). Citizens and leaders should feel good about trying to help messed up individuals work through their problems. Moreover, it's very desirable that analysis is done to check out the roots of crime and figure out how to prevent lawlessness from taking root and spreading. As agonizing as it is to be hurt in a criminal act, it's necessary that law-abiding citizens eventually get beyond their desire for punishment and retribution in order to save future victims the turmoil and disaster. It may well be that rehabilitated convicts could begin to make at least some form of restitution and at minimum express clearly and thoughtfully regrets for their crimes. Imagine the possibilities of criminals and thoughtful members of communities getting together to try to heal the pain of serious anti-social behavior as well as to function as teammates in preventing it. With such experiences on the increase, healthy respect might begin to develop among different classes and races of people as former adversaries learn to understand the weaknesses and struggles of others.

Just as society might not easily and quickly adjust to a different approach to our system of justice, likewise incarcerated people might not be easily and quickly won over to a new way of life. Certainly we know that smokers and drug addicts can quit, alcoholics and gamblers can learn to abstain and criminals can be rehabilitated. Yet it's hard… and maybe more than doubly hard if the vices are many. Education, patience, persistence, discipline, motivation, training -- all are necessary to the realignment of a life that is twisted and deteriorated from troubles and turmoil. No doctor would consider delivering anything but "tender care" to a person torn up in an automobile accident. Care-givers in prisons would need to gain real insight into the generally deteriorated condition of those so hazardous to their own well-being and the welfare of others that they desperately commit crime... with all the risks that entails. Desperation can bring out the worst in any human being. Each individual within the prison system would be "a special case" in ability to change and in potential for fighting crime outside the prison walls. Part of the reason today's prison is helpful in determining both this ability and potential is that careful observation can be done in checking out a prisoner's seriousness and reliability under relatively controlled conditions. If success is not evident inside the walls, society would never risk a convict's proposed activity outside the walls. A lot of personal factors would need to be taken into account in determining the sincerity of an inmate desiring to switch sides. In fact, the way we understand how healthy change happens pushes us to see the convict's choice as not so much a moment's decision as a process of commitment over a period of time.

The factor at dead center of commitment to the program of becoming a crime fighter is "motivation". If the commitment we seek is understood to flow from a process of words and deeds as well as an evident life-style change, then motivation doesn't need to be offered or developed all at once. What is necessary is to get the process of a turnaround moving in the right direction. Most people have trouble just getting started on a project or a change in their life. That's rather natural since we are creatures of habit for the most part. We need to get over the difficulty of beginning something, so the major push needs to be "the initial one"... to get some momentum started. What might be incentive enough to get an inmate started "opening up" and "getting involved?" Remembering that individuals will differ to a certain degree, practically all inmates desire the things that have been withheld -- freedom, self-esteem, material possessions, good living conditions, closeness with family and friends, hope and practically anything enjoyed by any of the human senses. Realizing that convicts are not much different from the rest of us in terms of human desire, most individuals would like to envision an overall better life for themselves. That is something that society, prison personnel and change agents should be able to offer and deliver. All the specifics could be discussed and then implemented as small steps are accomplished. Think of the motivation to learn a new way of life... being given MVP treatment (starting behind the walls), free treatment for any addictions, problems or hang-ups, education to accomplish change and help others to change (to become a change agent), better living conditions within the prison (from food to entertainment), privileges within the prison, more contact with the outside world, respectful praise for crime fighting contributions, rewards or bonuses for rapid progress within the program and eventually after "graduation" the possibility of paid, crime fighting, job security outside the prison. There is good reason to believe motivational inducements could be found for reasonable, tailor made, sensitive, encouraging, careful, steady, small steps toward reachable goals. Yes, incentives are critical for starting movement toward the excitement and satisfaction of a new life. Remember that such encouragement should be contrasted with all the usual negatives of present prison life. On the other hand, it would be foolish not to use all the tools available to turn around convicts and help them see the goodness and satisfaction of life on the other side.

After initial insight into the advantages of a changed life, the serious work must begin. Let everyone understand that this "work" does not need to be anxious, exhausting or even trouble-some. It can be joyful, exciting and rewarding… and in the end it should be. Enjoyable work will definitely accelerate the training process. Proven scientific methods can be used to move inmates toward goals they ultimately desire. For example, a person might be willing to undergo a safe, painful but brief electrical jolt for a thousand dollars. In the same way, a convict may very well agree that suitable techniques of behavior modification would be acceptable to attain certain strongly desired rewards. Of course behavior modification can be as simple as teaching a person to say "thank-you" after receiving a gift… or as terrifying as redirecting a person's loyalty and personality under torture as a prisoner of war. With the encouragement of society and those in prison, a helpful conditioning process could take place with both positive and negative incentives. Unlike present prison conditions, which emphasize all kinds of hurtful treatment, the focal point of changing a convict's behavior would be on correction with healthy, helpful, positive rewards. Alongside enthusiastic support from prisoners living in a controlled environment, even significant personality change could begin to take place within months, depending upon the seriousness of the convict's condition.

Other proven techniques might be used quite efficiently and profitably in early stages of conditioning and training. Alcoholics Anonymous group therapy sessions are well known for their success in dealing with drug addiction. Many positive features include the regularity of the sessions, peer pressure, family involvement, orientation to successful change, discussion of shared weaknesses, acceptance of others, personal help for a variety of problems and highlighting the value of contractual agreements. These helpful and healing methods can be extremely useful to almost any inmate involved in the process of switching sides. Another useful tool for healthy change is mentoring. If caring members of society would rise to the challenge of mentoring convicts in the process of change, the individual and community rewards would be great indeed. We probably could say that all human beings need other people to admire and imitate. People who have committed crimes may not have had the advantage of a meaningful relationship with both parents, outstanding community leaders or even respectable friends. Mentoring might be just what the doctor ordered for a caring, inspiring relationship, friendship, insight, analysis, encouragement and support. It might be just what is needed for helping communities come to terms with criminals becoming crime fighters. And finally, mentoring might be another reassuring aid in monitoring the lives of convicts outside the walls.

Convicts who become successful in switching sides will certainly prove their great value to society. Any society that gradually gets drawn into the morass of great wealth and extreme poverty, personal justification of immorality, environmental degeneration, violence and apathy is on course for national degradation, destruction or suicide. When so many people are prosperous and busy trying to get ahead, it's tempting to look past desperate individuals or those who are broken down at the side of the road. In other parts of the world, where the conditions of life are not so nice, it takes people who are hurting to identify and help other people who are hurting. It becomes quite relevant to ask where a society might look for "perspective" and an analysis of business as usual. Will religion or spiritual leaders cry out a warning to correct the inequities and reestablish virtue, generosity and humility? Not when "spiritual leaders" are in the hip pockets of the power brokers and special interests. Consequently, it may take the perspective of "those who have been there" to straighten out where our culture has gone wrong. What are the temptations that are so enticing to us and yet also so destructive? What are the weaknesses of a modern culture such as ours? In truth, people who have been "convicted" can be the source of our hope, for they have had to face the final results of our corporate greed, egotism and self-justification. Truly, prisoners in service to society can be the VIPs of cultural renewal and stability, if they can be recruited to help our communities refocus and reestablish healthy roots in our healthy beginnings.

What can changed convicts do to fight crime successfully? Convicts as VIPs can show communities that significant personal change can be accomplished. Each individual who moves from prison into the mainstream of society as a new person is valuable and important evidence of a successful strategy. Freedom from deterioration and bondage can be possible (for people inside and outside prison walls) with education, motivation and training. It's critically important that average citizens listen to past prisoner's declarations and warnings, since they have extensive expertise and background in crime. They can be society's protectors and agents against crime and the circumstances that lead people into it. Think how families who have lived in shame because a member has been incarcerated might experience a whole new feeling of pride in watching what change can do for those led astray. As criminals learn how to help ordinary citizens escape from hang-ups, addictions and unlawful temptations, these inmates may well find a very satisfying vocation after life "on the other side." Criminals turned crime fighters could turn out to be a source of great satisfaction in each community where they carry out their daily activities. After all, community inspiration and commitment to the possibility of change... plays a significant role in the new sense of freedom convicts come to know in their new work. So this is something special -- something to be proud of: Hurting, condemned, tragic individuals become VIPs in communities which request their expert and perceptive help. How wonderful that these crime specialists point the way toward freedom, satisfaction and joy for all.

Naturally there will be skepticism that "bad people" can become "good people." It also takes quite a while for some people to understand that the stuff they throw away can be recycled into very valuable products. Most of us need to see the "proof," and no doubt that's a good thing. Enthusiastic fans of sports teams are pretty skeptical about a good quality player coming in from a rival team. On the other hand, they are quickly won over by dedicated play and productive results. Likewise, any new prison program focusing on change will be watched carefully for the results. Teachers, trainers, change agents, mentors and the criminals themselves should be quite certain that skeptics will be ready to "deep six" almost any attempt to liberate society's troublemakers. Obviously there should be great demand that convicts do not regress back into criminal activity. Furthermore, convicts should be able to lead troublemakers and lawbreakers away from detrimental activity. Yes, changed individuals should give evidence to the social structure they hurt that they have what it takes to help.

When all is said and done, here are a few very obvious opportunities for winning public support. First of all, criminals will need to show how a prison can "change" with proper incentives, training and environment. Everyone within the prison system should be positively impacted. A decline in prison costs would probably win converts quickly to any new rehabilitation approach. Second, leaders and news media could reveal to the general public how everyone would benefit in many ways through prison transformation -- financially, physically, emotionally, socially, politically, spiritually and corporately -- in essentially every way. As citizens become informed about their advantages, the "lock em away" mentality might gradually be replaced by gratitude. Third, prisons could command new respect and become a source of cultural pride. With a strong shift in methodology, they could become "inspirations" for society rather than sources of unending deterioration and destruction. Impartial documentation of successes in communities would be crucial. Hopefully "news accounts" would show that prisons could become creative, hopeful, healing places... with ongoing "injections" to help cure society's ills. Fourth and finally, the divine shift from spreading an environment that nurtures crime to multiplying an environment that fights crime should be noted as a gigantic cultural reformation. Individuals could begin to align themselves with development of a healthy community and healing practices in contrast to promoting self-glorification and working to diminish others. These four advantages for prison transformation, if presented sensitively and insightfully, should help a skeptical society overcome its natural judgments and reservations about criminals switching sides.

Success won't come quickly for most incarcerated individuals who enter the process of change. Just as most criminals have slowly and rather naturally proceeded into a life of crime, so it will take some time for them to make their way into the new experiences of warning others and pointing the way to happiness and fulfillment. Certainly many steps will be taken within the prison -- from introspection to training to concern for others. We know that "practice makes perfect" and practice within the walls of the prison will reveal the sincerity and the fortitude necessary to carry forward any life-long task. Since there never is an end to the process of change (for more complete accomplishment and success), a critically important step in the inmate's development will be the determination of when he or she would be ready to move outside the prison walls into the challenging environment of a struggling society.

Surely careful analysis would be necessary with regard to the progress of change made by inmates. Have they successfully overcome their threat to society? Have they made adequate progress in overcoming some of their weaknesses and addictions, etc.? Have they become enthusiastic about their ability to help others move away from being detrimental to society? Do they have the ability to be shining examples of healthy living to average citizens? Are they willing to be scrutinized for signs of recidivism and for the insight they provide to vulnerable people? Such analysis probably would need to originate from a diverse group of people... coming from within the prison and from the communities within which the former inmates might work. The safety and reputation of all parties involved would be of utmost concern. A careless action by an inmate out too early could risk the opportunities and happiness of countless people -- the politicians enabling prison reform to proceed; the teachers and trainers encouraging change; the prison officials and staff offering opportunities; the society risking repeat offenders; even the remaining prisoners cut off from trust and future possibilities. No program is perfect, but great care would need to be taken to insure that convicts have truly switched sides and learned how to benefit society.

Whether prisoners can be motivated to switch sides and help communities fight crime by preventing crime will be determined by how much society is willing to change. If the majority of people are happy with conditions as they are and where they are headed, then there will be no need for rehabilitated convicts and no need to research ways to get troubled people involved in beneficial activities. On the contrary, good leaders in our day are smart enough to know that the world's resources need to be treasured, conserved and even recycled. Human beings are not the least of such resources worthy of thought and consideration. Yet just as a sports team needs to figure out whether last year's team is good enough or whether to go after some potential "free agents," so our society needs to ask the same kind of question. "Free agents" will play the game for one side or the other; that's really determined by where they are felt needed and where they can find adequate compensation.

Very few people on our planet in this new age are willing to work for free. By trying to do so they would be risking elimination from the game of life altogether.

Isn't it really "a no-brainer" to try to get the help we need to fix up the vulnerabilities our team has revealed under the spotlight of history? What good person is really happy to waste what can be useful and helpful? Do we honestly want our species to survive over the long haul? Will we need to adapt eventually, and if so, is it in our interests to do so now? Of course the answer thinking people should have is in the affirmative. We obviously need to let our "competitors" know that we can use their help and expertise. In any case, certainly we don't want them working for the other side. Is there something we might offer them to switch sides, especially if all of our necessary conditions are met? At minimum, they need our enthusiastic support and encouragement. We just might be surprised at what a difference they might make for inspiring a friendly, gratifying society.

CHAPTER 14

"Community Rehabilitation"

As we enter the third millennium, it's natural for us to be concerned about what might be ahead for our society. Since we do not know the future, we generally draw from our past to make speculations about it. Will the environment hold up? Will there be a recession in the near future or maybe even a depression? Should we expect more turmoil on the world scene or less? Each question arises out of our past experiences -- environmental deterioration, the depression and recessions of the last century and terrible wars being fought almost continually. These are some of the big questions that probably will affect our lives to some degree. But then there are the more personal questions. Will I still have my job next year? How heavy will I be five years from now? Can I expect my wealth or health to hold up for the immediate and distant future? What's going to happen to my family as competition becomes more brutal and as pressures become more intense? Here are typical questions that will definitely have a strong impact on almost anyone's daily life. They too arise out of the events of past experience. It's clear that every person's questions about the future may turn out to be quite different. The thing that puts us all on the same level is that we can't control the events that will challenge our happiness and may even jeopardize our lives. Change just happens and sometimes it seems to happen at increasing speed. While none of us can stop change from happening, we can adjust to it -- we can adapt.

Adaptation has been occurring for a long, long time and will continue to go on as long as there is life on this planet. Humans have adjusted quite well over the time we have lived on earth. Maybe we have adapted too well, since we are causing some strain on our world's carrying capacity. Yet for most of us, we don't get too upset about population increases, the disappearance of the rain forest or what's happening on the other side of our globe. We've got enough to deal with in our immediate surroundings and in connection with our personal lives. Here too we adapt. We have to adapt or we find ourselves "out of the loop" and hurting. Obviously a lot of people born into our world can't adapt well enough and therefore don't survive. What is crucial to nearly every thinking person is how to adapt properly for a happy and meaningful life. All of us make mistakes in our adapting and adjusting, but we dare not make too many or we may get left behind... possibly to perish. The interesting thing is... no matter how powerful or proud or independent any individual might be, that person needs the help of other people to "survive" say nothing of do well. As they say, "No man is an island." We as individuals may want to appear to be independent and we may want to think that we can live apart from others and have a quality life, but we can't do it. We learn to adapt in relationship to our surroundings and other human beings. Since time began, our ancestors have taken care of one another, been productive and survived. We should do likewise.

Cooperation is paramount to successful living in any age. Insurance is a good contemporary example of people helping out others who accidentally fall into extreme need. Since the future is dark to us, we need to work out a way to handle any desperate circumstances that might confront us. Whether it's neighbors helping neighbors, paying insurance premiums or defensive alignments between bordering nations, people of all races, colors and creeds have supported others in difficult circumstances. There are significant risks to the powerful and popular "go it alone" approach and "survivor" mentality. Sometimes the smallest, most insignificant creatures show the greatest resilience and adaptability. The dinosaurs have revealed to us that the big and strong do not always survive. Today's very wealthy and powerful people cannot guarantee that they will live long lives say nothing about happy lives. Life is for sharing. Not so surprisingly some of the happiest people are those who have very minimal possessions. It's also true that in climbing to the top of practically any human endeavor, the only way to get there is on the backs of others. More than a little is lost as human inter-dependence is pushed to the side for ego-centric individualism. The ultimate fate or fortune of amassing great power and wealth is evident in a solitary person owning and controlling the whole world. As desirable as such power might seem, not many of us looking up from the bottom of the pile would envision this as successful living.

What do the above three paragraphs have in common and how do they relate to community rehabilitation? We have looked at the future, adaptability and cooperation and have noted how they can affect our quality of life even in a technological age. Common people can find meaning, happiness and healthy living standards when they can confidently face the future... and adapt to whatever change occurs in cooperation with others. Communities that function well are composed of people who care about the welfare of each and every person. There would be great social and moral risk to live out life in any other way. Who should live and who should die? Who should be rich and who should be poor? Every individual has an important role to play in the ultimate interdependence of life and consequently should be protected and nurtured as a valuable resource. No one should be left behind. Everyone should be urged to attain full potential. Basically this is the theory behind convicts moving into communities to subdue or root out crime. There may be high risks to such tasks, but these specialists are capable of handling the job and are important warriors on this critical battle-front.

The quality of society in the future will be determined to some extent by how well individuals adapt to the challenges they face. What is best for the individual within a cooperative community? Criminals who desire to become crime fighters will need to understand the consequences of uncontrolled individual desire. In fact crime is the inevitable outcome of people putting their selfish interests above the welfare of people in community. While personal desires are important, corporate interests are even more vital to healthy community living. Somewhere along the line convicted prisoners separate themselves from authority figures to carry out their own agenda. As time goes on, they drift more and more into conflict with the corporate welfare of others... until they finally get caught and are stopped. After being incarcerated, hopefully a rehabilitation plan moves the convict back in the other direction -- into seeing the great personal and corporate advantages of working for the benefit of the total community. While working to inspire the general public, changed convicts will undoubtedly need to begin their efforts facing individual desires and needs within the community. Yet the overriding emphasis will be on enabling people to withdraw from purely selfish motivations and begin to learn how both personal and community benefits are enhanced. As our world almost literally decreases in size year by year as a result of communication innovations, trade improvements, technological change, environmental fragility and political interdependence, all people are pulled more closely together in many ways. Individual inequities, personal weaknesses, flagrant waste, unrestrained aggressiveness and other similar "environmental problems" will need to be put under scrutiny for the smooth operation of "spaceship earth."

Communities will also need to evaluate their places within the larger society and culture. As individuals begin to grasp how to fit in with the people around them, so too countless communities should begin to comprehend what special offerings they might be able to present to the common good of humanity. Unlike individual people who find themselves in conflict with the law, larger groups of people don't feel very accountable to the welfare of the world. Since the human race has done little exploration of the intricacies of human motivation and decision-making, practically nothing has been laid out with reference to community outreach. The interaction and mutual support between the individual and community is in the process of developing even with this book. However, city or community responsibilities to the world aren't much more than a blank page. The challenge a community faces is not so far afield from the parent who looks in two directions -- at family as well as community obligations. The commendable stance is to try to work out a balance between the two for the sake of productivity and healthy relationships. Groups of people will function best as they strive for balance -- not only taking individual needs into account but also harnessing personal talents to compliment the world. As convicts are able to come into the mainstream of communities, not only showing how individuals but also groups of people can change to improve the welfare of everyone, then a more livable, workable and responsible environment will be shared by all. In the end, it is critical that creative minds are at work within prisons to help sketch out how communities can also adapt for a more perfect union with individuals.

Community rehabilitation like personal rehabilitation can only be accomplished over a process of time. Convicts will come to understand that they will never be completely "healed." For some convicts with no rehabilitation experience, the process within the prison will begin with their consent to "change sides" and will hopefully continue until their dying day. That's not a pessimistic outlook but a way of understanding our human condition. Since imperfection is not just found in prisoners but is an integral part of every person, there's always more work to be done or more change to be accomplished. One of the great "liberations" of convicts working with the public to prevent crime is the underlying admission that no person is far removed from violating the public trust. That means that everyone can use some help in comprehending potential pitfalls ahead. It also means that at every point in a person's life there should be an interest in better understanding human as well as personal frailty. The process of liberating change is meant to be carried out over a life-time of interaction with other people. Criminals are "the perfect people" to help at all levels of society in understanding how we can easily move in our daily experiences from a point of innocence to a place of condemnation. They not only have experienced the subtle, complicated and destructive process but also hopefully have come to know the motivations and forces that have caused it to happen. Who needs to learn on their own the ways to drift into places of trouble and turmoil? A lot of people will be quite pleased to have an experienced ex-con pointing safely through the dense fog of unexpected and difficult events close at hand. Never knowing what lies ahead in our lives, it's very reassuring to have specialists waving warning signals at us. The process of life and the process of change demands that we involve ourselves in the process of healthy adaptation to the circumstances we all face daily.

We all have a natural tendency from the time we are born to focus on our personal needs and desires. As the years go by, we begin to have more interest in others. We gradually understand that to be happy we also need to be concerned about the needs and desires of those around us. By the time we are adults, we know that our very survival depends upon how well we cooperate with family members, co-workers, neighbors in the community and even fellow citizens of the world. Yet there are difficulties in determining one's own best interests as compared to the best interests of others, who maybe even live in far distant places. In a balanced, healthy environment, how can we begin to figure out what's in everyone's best interests, maybe even around the world? Think of the conflicts we might have in determining whose interests should win out. Or might there be interests that serve the needs of all? With prisons as research centers and former criminals as resources and change agents, questions that have generally not been given much consideration in the present will have our attention and will be causes for discussion and debate. This would be a healthy environment where our limited resources and all peoples of the world would receive consideration. It would be taken for granted that citizens of the world would ask about the common good and what is best for everyone rather than simply look at personal interest and what is immediately desirable. Obviously there would be a need for more social, interactive education as well as training to help restrain personal greed and boundless lifestyles. Here again there would probably be too much "culture shock" to have such change happen too quickly. Thoughtfulness of others should be taught over a period of time and would be expected to take root and bear fruit over the years. Exemplary family training of children could be a good model for the challenge of winning over converts.

Imagine "change" being uplifted into a rainbow of light where hope and happiness run free! Unlike our present times, when people are generally defensive about mistakes, weaknesses and difficulties, such things might provide opportunities for commitment, dedication and great accomplishments. What a switch this new outlook could provide for personal satisfaction, for meaningful living, for community cooperation, for environmental sustainability, for resource conservation, for crime prevention, for cultural understanding, for terrorism cutbacks and for military reduction. "Change" as a personal opportunity to correct mistakes, strengthen weaknesses and overcome difficulties would supply hope and potential satisfaction to the weak as well as the strong. People on the winning end of any human enterprise would have no less challenge in curing personal addictions and overcoming social barriers. Contemplate the blessings for life in being open to all that life has to offer and knowing not only that one can face all possibilities but that it can be done with the support and encouragement of many others. Of course, as change takes root as a common occurrence among people living in desperate circumstances, eventually that practice will raise the application to a more moderate level of activity. Envision the possibility that eventually "crime fighters" become "personality shapers" as organized, purposeful, willful change takes the upper hand in people's lives. What a future for the human race… under the banner of a rainbow of hope!

We should further ponder the possibility of benefits gradually moving from personal experience into corporate areas of contemporary life. Individuals who find success in change will naturally pass on valuable insights to the many groups with whom they have association. Just as individual bad habits that have developed over a period of time eventually can and do infiltrate all levels of society, so positive developments also can make big differences at all levels of human interaction. Obviously, the experts working with criminals for the sake of change will be questioning, debating, analyzing and proposing activities with reference to all inter-personal enterprises. State and national programs for people that are conceived in the political arena might be some of the first to receive impetus from knowledge gained in transitional prisons.

Government initiatives to watch over extensive power and wealth might be equally as important as initiatives to uplift people in weakness and poverty. Educational systems from kindergartens to prestige colleges and universities could not only help society refocus on high priority subjects for a shrinking world but could certainly provide inspiration for education and training as well as moral and ethical propositions suitable for this new era. The business world might find a whole new agenda in providing for the needs of people within the limits of environmental sustainability, equitable profits and satisfying wages. Imagine profitable, healthy cooperatives or maybe even corporations finding ways to treat employees as "family members" and providing life-long security, support and encouragement. In a period of history where nations and peoples would be looking to change for better relationships, the implications for military forces around the world might well be downright "earth-shaking". Rather than the vast majority of the world's population taking steps deemed necessary to control a few "rampaging monsters", the urgent mission for the changing, caring majority would be to help "insecure tyrants" find the flexibility to relax, release and refocus for the good of the whole world. Finally, the world's religions could finally get back on track with a revival of the goodness of change. At minimum, the Christian religion (rooted in caring relationships, stewardship of the earth and high moral standards) could venture back to see Jesus Christ as an advocate for change in all of life. Christianity, as witnessed by Old and New Testament accounts, has always proclaimed change as a friend, as preparation for a new, uplifting way of relating to others, as a source of meaning and happiness and finally as a vision of what is a fundamental activity for all of life and death. At all levels of society, the creative use of life-sustaining change (passed on through the whole social chain) could certainly enhance healing, health and wholeness in all human endeavors.

A critical factor in enabling change to take root from a single prison and reach out to far distant places on our planet is how the media handles various events. Newspapers, magazines, radio, television and the internet are all a part of our present culture, of course. All segments of the media are affected by personal perspectives as well as by the ethics of the entire society. A good case could be made that various segments of the media have a large part in affecting (if not directing) the choices, priorities and morality of the people within their circle of influence. Therefore, certainly how fast or how slow change will take place will be determined to a large degree upon how quickly and efficiently the media will pass on breaking news about changing events. Literally millions of minute decisions are made within each public presentation that alter in very small but critical ways how members of society react to their surroundings. Factors from type style to tone of voice are inputs into human brains about the environment in which we live. Little things pile up into big things and so alter thinking patterns and life-style choices. What opportunity for a wide spectrum of the media to spread an uplifting "good news story" so that the general public can celebrate a deeper sense of hope and increase momentum toward a truly civil society.

Maybe no example of change is so dominant and clear as the change achieved (or purchased) by the entertainment industry. Our whole culture has been moved radically toward individualism and materialism in a relatively short period of time. Very few people in our age of televised movies, sporting events, music events and other forms of entertainment would suggest that our society is better off morally, physically, mentally or emotionally because of the broad influence of such public presentations. We know very well that change is not always positive. But how do we turn around the awesome influence of hours of televised "brainwashing"? Certainly media advertisers understand the vast temptation and transformation possibilities associated with instantaneous bursts of words, images, sounds and even manipulated emotional excitement. It doesn't take much common sense to begin to grasp the enormity of what flashes into the human brain on any given day, especially when individuals strongly desire the mental and emotional "hit" they receive. That same "brainwashing" influence, however, can serve to move large segments of a society's population back in the opposite direction... toward healthy, beneficial, uplifting change. A momentum shift needs to take place before a positive effect will offset the present negative effects of sedating, seductive, ego-centric, materialistic, television addiction.

Shifts in momentum don't happen overnight. The ongoing process of community rehabilitation should help everyone realize that most transformation or rehabilitation takes a lot of time to solidify results. A person doesn't need to be a biologist to grasp the idea that change has made its effects known over millions of years. True, under controlled conditions that are arranged for particular results, desired change can take place much faster than what biologists have been able to document in evolutionary steps. That should mean detrimental transformation can be stopped and in fact reversed before too much damage is done to human personality, cooperative interdependence and moral integrity. This will take insight, dedication and a desire for the best in community resourcefulness. Yes, there is no doubt that our U.S. Constitution guarantees the right to "free speech" among other privileges. Yet that should not obligate the vast majority of people in even a country such as ours to cooperate or play along with the lowest common denominator of public display. Change agents from prison basic training centers will carry the responsibility of helping the public understand how important it is to "stay the course" in opposition to the little things that diminish the chance for great initiatives by the human spirit. Such initiatives include forgiveness of the enemy and criminal... love for the hated and dispossessed... faithfulness in mission and hope... and self-sacrifice through inspiration and action.

Getting back to reality just a bit, the future does hold

great opportunity for the human race, if it's on the right track. The flip side is that certainly the future will hand us all great challenges (hopefully not to our demise and destruction). So who will appreciate life in all its fullness and who will not? We know that even as we contemplate these words, individual people are overcome by certain circumstances that they are unable to adapt to and are being wiped out. Within the context of our history, help should be available from experienced people. Interestingly enough, today's prison population can be equipped to do the job of revealing the way to change, liberation and success. On a larger scale, society as a whole may never be relegated to the scrap heap of history; yet that does not mean that people will necessarily enjoy quality life. Mere survival does not make life worth living any more than does clinging to a twig over Niagara Falls. What's ahead in our lives will require perspective, innovation, education and training to enable us to live with dignity and grace. How will we prevent ignorance and foolish mistakes? Will we overcome apathy and near-sightedness so that valuable human resources and talents do not fall by the wayside? Can there be a new climate of cooperation, concern and respect between present day antagonists for the purpose of rescuing and liberating all people? Decisions made inside and outside the walls of today's prisons will determine what the future holds for countless people and for society as a whole. No item on the human agenda for the next millennium should have higher priority than the issue of how we humans handle change and work out our relationships with one another. Whether we want to believe it or not, the sights and sounds of impending deterioration and destruction are within the range of our human senses. We must quit drifting, rev up our engines and reverse course before it's too late.

CHAPTER 15

"Cultural Healing And Health"

The first book of "The Bible" -- Genesis -- has an interesting account of life in "the beginning." People had ideal relationships and a wonderful place to live in "The Garden of Eden." A stream watered the garden and beautiful trees grew to provide plenty of good fruit to eat. It seemed like "Adam and Eve" had the perfect place to live, since they didn't have any rules and regulations to complicate their lives. However, they did have one restriction. They were not to eat from the tree that gives knowledge of what is good and what is bad... because that was the domain exclusively of the creator God. The story goes that they desired to be wise like God, so they ate of the forbidden fruit and immediately were given understanding. The consequences were disastrous. They were sent out of the abundant garden of life... to work hard, wrestle with the elements and eventually die. Although they would cultivate the land and produce children, obviously bad and hurtful choices became a part of their daily lives. A killing even took place between brothers and the results were calamitous for generations and beyond.

This Genesis story of human beginnings is interesting

and rather remarkable for focusing on the heart of our species' weakness, vulnerability... or possibly even prominence. From the earliest days, people were given the ability to choose. What shall we do? Shall we be satisfied with plenty in the garden (enough) and carry out our purpose in the creation as God's guardian? Or shall we "go for broke" and see if we might be able to get just a little more (rich)... and maybe be like God... with knowledge and power? We know and can understand the decision, for the decision is in every man's heart and soul. As the account states, "Then the Lord God said, 'Now the man has become like one of us and has knowledge of what is good and what is bad'...." Ironically, but not so conveniently, in the man's choice "he has become like one of us...." What does this mean to be like God? Would man be like the Triune God -- Father, Son and Holy Spirit?

We have desired to be like God. We get our wish. Without man's bad choices challenging ultimate authority and hindering interpersonal relationships, all might be right with the world. But we can also choose what is bad. The heat is on and the responsibility is overwhelming. What will be the results of bad choices on our neighbors and the environment that surrounds us? Since the beginning, relationships have been at the heart of good choices and bad ones. It might be interesting to speculate what the creation would be like without evil or bad choices. But speculation is as far as we can go, since decisions are made continually for what is forbidden and hurtful to ultimate authority, creation and people in general. We can't seem to locate "The Garden of Eden" and we can't reverse what has been done in the roots of our humanity. History tells us that as man's predicament went from bad to worse, "The Ten Commandments" were passed down to give rebellious people some restriction to their free but detrimental decisions. And finally, Jesus came on the scene to share insight as to "the path" leading back to the garden of Eden. Choices remain as we enter an era nearly 2,000 years later.

Frankly, our choices have put us in a bad predicament. Close up, and in the midst of partying, many of us can't seem to see the hurt of "being seduced to take a little bit more" of what should not be ours to take. Then along comes responsibility for our decisions together with some frustration and grief. We can see some aggressiveness and egotism in our acts and in the acts of our loved ones and neighbors. And then we are left alone to play God -- just what we thought we might want, in the beginning. Now things are not so simple. We labor and sweat and stew in our own juices… and die inside, if not physically, as a result of our bad decisions. The really terrible part is that we can't see any help on the way. Who can show us the light at the end of the tunnel? There is no light; we only feel frustration and grief as we fight the elements and even other people who primarily seem to be looking out for themselves. We slide deeper and deeper into the quicksand of our society or culture. We begin to feel some panic, for the more we struggle the deeper we sink. Can we find a way back to the beautiful, peaceful garden? Could there be such a thing as cultural healing and health?

Culture is defined as the concepts, habits, skills, arts, instruments and institutions, etc. of a people in a given period of time. It must be acknowledged that the culture of the United States is the envy of nearly all nations of the world… or at least it has been in the past. Today there are a few more doubts about our advantages, possibly do to the fact that even we as U.S. citizens are a bit concerned about our overall life-style and where our nation is headed. Why do we have so many more incarcerated individuals than any other country? Why do we live in a nation where there is so much violence? Why do we waste so much of almost everything? Why is "the family unit" suffering so much these days? Why are political and even religious leaders increasingly letting us down? Such questions are on a lot of minds as we step into this new millennium; and there are not a lot of simple answers. It's true that we Americans have been a creative and innovative people throughout our history. This may result from the wide diversity of our people or because we have been blessed with such things as great natural resources and a superior political system. Whatever the case, in the past, we as a united people have solved problems, faced adversity and created opportunities probably like no other people in history. We have much in our culture to inspire pride. Still, we also know that even the most gifted and powerful cultures of the past have either been destroyed or faded away for some just cause. Obviously, it would wise to note what has happened in the past and learn from the mistakes of others. We think about misguided convicts, who not only need their thinking set straight, but in most cases are even more seriously diminished by their prison experience. Whether criminals have been rehabilitated or not there is much to learn from these "mistaken people" produced within our culture. How good it would be to take notice of how easy a person can fall into seductive traps and be victimized... before it's too late. And how easy it is for a society to overlook vulnerable and sometimes helpless people before they are legally doomed for a hopeless future. History can teach us a lot of valuable lessons -- even recent personal history. Current facts are showing us increasingly that we are sinking into serious trouble. If any one of us could try to look at our culture from an impartial viewpoint, we no doubt would see that at least some of our bad habits should get stopped or "arrested"... before our choices become very limited or we start suffering too much.

We like the power to choose whatever we might want, but the responsibility that goes with our choice is another matter. Who is willing to take responsibility for our present condition? A parallel question relates to how much personal responsibility a convict might want to shoulder for being found guilty. The tendency of people personally and corporately is to pass blame on to others or onto the system or circumstances or even fate. Adam blamed Eve and Eve blamed the snake. Pass on the blame, for then it seemingly can be hidden. It's quite true that neither responsibility or guilt (whether individual or corporate) is directly caused by any single condition, force or circumstance. In the absence of being able to place blame and take out any offending element, it may be helpful in our present situation for us to label our cultural problems as a kind of "affliction" or "sickness." At least that won't evoke a reactionary response. Not too many of us start feeling guilty or responsible because we get sick. We know or at least want to think these days that sickness just happens. That may very well be the case with the struggles we are experiencing within our culture. There are just too many causes to be able to label any one, two or three as being the culprits. Rather like ripples on the water, everything moving outward with even diminishing impact affects everything else.

Now while sickness happens, that doesn't reduce the seriousness. In fact sometimes, small sicknesses, if not cleared up, can lead into quite serious afflictions… with all the complications a person might envision. Multiple sicknesses arising at the same time can be critical or life threatening. Whatever the case, the cultural problems that infiltrate practically all levels of our society need to be examined before more serious damage has been done. What present day person is going to quarrel about getting immediate help? Almost out of control medical costs these days show American readiness to see the specialists who can get us back to normal functioning. It's a pretty desperate and hopeless society that doesn't want to continue as a world power at least a while longer, at least if life still seems to be good and rewarding. Not so strangely, we probably should count our culture and people as being willing to rise to the occasion of an "examination," especially when we aren't feeling just right. Such an exam can be instrumental, for example, in "finding spreading cancer" within... and encouraging us to accept a prescribed remedy to stop our very contagious disease.

The cultural sickness we face today is not something that just hit us yesterday. In some form or other it probably has been with us since the beginning. A further complication is that there aren't many illnesses that show their symptoms immediately. Finally, we can be almost one hundred per-cent certain that we didn't plan to catch what ails us... nor did we get lured into our illnesses while fully comprehending the terrible consequences. (Might there be a parallel here with regard to criminals getting caught up in contagious crime?) We do know that illnesses can intrude upon our lives when we aren't taking good care of ourselves or when risky, dangerous or damaging elements infiltrate our weaknesses. There is at least some measure of accountability for us, of course, in forgetting beneficial exercises, losing sight of priorities and giving up standards in order to grab immediate satisfaction. This is essentially the situation that faces us within our culture. Over a period of some years (maybe even since the great depression), we have been led down a path toward softness and decadence. Society in the U.S. has relied heavily on Christianity to establish personal restrictions, proper balances and worthy goals. However, in the Church's desire to be loved by all and in her desire for structure, power and wealth, the Church has conceded her ability to lead and inspire. Left to go our own merry way, our society has fattened up on its resources and profits, sacrificed its strength with addictions, lost vision with its entertainment and deleted admiration with egotism. At the heart of our nation, there's plenty of increasing frustration and grief to nudge us to go see a doctor or specialist. Tests reveal a troubled culture that is overlooking its responsibilities and capacity to cope.

Our level of frustration is rather intense these days. A lot of people are messing up their own lives as well as the lives of others, whether they are national politicians, sports heroes or experimenting teenagers. Moral breakdown has run rampant. Violence is not far off the pace, whether it's increasing or decreasing. News media gives us contact with literally the whole world, so we don't miss much of the violence happening nearly everywhere. Where the basics of food and shelter are at issue, it's not too hard to understand the urgency of violent actions or going to war. The issue of continued violence in the richest society the world has ever seen… seems to be a lot more questionable. Maybe it's no wonder that violent acts occur frequently. Violence is close in the availability of more weapons, the continuing emphasis in entertainment and the news, demonstrations and highlights in sports events, games and technological advances more intimately connected with children and rising tensions in the workplace and the home. Extreme personal circumstances seem to be often followed by extreme violent counter-measures. So from Cain and Able, what's new?

Stealing also appears to be a frustrating common occurrence. As we think about the attractive advertising all around us... trying to encourage us... giving us the desired connections... showing us the rewards... we can't help but understand that vulnerable people will be seduced. It will be natural for them to use whatever methods they have available to take whatever they desire. After all, they are continually being bombarded with seductions from their peers as well as from the society at large. As we think about what some people go through, it's doubtful that even the best of us would crave less in material goods as we feel cut off from more. (Usually we crave more as we are deprived of more.) When people watch others get away with "criminal acts," it's rather normal to be drawn into the same or similar activities. If morality is left to individual whims or is relegated to the back burner, so to speak, many actions are often justified under what might be considered special circumstances. In times like these, when the temptations are so great and the deterrents are so small, it's no wonder that most people steal what they can comfortably -- a jacket, a bike, a piece of jewelry, a few miles per hour over, a few bucks off the income tax, some little things from the workplace. The items seem small but the "cancer cells" spread little by little... with no noticeable difference in society's overall health.

Individualism can easily be intimately involved with

stealing, for individualism seeks its own personal rewards. One of the weakest and possibly most detrimental features of our culture is its distorted focus on personal rights at the expense of the public welfare. Here are a few examples: A sports hero has the right to as much money as the market will bear while the most honored public servant is paid a small fraction of that amount. Individual wealth means power in our society, where poverty usually yields injustice and few opportunities. The most despicable personal acts can earn fame and fortune from a sensation hungry society. A self-centered citizen can either bankrupt a vital service industry by suing in a court of law, destroy countless lives in selling legal drugs or terrorize a town with prank calls or notes. Yes, individuals with big egos can command a lot of society's attention and resources without much regret. So as long as we hold "big shots" in high esteem and desire to be like them, the majority of people in our communities will be short-changed in their daily efforts to live healthy and peaceful lives.

Maybe there is one feeling we get inside that can send us off to the clinic to try to get some help. The feeling that seems to hit home the hardest is the grief all of us go through as we face "daily confrontations" all the way to "total war." The inner grief of the workplace, the home, the crowded highway, the verbal or physical challenge, the threatened lawsuit or the battle-field casualty has nearly every person propelled back in anguish. The wide gap we experience between "The Garden of Eden" satisfaction and the gut wrenching view of starvation, between the good choice of living in love and the bad choice of instilling hatred -- this wide gap of knowledge in our day by day lives can send us over the edge towards seeking to get ourselves straightened out or healed of our sickness. We all know too well the confrontations and wars we put ourselves through in the bad choices we make. But they are so hard to look at and so hard to acknowledge. So let's try to envision ourselves in a rather removed sort of way. The following illustration provides an overall look at what we grieve about in our personal lives moment by moment.

From the time we are born as a nation, we are created to be a prominent, forceful, defensive entity. In the world as we know it, we are taught the basics for survival. Aggressive tactics are generally regarded as the best for getting what we want. On the other hand, defensive tactics are sometimes even more powerful and self-sustaining. Proudly we export our "principles" or methods of living the good life, as long as we are in the driver's seat. Our corporations take what they need at the prices they can afford. At this point we try to use subtlety and charm to win the resources and increase low-cost production capacity. Soon our neighbors realize that we take too much and give too little, so friction develops. For wise, manipulative minds there are always legalities to use in order to overcome any power our adversaries might hold. As a powerful nation we have more than enough force to make others do our bidding, for we have by far the greatest military might the world has ever seen. The wealth we have chosen, taken from others and worked hard to attain has given us awesome power and made us nearly invulnerable. Not only do we have the best minds to create vast weapons of destruction. We also have been able to sell these weapons to the perpetually fighting little nations of the world. We can remain aloof from the mundane problems of the world. Who would dare threaten us? Still, fear and the threat of future competitors drives us on to make ourselves still stronger and more invulnerable. Meanwhile we watch as the immature, young and belligerent nations tear at one another for "the scraps" the world has to offer. Although we seem to have everything going for us, in the end, it would be instructive for us to remind ourselves that all peoples and nations have "feelings." We look at them. They look at us. And we all grieve.

Isn't there a pill that we could all take? Some religious people might even suggest that we try to locate "The Garden of Eden" and get back to God. For better or for worse, there is no going back. It's forward all the way home. And there's no magic pill to make things right. After all, there is some important, basic truth to the story that the human race has decided to take on the knowledge of what is good and what is bad. It's sort of like the ultimate challenge -- maybe even beyond "survivor" -- for there is something close to God in having to decide what's good and bad. Furthermore, responsibility goes with all the choices that have been made and will be made -- it can't be avoided. Here is the center of what each individual wrestles with day by day -- choices... and responsibility for them all. When it gets right down to it, most people probably will acknowledge that our human race has drifted slowly and methodically into some pretty bad choices. Our decisions look as though they may eventually give us a bad ending. Yet we just put one foot ahead of the other and keep on going... downhill. Basically, we desperately need something to stop us cold and get us moving in a different direction. Some radical change is the prescription we need for the "sickness" of our human choices. Or will we wait until disaster strikes, as it most certainly will eventually.

The answer to our predicament is surely to take action... and "stop the bleeding" or "take our medicine," so to speak. The only question that remains on the table is how to begin to make some good choices in place of the current bad ones. It's complimentary to be able to say that our culture has not totally lost its vision for what is good, moral, ethical, healthy and right for people in general and the creation as a whole. Religion, philosophy, ethics and history have all played important parts in our roots and potential as caretakers of the creation as we know it. Most of these disciplines and the specialists that advance them could make important contributions in pointing out good choices for the future. Specifically and critically, we need to turn to good leaders, begin to listen to inspired insights and start to act for the healing, health and wholeness of our planet. The understanding is that everything affects everything else. There's no choice but to see the world as "a single entity" that contains a lot of vital and interdependent parts. As a united body, the peoples of the world must begin to sense a new way of living in order to get our species off the critical list.

Together two groups of people can begin to "show and tell" the world how to get into the process of healing as well as find health and wholeness. The divine and indispensable advantage of these two groups can be not only helpful in nursing cultures back to health but also re-creational in revealing a vision for the future. The Christian religion fundamentally has a critically important perspective that can give "new life" to the world. That insight is about change. It's true that the followers of Jesus Christ have often lost sight of the need to be in the process of change toward Christ-like living. Instead of being vitally involved in providing the world with a fresh new look at a renewable, healthy life-style, "the hangers on" around Christ have been conformed to the world's disturbing and harmful standards. Instead of the Church giving of itself even to its own detriment in the pattern of its Lord, the Church over the centuries has been very busy in striving for comfort, serving its narrow goals, taking pride in its materialistic structures, giving glory to it hierarchy, and even worshipping its own superficial models of praise. That is not to say that the Church has not made some good choices, at least for appearance sake. One is reminded of the poor man who did get to eat the crumbs that fell from his master's table. Still with all that on the negative side, the Christian Church does give credit to Christ and to his actions on behalf of the world. What has been overlooked or maybe even intentionally relegated to the dustbins of history are his life-giving words, "Follow me". For all his followers that means a radical change in direction. It also means providing insight to the world about what is truly valuable and worthwhile for ongoing life, health and happiness. With knowledge of what is good, different choices and a reformation of Christ-like activity, the Church in today's world could provide the needed inspiration for cultural healing, health and wholeness throughout the world.

It's a humbling experience to be a convict. Of course that was the intent from the beginning... that people experience humility before the creator. Jesus came to re-introduce God to man in a personal way and to get the relationships right. Of course, without the acknowledgement of rebellion, law-breaking and heading off in the wrong direction there would be no need for a liberating Christ and no need for Christian converts. So put simply, Christians are convicts in need of change. In coming into union with Jesus, Christians in humility face the fact that they have been choosing what is bad and indicate their desire to live differently. That not only tosses Christ's followers in with the bad people, but it provides them with some humility in working with other bad people. As we begin to look at these fundamental realities, the brotherhood or sisterhood of Christ becomes more clear. People in the world who have been judged guilty and convicted and imprisoned are potentially members of the same family or group as Christians. Prison convicts who have not accepted their guilt are like fake Christians who do not recognize their guilt or feel humility. Both are rather worthless fakes in the sight of the world and have little to offer others except a way to live badly and sadly. But look what's on the positive side. Christians who know they have strayed and take off after their Lord are powerful witnesses to everyone. They testify to a life-giving way for the planet to find peace and harmony. These disciples of Christ know what it's like to be in violation of what is good and right. They can tell others about frustration and grief and how not to live. Now imagine Christian convicts joining forces with prison convicts to cut crime and strengthen one another in their attempts to make the world a better place in which to live. What a powerful team to point to good choices and the benefits of change. Both groups in exemplary, humble living could show the world that fundamental change is not only possible but also critically important to every person seeking significance, meaning and happiness. Criminals become crime fighters could start individuals thinking about cutting down on bad choices, while Christian actions based on spiritual perspectives could help people grow into fundamentally more healthy and whole creatures. Today's crimes indicate rather gross violations of individual freedoms and infractions against the welfare of organized society; but tomorrow's crimes might have more creative insight into how people should function together for the enhancement of all of life in the universe. Helping people get into the process of mutually uplifting, transforming change would set societies on the right path.

All the dreaming in the world will not make any good choice or inspiration happen. Very little of what has been of real value to people down through the ages has happened quickly. In a culture like ours that features immediate results and satisfaction, the temptation is to brush off long-term possibilities as unrealistic or fanciful. But the steady slowness of change is really the hope of a cooperative and caring world. As common people realize that properly executed goodness is "a walk down a beautiful path" and healthy change is "a liberating, dedicated, careful process," then almost anything is possible and there is exciting hope for all people. With radical change it's necessary for individual people to take their first steps deliberately… and simply begin what they believe to be right. There is no magic necessary to make things happen, but the miracle of newness can flow out of what was desperation and deterioration. Clearly skeptics abound for many reasons, not the least of which is to insure that the status quo remains. Some people persistently believe that bad and fearful choices remain the only rational options in a world gone bad. Since mankind has the power to make both good and bad choices there is no guarantee that the good will win out for any of us, say nothing about for our culture or society. Yet merely a few courageous, hopeful people joined with others can make the difference to sway the course of history and send our species off into a new, enlightened, life giving experiment.

Healing, health and wholeness will only become a part of our life together as people give one another encouragement to carry out the exercise of change. When individuals develop bad habits, take in substances detrimental to their health, let themselves get run down and don't exercise properly they become very vulnerable to sickness. Likewise, our culture has over consumed, absorbed all kinds of corruptive elements, become apathetic about the environment and yielded to sloppy if not flagrant immorality. From only a little distance away in time or space, we probably could recognize that we are not at all well. Really the only way out of our "sickness" is to start to rehabilitate by going through the exercise of change… individually and corporately. Of course change can proceed down any wrong and hurtful road. Our natural instincts, coming out of a jungle mentality, is to go with the flow of self-interest, aggressiveness and egotism. Beneficial change will consequently send us in the opposite direction -- the direction of self-giving, encouraging others and humility. Initially, most people in our culture would probably react and argue about the losses such change might cause. What an outdated way of life…you're taking all the fun out of living… that's only for the prim, proper and pious people… they might argue. Sadly such people are not aware of the eventual fate of hedonistic, selfish, egotistical living… until often it's too late. On the contrary, getting into the exercise of change toward a caring, sharing, self-giving mentality will produce unimagined benefits. Through the process of time, positive, healthy change will bring strength to our species personally and corporately as well as provide lasting satisfaction, meaning and happiness. True love, sacrificial giving, insightful guidance, long-term commitment and cooperative adaptability are all critically important to sustainable, peaceful and happy living on this planet. In essence, we need to exercise change wisely for quality living now and forever.

In putting change into practice, a valuable goal is to try to attain the highest degree of efficient, productive living. Looking at the whole creation, we can take note of how intensely efficient each part is in its living and giving. Each part survives not only in its disciplined "lifestyle" but also in its contribution to the interdependence of the world. More pointedly, each part survives for another part or it doesn't continue to survive. People, however, in being able to choose what is not in their own best interests or in the best interests of the rest of creation, have chosen to be self-absorbed and inefficient. Look at the extremes humanity displays in the world today -- the extremes of wealth and poverty, fat and thin, wise and foolish, productive and unproductive, sedentary and athletic, passive and aggressive, rebellious and conformist... and the list can go on and on. There certainly is a great amount of room for variations and differences. Yet the wild extremes our human race exhibits... is to the detriment of all. One of the most awesome contributions that human beings could do to advance the quality of life for the whole creation, forever, would be to start to lower consumption of everything the world has to offer. The advantages would soon become obvious to every living creature. Imagine the short and long term gains for everyone, if the largest consumer of the world's resources spread those resources out to people who consumed the least. Consider the increased happiness in the world if the most efficient and happy person in the world would share his or her secrets with those who don't enjoy such living. As people think about the simplicity, satisfaction, benefits and joy of change, they also can pass on the goodness of great goals.

One of the greatest accomplishments for the human race could be in bringing antagonists together in mutual understanding and cooperation. This might be considered the most outrageous and ridiculous suggestion the world has ever heard... with regard to realistic possibilities. Still, what we humans can understand as creatures viewing the past... is how so much has already changed so rapidly. For example, the technological change the world has witnessed over just a few decades is quite awesome to contemplate for even the most knowledgeable person. Of course, highly specialized, trained and sophisticated human beings have focused on these changes persistently and patiently for relatively long periods of time. Unbelievable change can and does take place over even a single life time. The key, of course, is the direction of change and how it is intentionally manipulated. It is completely feasible for our species to begin to move away from creating new products to focusing our attention on change within the human soul -- body, mind and spirit. What a re-formation of life might be in store for our world if we were to begin to take entirely conceivable steps within the human psyche toward sustainable, cooperative, healthy living. A way or process could be found to reduce… tensions within individuals, conflicts between individuals and hatreds between peoples. Along the way, maybe an even greater objective might begin to take shape in all races working harmoniously as "caretakers of the universe." What a radical reversal in direction that would be from directing our world down the path of destruction. However, it must be said that some fresh and new steps need to be taken soon.

If it is our desire to find cultural healing and health, the process might begin with some simple personal assessments. What person doesn't need some inspiration now and then? Every person on the face of the globe could use regular and at least minimal soulful tune-ups… with change as one valuable prescription. What would I like to do with my life? What would I like to change to enhance my life and the lives around me? Who might be inspired to enter my life, help me do better and so find some fulfillment in giving? What small things could I do to grant liberation, encouragement and support to others so that they might grow into fullness of life? How could I be a part of the big picture of setting my race back on the right track toward a divine and ecstatic future? Every person could pick even one question, seek out an answer and take a first step. What a great opportunity to enhance living. What a big shift and what a big accomplishment this might be after "growing up" in a culture of defensiveness, under the fear of change and bogged down in self-satisfaction. Each and every individual could experience a brimming sense of excitement while heading off in a new direction. Yes, we could travel together on a long, inspiring, meaningful and friendly journey into a well-balanced, wonderful world.

CHAPTER 16

"Being Inspired To Give Blessing"

Blessing is not a word that is commonly used in our secular world today. Way back in the 1970s and 80s I gently suggested to my two boys that they should pray a blessing before eating their meals at school. Obviously that was quite difficult for them to carry out in front of their friends. I would guess my suggestion was disregarded. Blessing after all has been primarily a religious term, except when politicians or presidents feel the need to have their speeches sanctioned with a "God bless America." What does it mean to bless? The dictionary definition says that "to bless" is to make holy, consecrate or set apart for a holy purpose. "A blessing" is a statement of divine favor, a benediction or a grace said before or after a meal. Both bless and blessing have their roots in religious terminology. Generally the world of the marketplace and politics isn't comfortable with serious bowed head humility, grace and consecration for God's purposes. Similarly, public school students generally have their fun teasing or irritating the special child trying to be different. We also know that children are good imitators of the popular, secular world around them. They quickly learn to take charge, get what they want and follow their peers. None of this is new to us.

It's all a part of our recent past, which we know almost too well. Furthermore, it has brought us into some difficulties in our world today.

Is it so strange that as we train or permit our children to grow up with "a jungle mentality," they turn out to be little animals -- cute and funny and instinctive, but little animals, none the less? Many children are left to educate themselves from whatever environment that surrounds them. "Do whatever feels good" is the typical entertaining interplay for our day. It's a directive that's learned quickly and thoroughly especially by all the aggressive ones that want to take charge. Your basic animal of the jungle looks out for itself, considers nearly everything a threat, seeks to meet its desires immediately and lives to propagate as much as possible. On the other hand, human beings have the capacity to choose to act at a "higher level", but only when taught to make different decisions for different purposes. Careful and persistent teaching really does make a difference. There really is reason for people to take action contrary to "the law of the jungle." Since most people are aware of inspiration beyond the jungle, they are acquainted with different if not higher ethical and moral standards. As an illustration, some people believe that there is a greater good in looking out for others than in simply looking out for self. Some people believe that many personal desires do not need to be met immediately for true happiness. Some people believe that love is the way to overcome hate. Some people believe that our environment and resources should be preserved and treasured for future generations and not trashed in our own lifetime. Some people believe that happiness can be achieved with very little material goods. Some people believe that they do not need to propagate the species in order to leave a rich legacy. Some people believe that "humble living" is for the greater good of all, since there is a greater power to be praised. Some people do not choose to live in defensiveness and fear but with open handedness and courage for the sake of others. Some people believe that there is something beyond the jungle and the materialistic world -- something worth sacrificing for in order to be uplifted and blessed. These beliefs are not found in your basic "animal" living in the jungle. Furthermore, these beliefs do not come to us instinctively. They need to be taught, caught in training and exemplified. Essentially, they are what some might call a blessing to the world from the Gods.

At this point an argument will be made about our exemplary children, since they are so much a part of us and we are so much a part of them. Certainly we and our children are not mere animals, for we are educated, skillful, prosperous and strong. But think about it for a moment -- do these four attributes move us very far away from the instinctive and selfish crowd? Our innermost desires are made evident within our culture, which is highly institutionalized. One of our most influential institutions -- the college and university of our day and age -- is symbolic of some or our highest aspirations. It takes pride in some of our brightest educators, our most ambitious students and our most sophisticated teaching resources. Maybe it would be instructive for us to look at the atmosphere of today's college dorm room and see what is treasured by the coming generation. Within the "back woods" of the northern mid-west... an article headlines that living in a dorm obligates students to have all the right gadgets, toys, pictures and displays. In 2001, dormitories are full of youthful treasures -- a few of which are stereos, powerful surround sound speakers, big screen T-Vs, VCRs, CD players, DVD players, PlayStations, computers, laptops, refrigerators, cell-phones, answering machines, grillers, clock radios and mood lights, along with the liquor bottles, posters, stylish clothes and jewelry. Many students claim to need continual internet access, cordless phones, and a wide range of electronic goods to be happy going away to school. Check out a few current dorm rooms. Most young people claim to simply try for an extension of their rooms at home. What does all this say about what the most sophisticated and envied members of our culture need for happiness? What does this say about future consumption on our planet? What is our hope for future harmony and happiness between the nations of the world? Do we have time or courage to stand back and take a long look at who we are, what we want and where we are headed?

Let's step back and look at another illustration of who we are, what we want and where we are headed. One of the big attractions of the internet these days is the proposed invention of Dean Kamen who is a prolific inventor. Having more than 90 patents, Kamen recently

introduced the wheel-chair step climber named IBOT --
nicknamed Fred. Fred is certainly high-tech and worthy
of high praise in our modern world. It certainly might
help a lot of handicapped people. Kamen's most recent
invention simply known as "It" is widely anticipated
and is represented as so awesome that it will change
the world. Dozens of pages on the internet are filled
with speculation about what "it" will it turn out to be.
Probably the most reasonable guess is that this invention
will be some form of personal transporter, which will
transform the way cities operate throughout the world.
In any case, our culture is caught up with "It", what
technology can do for us and how it can change our
lives. Not unlike the way many who are entering the new
millennium see drugs as an almost immediate fix for
our physical and emotional problems, so also many look
to technology to correct the social and environmental
problems that confront our world. Is this really where
we want to put a major part of our emphasis as a society
or as a rational species? Will we be content to go to our
personal or corporate destruction playing with or even
working with the latest gadget? Is the success of the latest
piece of military hardware more important to us than
living in peace with one another? The toughest question
of all -- Would we rather be in the process of building
personal wealth, power and security than in putting our
minds and hearts to work in changing the world into a
place of cooperation and harmony? These are two quite
different agendas for the present and future. Again, how
will we spend our time and efforts? Will we work hard
trying to possess the latest red-hot device or will we

try to spend our time and energy on changing human behavior? The choice is ours, for we know that we have the power to choose for good or for bad in every age.

Speaking about choices does not translate into an easy subject for people living in this most wealthy and materialistic culture since the beginning of time. Almost all of us are addicted to our materialistic, comfortable, egotistic life-style and it would take a radical change in perspective to get us on the road to healing. Addiction is really quite simple. It's being devoted to or consumed by some habit, especially to a bad habit like the use of a drug. Essentially we are hooked on our desires for more and more of all the things that tempt us in our culture -- money, fame, power, prestige, toys, gadgets, clothes, food, drugs, entertainment, and whatever else our little hearts desire. Try to withdraw from any of these "things" for something more important and see what power lies in the addiction. The reason that there are so many possible focal points for our habits is that their roots lie in our selfish and egotistical instincts. The proof lies in the fact that we as addicts can't get outside our personal, habitual desires. Otherwise, how could we be quietly content with our luxuries... as millions of our fellow human beings starve? How could we permit the existence of the torture chambers we call prisons... with all the social science, motivational tools, training techniques and spiritual ideals that reside at our fingertips? Addiction is pervasive throughout our society and culture and almost no one is able to see the truth of our condition. As for escape, what mere mortal can swim against the tide of the ocean? We have heard that no one is perfect, no not one. Still, it's ridiculous that there don't seem to be even solitary voices who question the zombie, apathetic life-style that is our daily routine. Of course there is the sadness of not being able to take on changed lives... when we do feel even a faint wish to think and act outside of our addictions. In very rare moments, we may even wonder if our sickness is too advanced and if we as habitual consumers are beyond saving. What is our hope? Who can help? Can anything be done? If we are to have a healthy future, the absolute first step is that we candidly face the truth... of who we are, what we want and where we are headed.

It might not hurt too much to take a quick glance in the mirror and see if we can face our unhealthy condition as an addicted culture. Health is usually quite evident in generally satisfied, well-conditioned, happy people. The average person today doesn't consider any serious conflict to be healthy. Moreover, health is not associated with doing detrimental things to the environment. Health is not evident in the loss of physical, mental or emotional fitness. Health doesn't rely on risky, outside stimulation for meaning and happiness. And healthy living is not jealous or conceited living. Our "national arrogance" may indicate one of the saddest aspects of how unhealthy we look to other peoples. Instead of being apologetic about using foreign labor and the planet's resources for our own pleasure, we gloat about what a good time we are having. Rather than being ashamed of our outrageous consumption and waste, we brag about what a successful society we have become. This is not healthy living. Simply because almost every family in the U.S. seems to be able to afford several modes of personal transportation does not make that advisable for every family on the planet. Or look at food. The use of food in our country is not only shameful but could be thought of as revolting. Yes, we eat too much, we eat what's bad for us, we waste what's been given to us, we neglect and corrupt our capacity to produce it, we take what is good out of it, we use it as a weapon and we neglect its proper distribution. This "quality of life" is not much to brag about.

Another important condition of our addicted culture has to do with the greed that we rather innocently put on display for the world to see. Have we no shame? We must face the fact that we live deeper in materialism than any other people in history. A fundamental assumption is that we need to spend more and faster to keep our capitalistic system moving along. It has been documented time and again that the rich get richer, while the poor get poorer. Natural resources like the rain forests, farm land, oil, natural gas, clear water, plant and animal life and even oxygen are being corrupted or depleted at alarming rates. So who cares except "the environmentalist"? Who cares what is left over for any of the coming generations, as long as we can have what we want and get it soon? We are an addicted culture and we are so caught up in our habits that we have lost our ability to think rationally and conscientiously.

The amount of money that is paid to "the most popular and productive" people in our society is almost beyond belief. How can a sports hero, entertainment celebrity, rock star, or clothes designer get paid what multitudes of the world's poorest people could find "enough" for basic needs? Of course, business executives and dictators from around the world are the proven champions of siphoning off the wealth of the world. Each wealthy manipulator has his own moral justifications, legal techniques and cheering sections… so the rise to the top is "smooth and legitimate." Even if we are nearsighted, is it acceptable that our capitalistic system permits such hogging of our nation's gross national product? What kind of government sanctions "highway robbery" because its citizens are ignorant, apathetic or don't know how the bandits operate? Will the whole world be destroyed in the name of freedom for a few? It's downright amazing that we as individuals are so caught up in our addictive habits that we can't see what's happening on just a little more advanced level of desire and greed. But wait just a second, here's a surprising turn of events. As these words are being written, a few of our nation's richest people have joined in stating their interest in preserving the estate tax. Could this signal an interest in cutting down the massive asset accumulation of the wealthiest people? Give credit where credit it due, if this unusual and maybe controversial statement is intended to benefit the poor, we should all pause to stop and think. If exceedingly wealthy people are willing to pay more, other people will pay a little less. Could these leaders be consciously or maybe even unconsciously pointing us in a hopeful, new direction? In our wildest imagination, what might living on earth be like if our reference points were not those who have more but those who have less?

One last flagrant example of our addiction to material things can be seen in our "Who Wants To Be A Millionaire?" mentality. The assumption is, of course, that everyone wants to be a millionaire. What can we learn, what can we say, what can we do… to get money, fame, fun, security, leisure and all the things we want? Compete, have a grand time, take center stage and just maybe win a lot of money. Better yet, today in our country many of our seduced citizens want to take their chances for securing "the good life" through mere games of chance. Lotteries and casinos target our greed with advertising to the most vulnerable, weak and ignorant people among us. Billed as "entertainment" in an addicted culture, games of chance continually take from those who have little… and in effect, give a semi-load of alcohol to an alcoholic. Who is "a better person" for cashing in on a fortune… which "liberates" from normal living, drains gaming money from addicts, piles up the wealth of a few and intensifies greed all in one delirious event? Meanwhile, the people who desperately need this "extra cash" go without basic nutrition and die with bloated stomachs. We have become addicted and we have sold out our souls for the bad choices.

The ultimate irony is that we have become a fearful society in the age of superficial security. There has never been a culture with more food, shelter, clothes, medical care, police protection, dead bolt locks, military power, economic strength, political expertise and even spiritual resources. But we don't have enough to give us peace. Not so strangely, our addictions have made us anxious and apprehensive. As we try to accumulate more, we need to protect more, insure more and pay attention to more. Since we never get enough, we need to work and strive harder for what we think we might want. We run as fast as we can to try to keep up... with buying and payments... over and over again. As our neighbors watch us consume they don't want to get left behind. They naturally seek a bigger piece of the economic pie. That prods us to try to "squeeze more blood out of the turnip" of economic life. So the level of greed and accumulation raises up a notch and the process continues. Why shouldn't we be fearful? We know that there's a lot of our stuff that could be taken away. Since we are caught in wanting, it's understandable that others are caught in wanting too. Will the Russians come over and take away our toys? Or will it be some tin-horn dictator? Maybe the Chinese will want to expand their horizons. So we build more fighters, warships and weapons at a terrible cost... all because we are filled with insecurity and fear. Yes, it's hard to stay on top of the mountain without fighting off a lot of foes... in our imagination at least. On the local scene, it's the mugger, the robber or the gang member that seems to be the threat to our security. So we try to keep them as far away as possible from the things we need to sustain our habits. Then we need more jails and prisons and longer terms and more police on the streets. There's no end to trying to reduce our fears, and it costs us dearly. Maybe insurance will fill our need for peace and contentment, but how much and at what price? We insure our cars, our homes, our lives, our businesses, our partners, our children and sometimes even our talents and our toys. It does cost us though… all because of our addictions. The evidence seems to indicate that in the midst of all this, we have not secured healthy or happy living.

There's no question even the most enthusiastic supporters of our economic system can begin to see (if they look hard enough) that we not only have some present difficulties on the road we travel but that there are increasing troubles ahead. We as a people are a bit like that chain smoker who is continually taking more and more puffs while getting less and less oxygen. As the lungs get clogged with more and more smoke they are less and less able to supply the body with fuel for life. It's obvious that the faster the treadmill moves the quicker it will come to a halt. It's just a matter of time. It is true that many chain smokers don't care and claim that they need to die sometime anyway, so they might as well go satisfying their desires. Such people who feel that they "own themselves" and do not care about the impact of their activities and lives upon others, can make some case for destroying themselves as they see fit. However, as a society… and as a culture… and as a grand political experiment… and as an important part of the human race… can we culturally turn our backs on our long-term health and happiness with the shrug of a deteriorating and dying addict? Yes, sadly, we can… for we can choose. On the other hand, we can also choose the good, the better and even the best.

We have spent time trying to look honestly at ourselves and at the source of our addictions, unhealthy living and deteriorating future possibilities. We should also spend some time thinking about other more healthy and hopeful possibilities. Like the chain smoker, our culture can begin to withdraw from what is killing us or we can even eliminate our addition altogether. Imagine the benefits of a little less smoke each day -- the increasing lung capacity, the goodness of heading in a new direction, the increasing care for the welfare of others, the example to others of being able to carry out positive change and the transforming energy of increasing health and hopefulness. What a radical and positive development for any individual. Would the situation be any different for our culture or society? With some inspiration from outside, our society could also find a new path... to travel away from addiction and eventual catastrophe. Imagine the benefits of a little less materialism each day -- the satisfaction of moving away from addiction to freedom, the goodness of people with too little getting more of what they need, the joy of getting out of the rat race to the top, the excitement of leading our fellow human beings in a healthy, new, direction, the benefits to the environment of less consumption and the enhanced harmony for all of life on the planet. Such advantages for healthy living should not be minimized in the least, since these positives are 180 degrees from the disaster of addiction and deterioration. What a difference in the way of life for people on the planet -- from bad and sad consequences for the poorest as well as the richest... to moving toward fullness of life for the whole creation.

"The difference" between what is good and bad seems motivation enough to begin to move from negative to positive living standards in any culture. Yet as any addict knows, rational thinking does not easily break well-entrenched habits or bring about change. How shall a society or culture such as ours escape the clutches of the addictions on which we are hooked? A key word for answering such a question is "inspiration." In a very real sense, to be inspired is to be infused with life -- quite literally, to have breath blown in. Inspiration is a stimulus to creativity, thought or action and so rather naturally is linked with divine influence upon human beings. Consequently, human beings who have been caught living under the natural "law of the jungle" need to be broken in upon by a higher power -- simply to be inspired. The success of the Alcoholics Anonymous program for alcoholics and other addicts is undoubtedly strong testimony to reliance on help from "a higher power." The flip side of the coin is... as our culture has drifted away from being inspired on a higher plane of morality, ethics and spirituality, we have become entangled in our own web of selfishness and conceit. We find ourselves sinking desperately into exhaustion, which will lead to our eventual collapse. As usual, the results of addiction become quickly obvious for the whole world to see.

As we enter this early stage of our new millennium, every person on earth can be inspired by great, spiritual leaders in order to begin to walk down an exciting path of healing, health and harmony. The Christian tradition presents Jesus Christ who may be the most creative and influential person the world has ever known. Born humbly, Jesus saw himself as the Son of God, entering the world to personally make known the Creator, Redeemer and Comforter of the universe. His mission to raise up the broken-hearted, free the captives, love the enemy and point the way toward The Kingdom of God inspired his disciples to leave their past behind and follow him. Maybe the most simple and loved Bible verse speaks to the core of this divine man: "For God loved the world so much that he gave his only Son, that everyone who believes in him may not die but live forever." Jesus came asking those who took him seriously to follow him and find a new way of life carrying out his teachings. His message involved calling all people to change -- to give up their old selfish ways in order to make self-giving love the eventual victor over all that is bad. He was not interested in earthly power but was interested in a greater and higher power... encompassing the way to forgiveness, the truth of divine redemption, and the life of sacrificial love. Jesus eventually went willingly to a tortuous death on a cross at a young age for the sake of all needy people, or as he put it, for "the least important of these brothers and sisters of mine." His sphere of influence reached out and continues to reach out to all those people who humbly acknowledge their need of a savior or even inspiration -- the poor, the mourners, the humble, the merciful, the pure in heart, the persecuted and those who work for peace. For all these, Jesus revealed the way to true happiness and new life.

Known by many as simply The Lord, Jesus Christ offers unlimited inspiration for people living in this twenty-first century. People of all persuasions can be moved to powerful, refreshing actions by this "Chosen One" who steps in to help lift the burden of every troubled soul. Even atheists can be moved by unselfish love. And what can be better for people who live in our time and place than to receive forgiveness, a forgotten past and the gifted motivation for change? Throughout the ages, Jesus seeks to speak and act through his enthusiastic followers so that people of all times and places can experience peace, renewal and meaning. Addicts in our culture critically need a new watchfulness and connection with others to begin to step away from their habits and what ties them in knots. This Lord not only commands our attention because of his great action on behalf of all people, but he also reveals the fantastic rewards of carrying out his loving and satisfying policies. Imagine the boost to our national reputation if our society began "loving our neighbors" and equally distributing the world's wealth. Or what would be the overall impact on the world if U.S. citizens would begin to work with convicts to bring vast cultural changes into our economic and political system? Christ's servant role is finally "the frosting on the cake" for thinking people who are looking for inspiration in our times. There just aren't that many true servants around these days to minister to the desperate needs of our world. Think about what a nation of servants might do to clean up and change the mess we've created. If you can begin to think about something like that… you've most certainly have found inspiration and blessing.

Another wonderful inspiration for contemporary people is the great, nonviolent leader Mahatma Gandhi. Gandhi was born in the late 19th century and was the mastermind behind India's freedom through nonviolent revolution. His character was strongly affected by his deeply religious mother. An event early in his life -- where he was pushed out of a first-class section of a railroad car in South Africa by a white guard -- played an important part in his future activities. He was quoted as saying, "There was a white man in the room; I was afraid of him. What was my duty, I asked myself. Should I go back to India or should I go forward, with God as my helper, and face whatever was in store for me? I decided to stay and suffer. My active non-violence began from that date." In his writing of 1909, Gandhi set forth a goal of "an exploitation-free society in which the ordinary individual can claim and defend his rights." In 1915 he took vows with 25 inmates to observe truth, nonviolence, celibacy, fearlessness and to practice self-control. After periods of fasting and prison terms for civil disobedience, in 1932 Gandhi identified himself with the untouchables, whom he called "children of God"… for "the most despised people are the most favored of God." In 1940 he pushed for individual civil disobedience to win freedom of speech against war. As he was on his way to attend a prayer meeting in 1948, he was shot and killed by a Hindu fanatic.

Gandhi's deep humanity insisted that people fighting for their rights (as individuals or as groups) should never violate their basic obligation to respect life. "As man has not been given the power to create, he has not the slightest right to destroy the smallest creature that lives." And he put no limit on his humanity: "My life is an indivisible whole, and all my activities run into one another; they all have their rise in my insatiable love of mankind…. I do not know any religion apart from human activity. It provides a moral basis to all other activities…. We needlessly divide life into watertight compartments, religion and other; whereas if a man has true religion in him, it must show itself in the smallest details of life. The smallest irregularity in sanitary, social and political life is a sign of spiritual poverty." In the final analysis, Gandhi showed himself to be one of the greatest thinkers of the recent past. He was an extraordinary composite of east and west, ancient and modern and his life and thought went through a continual process of evolution. Gandhi laid no claim to superhuman power, but simply, for him to know was to act. He would have made Jesus proud. Albert Einstein said, "The moral influence which Gandhi has exercised upon thinking people may be far more durable than would appear likely in our present age, with its exaggeration of brute force. We are fortunate and grateful that fate has bestowed upon us so luminous a contemporary, a beacon to generations to come." Might Gandhi be an inspiration for health and harmony and the process of change today? Rest assured that the inspiration "to know and then act" would most certainly bring us blessing.

One last contemporary figure that can provide us inspiration for change (or show us how to move away from our worldly addictions) is Mother Teresa. Born in 1910, as the youngest child of an Albanian builder, she took her vows as a Roman Catholic nun at the age of 27. While riding a train into the mountains to recover from suspected tuberculosis, she said she received a call from God "to serve him among the poorest of the poor." After moving to India, one day she faced a woman "half eaten by maggots and rats" lying in front of a Calcutta hospital. She stayed with the woman until she died. In 1950, Mother Teresa founded the order of Missionaries of Charity. Around the world she and others devoted their time and energies to the poor, the blind, the disabled and the aged. Schools, orphanages, homes for the needy were opened. "I see God in every human being. When I wash the leper's wounds, I feel I am nursing the Lord himself. Is it not a beautiful experience?" she asked. Mother Teresa won the Nobel Peace Prize in 1979, and in accepting the prize commented… "I choose the poverty of our people. But I am grateful to receive (the Nobel) in the name of the hungry, the naked, the homeless, of the crippled, of the blind, of the lepers, of all those people who feel unwanted, unloved, uncared-for throughout society, people that have become a burden to the society and are shunned by everyone." This frail woman who had many physical setbacks would sometimes quote statistics about people in poverty and ask why there was no large-scale investment in human development. Like Gandhi she had great spiritual resources and spoke for the poor everywhere. Her work in the slums of Calcutta illustrated for "the concerned" that the way to pull people out of poverty is to first give them self-esteem. Then the down and out need hope that change for the better is always possible. As Mother Teresa's experience asserts, she knew that many small steps by individuals can be more valuable than huge governmental anti-poverty programs. And so lived a small woman in simple clothes, who had little time to talk but walked out into a world of need and little by little changed the lives of millions.

Can Mother Teresa inspire us and move us to act for others? She doesn't challenge us to turn the world upside down immediately. She shows us how to care… and sit with a forsaken one. A common human being like the stable born Jesus and the toilet cleaning Gandhi, this woman who received "a call" started with "a sickness" but was open to change and persisted with good, self-giving choices to the end. She so desperately wanted healthy change for others that she kept putting one foot ahead of the other until she dropped. Commenting on her life's work Mother Teresa said, "The other day I dreamed that I was at the gates of heaven. And St. Peter said, 'Go back to Earth. There are no slums up here.'" In our personal lives, is it possible for us to turn around, kick our bad habits and take on a piece of that action the little lady left in 1997? Yes sir, St. Peter.

There is a real, honest to goodness nucleus of people in our world that can be inspired to give blessing. Not everyone will jump on the bandwagon all at once, however, for there are always leaders and followers. Not only are some people inspired quicker, but some also feel more blessed. Even the Christian Church will not be re-formed into an action oriented Body of Christ in the next few years, even if the clouds were to open and Jesus himself would make another entrance. Yet there are those people who will get that vision… or that call… or see the light of our spiritual forerunners and counselors. Today, within the Church there are those who remember what God has done… and what it means to choose wisely and reverse course before it's too late. There are those who know what it means to be a convict like other convicts and join them in humble, worshipful work for the Kingdom of God. There are those who truly care for the future of God's world and want it to flourish… more than they want to satisfy their personal desires. And there are those who want God's will done… on earth as it is in heaven. Such people will begin to take their little, persistent actions for God's sake and for the sake of others. Yes, the addictions will have to go, but with the help, support and encouragement of fellow convicts there will be victory over those obviously destructive habits… inspired by the grace of God. Certainly, we have been inspired to give blessing.

CHAPTER 17

"Renewing Commitment"

Are we ready... for commitment? That almost sounds like a dirty word. Over the last few years, haven't we as a people been trying to get away from of a lot of our commitments? Hasn't our culture been stomping on marriage commitments, lawful commitments, family commitments and even health commitments? Don't we really have trouble with New Year's Eve commitments and especially spiritual commitments? It's true. This has all been part of our addiction problem. Commitments essentially have fallen by the wayside. A part of the reason is we become sold on the idea that there's something better or more fulfilling than what we've pledged our loyalty to in the past. After all, there's just so much more to go after. We suggest to ourselves that we would be more happy and satisfied with a different mate, or driving at a different speed, or taking on more work rather than spending more time with the children. Then there's the slide into apathy that takes us away from commitment. We get so taken up with other things, work, entertainment, people and outside interests, we lose our focus on past promises. To make matters worse, the problem of selfishness also raises its ugly head... together with wanting our desires met almost immediately. It's pretty natural in the land of multi-level advertising to want to quickly grab what other people seem to be going after… and try to get "whatever" before it gets out of reach. We want sexual relations, food, cars, drugs, parties, tech toys and exciting entertainment as soon as we can get it. There's no wonder that the pledges we've made in the past suffer under this barrage.

Of course, whenever we fail to honor a past commitment, we set up precedent for not honoring future commitments. Drifting more and more deeply into apathy and broken promises as well as telling ourselves that everyone else is doing whatever they feel like doing -- all this moves our morality, principles and commitments into a pretty negative spiral over a period of time. People around us seem to be letting us down more and more frequently, so again it's natural for us to just let things slide. And the momentum keeps increasing. What's to be gained by "keeping one's word" these days? The growing consensus is that you just loose out on some of the fun. We find out that "fun and games and excitement" packed in the midst of "a lot of work and stress and running" is what the life of addiction is all about. We further come to understand that addiction is pretty close to the opposite of a commitment. To commit really means to bring together, deliver for safekeeping or to pledge, bind or engage. So addiction is being devoted to a bad habit while commitment is being devoted to a pledge. There's a real struggle going on here between personal desires and promises to others. When personal desires win out in the life of an individual, then commitments often are broken and society suffers.

One of the real sad developments of a selfish and addicted age is that social links get very weak and society becomes terribly vulnerable to terrorism, deterioration and eventual death. The Roman Empire is one of the most glaring examples in history. Think about what happens when a society such as ours begins to splinter into smaller and smaller parts for lack of strong ties between the races. As families increasingly disintegrate, education, morality, health and insight are all reduced. When the rich get richer and the poor get poorer, when the wealthy have too much to protect and the poor have too little with which to live, when the separation is overwhelming and growing between the haves and the have-nots, when the military and dictatorships try to control the masses who are in desperate need, when tremendous resources are used to defend the interests of a wealthy few, when prisons and jails are used to try to control the minds and spirits of hurting people, when apathy runs rampant among spiritual, educational and political leaders -- when these kinds of situations begin to develop on a small globe such as ours, then commitment is in need of serious revival. As a society, how close are we to deterioration and death? Did the Romans ever see it coming?

We desperately need commitment to change. Terrifyingly, terrorism is real commitment to change. Even within our society we have become aware of terrorist actions.

Yet it's no more than right and wise on our part to ask what kind of desperation leads to such acts. What leads a terrorist in Palestine to be willing to sacrifice his life to commit a terrorist act? Maybe it would be good to ask if we could ever be so committed that we would give our lives to make something happen? What if you witnessed the torture of your children? What if everything you had was taken away from you? Would you become committed to a cause? What would you think of someone being apathetic in the face of such acts? Then there's the case of a mind drifting off by itself in our own addicted society... and becoming so warped and twisted that there is a horrible commitment to destroy a school or an office building. What kind of sadness and sickness in a life leads to such a terrorist act? Consider the power available in real commitment -- to destroy. Yet more importantly, the same power of commitment is available to help, heal and revive people for new and abundant life. Now that's something much better to think about. Should the only really committed people be the terrorists or the destroyers? Think of the sadness ahead if only terrorists worked with commitment, and wealthy, comfortable people worked only with apathy. What if the wealthy and powerful people in the world were not forced by deadly circumstances to change but were willing to change... for the sake of others and for the welfare of the world? The power of commitment to change for the "health of all people" would undoubtedly be the greatest revolution in the history of mankind. Imagine "addicted people" willingly kicking their habits in order to raise up the forgotten and destitute peoples of the world. Imagine a "sacrifice" of greed, materialism, apathy, defensiveness, pride and pollution for the purpose of harmony and happiness among all the nations. That could be the overall goal of committed change. It would need to be contemplated as a never ending process -- possibly an evolution, if you will, inspired by the Gods... back toward the abundant and harmonious garden of Eden.

What kind of commitment would it take to start to turn things around and begin to accomplish health, healing and wholeness for all? Let's take a current example out of our culture in order to try to identify how serious commitment can truly happen here and now. Nearly everyone in the U.S. has probably heard of the "Back To The Future" movie star, Michael J. Fox. More recently "Mike" had the lead role in the hit television series "Spin City." There are some other more recent facts, however, some people might not have heard or do not realize. Sometime after his movie career, this extremely popular young Canadian actor became aware he had Parkinson's disease. After he left the show "Spin City," he decided to throw himself into the battle to find a cure for P.D. -- a disease that affects an estimated one million Americans. This incurable degenerative progressive disease slowly eats away at him and erodes his motor skills. Being a person with a strong sense of humor, he jokes and treats lightly his condition, although he's deadly serious about his ability to cope with the illness and fight for its cure -- hopefully coming in the next 10-15 years. At slightly under age 40 as the new millennium begins, he is part of only five percent under the age of 50 with P.D. Yet he takes it upon himself to be a full time advocate for the people who suffer, often quietly, including high profile people like Janet Reno and Muhammad Ali.

These days, the real note-worthy item on Michael J. Fox is that he has committed himself almost completely to the elimination of Parkinson's. He wants that to happen at the earliest possible moment, for his own sake and for the sake of so many others. Recently, Michael became a U.S. citizen and voted for the first time. It's known he would like to get government money involved to help research a cure. For this purpose, he has raised over one million dollars with his "Michael J. Fox Foundation for Parkinson's Research." But he also wants precious research dollars spent on better treatments. Here is a disease where certain brain cells start to die for an unknown reason. Over the years, the body gradually becomes rigid as movement become awkward and shaky. Eventually there is paralysis. Does this young man complain and wish this incapacitating disease had never hit him? Not on the surface at least, for he considers himself "lucky" to be doing the most important job he has ever had in his life. There's no restful vacation for this superstar. In many ways, he works harder than he did on the set of "Spin City." Critical priorities are at the center of his life now. Although he has been missed immensely, his old friends from "Spin City" are nearby to support him in his work. The television advertisements that they present together are critically and somewhat humorously to the point in their attempt to raise more money. Michael knows that real people who are really hurting are counting on him to fight for their cause, and he is honored.

What can we learn from Michael J. Fox about commitment? First, he has "a cause" in finding a cure for Parkinson's… that's worth every bit of time and energy he can devote to it. He lets it be known that this present highlight of public interest is more important than anything he has ever done in show business. Parkinson's disease is not only at the core of his being, but going after a cure is meaningful and satisfying for his soul. We should all be as lucky as Mike to find a "passion" or truly satisfying goal in life that gives something significant to the world. It would be so tremendous to be committed to not only fight for our own lives but also for the lives of those who look to us for inspiration and help. Second, Michael uses all the help at his disposal as well as his own resources to carry forward a program for getting the job done in a reasonably short period of time. He wins over his friends. He does everything he can to convince others of the critical nature of his cause. He wants more relief now but he also wants an ultimate cure for the disease. Oh for commitment to a mission that would encompass our talents and the talents of our friends, which would not only solve many of our present problems but also provide hope for the future. Convicts can become crime fighters. World hunger can be cured in our lifetime. Military budgets can be cut. Foreign aid can be increased. Nations and peoples can work to revive all of life on our planet. And meanwhile, we will also work to find a cure for our disease. So let's set up the "foundation" to get the job going. Third and finally, the awesome Michael J. Fox humbles himself to the level of those valuable yet weak people he chooses to befriend, and in his identification with them will only be healed and helped when they are healed and helped. He becomes a believable, committed friend to the awkward, shaky and paralyzed ones. For people seeking to learn how to become committed to others, there's probably no better way than to search out and identify with others ("loved ones") in humbleness and humility. This is precisely what we see in Jesus, Gandhi and Mother Teresa. These three, along with "the lucky man," have shown us the way to commitment and some appropriate inspiration for change.

Commitments should always be carried out to enhance the lives of everyone involved. The commitment or pledge of marriage is a good illustration. When two people decide to be faithful to one another for a lifetime, the quality of life for many individuals in society is deeply affected. Of course the two people themselves have a lot riding on the pledge they make to one another. The manner in which each person cares for the other and loves the other will naturally affect their happiness individually and as a couple. Whether they are good for one another or bad for one another will also affect their economic, physical and spiritual well being, their self-esteem and mental health, their status and respect in the community, the relationships they have with any children they raise, how those children relate to each other and to society as a whole, the happiness, peace and satisfaction of the families they come from, the general success and security of the people with whom they work and many other "environmental" concerns. To put it bluntly, there's a world of difference riding on promises made on the wedding day. The ability to cut back on selfish interests and to develop ways of truly loving and giving has nearly everything to do with marital success. That's not always easy to accomplish in a society which encourages self-centered interests. So the divorces and unhappy marriages increase and the quality of life for a lot of people seriously deteriorates.

Renewing commitment can make an awesome difference in this world. Commitments can build up people and communities. They can strength the resolve of individuals. They not only can heighten the happiness, contentment and security of friends, family and loved ones, but can also make life much more predictable and peaceful for connected people. But how do commitments really happen? We must acknowledge they are often inspired by some excitement and usually influenced by past conduct. However, the key is that commitments (like those made in marriage) are decisions that are implemented permanently. Commitments should not be based on "emotions or feelings" since they are usually rather fleeting, but on solid, rational decisions that can endure through thick and thin. Maybe a commitment is a little bit like the decision most of us make with reference to getting out of bed in the morning. Especially early on a cold winter morning, who wouldn't really like to lay there, stay warm and go back to sleep? Yet most adults commit themselves to "getting up" and going about the business of the new day. Ponder what life would be like in your little world if you gradually drifted away from the commitment to get up and go to work. The consequences to your body, mental health, family, work, social life, resources, credibility and more would be enormous. You could feel perfectly justified staying in bed if you wanted to survey your feelings. You might chose to stay there because you just plain feel like it, or because some people aren't nice to you, or because the pressures are too great, or because you've already done enough, or because you've run out of energy, or because you're sick, or because life isn't fair, or just because. All that personal justification boils down to selfish and introverted emotional reactions, for the most part. From the standpoint of your family or community, however, most people would wonder about your emotional condition, if not your sanity. We know there are good reasons for an exception now and then. Still, there's not a lot of good rationale for giving up on a life time commitment once made with all sincerity.

Faithfulness (or commitment) in marriage is a little bit like getting up every morning to meet the needs of others. Essentially, faithfulness is necessary for a good, healthy and wholesome life. On the other hand, if we are not faithful in our relationships, if our commitments fall by the wayside, we will pay a high price. We are paying a high price these days because we are continuously competing with one another for pleasure and power. The high price isn't really recognized because we are so busy taking care of our own narrow interests. We can't see the people we have hurt… in our fighting for position, grabbing the goodies, running to get ahead and ignoring the losers. But in renewing our commitments to what we know are the good and right decisions, changes we desire will gradually take place in our neighborhoods and communities. Parents spending time helping their children understand how they can care for others and refresh the world, community leaders working with rehabilitated people to mend fences in relationships and to supply appropriate insight and direction for hopeful living, politicians sharing resources with their enemies and the most needy of the world to provide balance and harmony, the wealthy and poor of the world in dialog to help bring about sustainable living for all creatures on earth -- such ideas can come out of faithfulness and good stewardship of what the human race has accumulated in wisdom and inspiration. We have vast, untapped natural resources within the hearts and minds (or souls) of people lost in the jungle of competition and material addiction.

One other illustration might be relevant and helpful in looking at the importance of commitment. Generally speaking, we U.S. citizens live in a country with vast and even overwhelming resources of food. Our farms have been the envy of the world with regard to efficient production. It's not so strange then that we have over indulged and let our bodies deteriorate. Not only an abundance of food has caused our physical problems but also "fast food", fatty foods, addictive foods and unhealthy foods have gradually eroded our health. Since we have permitted ourselves to get away from proper exercise, along with being over weight, vulnerable to sickness, weak, dependent upon drugs and medications and vulnerable to environmental contaminates, with regard to our physical health we are getting into dangerous territory. Even an abundance of diet plans and gimmicky self-help programs have played upon our superficial concerns and have often led us astray. We want to look good, feel good and be healthy as a "quick fix." Very little of this is good for us, and furthermore, none of it gets us to what we should be doing for good health and fitness. Believe it or not, every human being should have a goal to be at a proper weight, get plenty of exercise daily and find a way to good health with the very minimal of medications. Carrying out that goal is important to the role of what it means to be human and a steward of the earth's resources.

Every capable person should be helped to realize his or her potential as a healthy, physically fit, efficient, productive and insightful human being. Of course this will take some commitment on the part of every individual. Commitment to self-interest seems to be somewhat instinctive since it's necessary to survival. But commitment to the best interests of any individual within the context of a healthy community that nurtures the world is not at all instinctive and needs to be learned. To begin with, a truly healthy person needs health in body, mind and spirit to be truly happy and whole.

There are at least three essentials for each one of these three parts of the individual. The first essential is to have adequate and proper nourishment for each part -- body, mind and spirit. The second essential is to have adequate and proper exercise for each part. The third essential is to check or test each one of the three parts of the individual to be sure it's on target with regard to its goal... or at least progressing properly. Wrapped up together -- physically, mentally and spiritually -- a human being that consumes, exercises and tests out positively is going to be able to draw from an almost infinite source of power, knowledge and inspiration for the benefit of not only human life but also for the sustenance of all living things. Every rational human being can and should be involved in some conscious, positive changes as an ongoing process to reach the greatest potential over a lifetime. The Gods grant us the potential for no less.

Getting down to specifics, let's look at one of the above three -- our human physical nature -- as an example of how we should be taking care of ourselves. It's convenient to be dealing with threes, since the triangle is used so extensively in architecture to provide strength... and maybe also since so many within our culture regard the Christian God as the Trinity. The first requirement for our physical wholeness has to do with the nourishment we take in as humans. At this time in history, we have an awesome abundance of food and enough nutrients for everyone on earth. How should food be allocated? Consuming a wide variety of nutritious substances would seem to be in the best interests of most people in most cultures. The greatest problem we have to overcome today is the political will to disperse the food production of the world fairly and economically. No person should be left without an adequate, pleasurable, healthy food supply. The most important factor for allocation is that every individual's consumption should be nutritionally adequate for healthy living. The second essential for physical health is that plenty of exercise should be important in every person's daily routine. Of course, exercise is critical for the wellbeing and even continued existence of every part of the body. Too little exercise and the body slowly ceases to function efficiently. Whether it's in normal work related activities or in planned exercise programs for enhancing various part of the body, exercise should have the equivalent attention of food consumption. In other words, the more a person eats the more that person needs to exercise. Put somewhat simplistically, weight should be maintained at the person's "ideal" by either exercising more or eating less. The final essential may be surprising and seem rather unnecessary. Yet it may be just as important as the other two because of our natural tendency as humans to become satisfied and lose focus. This primary element for a sound physical existence has to do with "testing or checking" the balance and sufficiency of the other two (consumption and exercise, for example). Naturally it would be quite important that food should be checked in many ways before it is consumed. Likewise, exercise should be done with guidance, carefulness and precision for best results. And finally, the interaction of both consumption and exercise in maintaining an ideal weight should be continually monitored for the purpose of making minor adjustments and not major ones. Once these essentials are implemented within the daily routine and practiced for awhile, the physical aspect of a human being can almost run on cruise control. Obviously the above illustration is also relevant for the mental and spiritual parts of each individual.

Renewing commitment to quite a number of neglected areas of our lives will certainly take some carefully planned changes. There's no question that such positive changes will greatly invigorate and improve our quality of life. The process of long term, gradual change will probably carry us forward to new, exciting levels of meaning and satisfaction. Still, we should have no delusions about attaining perfection no matter how long we live. What happens when our commitments crumble and we find that we no longer are in control or on the upswing in our lives. What happens when life offers us some hard knocks?

Envision a successful basketball team that wins most of its games. After a while this good team starts taking its success for granted and begins to play without good fundamentals and without serious commitment. A relatively poor team comes to town and aggressively takes charge from the very beginning. The successful team falls behind, but since it has usually been a winner it doesn't get too concerned. The feeling is that they will once again pull out the win at the end. Half-time comes and there's a trip to the locker room. So what will happen by the end of the game? There are at least two fairly reasonable possibilities for what might happen in the second half. First, if the team continues play like the first half and takes for granted that they can come back, they probably never will and they will lose a game that they should have won. On the other hand, if the talented team recognizes it has played poorly, if the players commit themselves to getting back to their successful style of play, if they have not fallen too far behind and if they really are inspired by each other and their coach, there is a very good chance that they will come back to win. The one qualification is… if they have fallen too far behind, no matter how committed or inspired they might become, they may not have enough to overcome their first half deficit.

We all can learn something from this simple illustration out of our common experience. We dare not fall too far behind in our daily commitments or we may not have what it takes to get back into the game. Our society and culture has slipped off the mark of our ideals and we have lost sight of good goals. We may not even recognize how grossly out of shape we have become and how little respect we have left in the world. Have we drifted too far to turn back? Or have we maybe become blind to what we could attain, as we find ourselves caught up in a miserable rat race? Little things really do count. We dare not slip away too far before we get back to our goals. Illustrating even more bluntly, as you are watching your scale with satisfaction, stick with your goals of good eating habits and good exercise. Let the scale please you as you progressively move toward your ideal weight. Then when you see yourself falling off the mark, work your way back before the task seems too large. That way, you stay under control, and it's always easy to remain a winner.

Good commitments… to family and friends, to good goals and ideals, to self-giving and caring for others, to simple and efficient living, to a healthy environment and generally to positive change -- these commitments are great blessings to not only our own neighborhoods and the larger society but also to the whole world. We deeply affect one another, whether we believe it or not. As has been stated "blessing" has to do with divine favor or being set apart for a holy purpose. That's probably not what is inferred when a president ends his speech with "God bless America." He probably hopes that the Almighty will continue to send us the goodies and keep us strong on the military front. Nevertheless, most religious or spiritual people do believe that God can bring about goodness or blessing through people. Our commitments to one another and to preserving creation would seem too high on His priority list, if we can take any inferences from such things as The 10 Commandments, from the words of His prophets, from the directives of His Son Jesus or from the many inspirational words and deeds done by disciples for "The Kingdom of Heaven." One of the signs of our seriousness to be about divine or heavenly business will be evident in how we treat the despised, rejected and lowly ones on earth… as well as how serious we are about sharing our blessings (or the worldly wealth we possess) with those who are poor. There's absolutely no mistaking where the prophets, Jesus, Gandhi and Mother Teresa stood on such issues. Maybe Jesus' words are the most direct when he said, "As you have done it unto one of the least of these brothers or sisters of mine, you have done it to me."

Of course for the Christian faith, the blessing above all blessings came to our race when Jesus humbled himself and became a human being… full of love, kindness and truth. When a famous person, say nothing about an Exalted One, gives up his life to "pass on a message" to his followers, they had better listen carefully. The Lord's great disciple and missionary said appropriately, "There's faith, hope and love, but the greatest of these is love." Christ's commitment to love for needy, mistake prone people is worth a long look by our culture in this new millennium. No one is without some serious flaws -- no not one. And when humility and forgiveness needs to be demonstrated, disciples crowding around Jesus will see some sincere foot washing and servant work. This is the stuff out of which God bestows blessings on the entire creation. Who can argue that inspiration has not been given to people over the last two thousand years? Many have responded with radical changes in their lives. They have renewed their commitments to great causes daily and have raised up countless multitudes for abundant life. It seems as though it's our turn.

It has been pointed out that communism has been a total disaster with regard to that which is moral and capitalism has been a resounding success with regard to that which is immoral. What a troubling statement that is for our world today. Where does the truth lie in that statement -- the kind of truth that Jesus held up before Pilate? We should dig deep to understand the kind of truth Jesus reveals. If we could find it, what could we do about it? Jesus stated flat out that his followers would do even greater things through the power of His Spirit than he accomplished. Christians can take those word of Jesus as Gospel -- as good news that there is great hope for inspired and committed people, even in our day and age. Consider the power in wealthy, blessed, committed people humbling themselves in the pattern of Jesus… to carry out the job of raising up the downcast and the dispossessed and to give of rich blessings to a world desperately in need. That would be capitalism on the mend and committed to love. What awesome power indeed. Such power would not rise up… out of finally "being forced to share" of all that we have been given, but out of the kind of love offered to all people -- love inspired and given by the Gods. Yes, self-giving love given freely and without expectations is true love indeed. What the world needs now… is love.

Renewing commitment means that everyone is "a worker" or one might say "a player" in the activity of self-giving. Oh "the unbelievable world" of even the great goal of everyone sharing of the wealth of what human beings can give and what the world has to offer. Think of the greatness of each person's particular talents being needed and thankfully received. Then add the totality of what people "made in the image of God" can offer one another in wealth, treasure and inspiration. In that tremendous positive for all living things on the face of the earth, exciting, dynamic, wonderful newness is stimulated each day the Son rises. "All that" proceeds out of a little change in direction within the souls of committed individuals, who truly want to make a difference for goodness sake.

When young lovers come to pledge faithfulness for a lifetime, it's in keeping with the wonder of the day that they consider this great but simple truth: When each of the partners is inspired and dedicated to <u>give</u> one hundred per cent to the other, both partners are blessed in <u>receiving</u> one hundred per cent... whether they need it or not. Renewing such commitment in the humility of facing and being forgiven personal imperfection is rather like "a daily baptism" -- a daily cleansing and uplifting shower with refreshing implications for offering blessings to the world.

CHAPTER 18

"Cheering On Change"

Are you ready to party? Who's up for a night out on the town? These two questions imply some fun and excitement coming up soon. And all of us are up for it, right? Generally there aren't many of us that do too much celebrating in our lives, partly because we see and experience so much that makes us sad and depressed. Certainly there's a lot of trouble and turmoil in the world, at least if we are keeping up with the news. We need the shot in the arm, so to speak, to keep us going. A long tough work week leads to a couple of weekend days to relax, enjoy some fun and get ready for the next work week. That's really a roller coaster kind of ride and it fits the life style that is very typical in our country. Where does a person get the energy and motivation to pass on some special goodness in all of this? It's pretty easy to get tired and cranky. A party just might lift our spirits.

In connection with raising our spirits, wouldn't it be great if we could move from "having to" to "wanting to" in our lives. We all remember when we were kids and our parents suggested we do some job that needed to get done. "Do I have to?" These would be our precise words, with a little sad face thrown in to help make the point. Then there were those times when we as children couldn't wait for some event to take place -- like going to an entertainment event with our friends or having the gang over for a party. It wasn't just that we "wanted to" but we almost "couldn't wait." What a difference in perspectives. Our adult world isn't so much different from that world of our early years. Our emotions run quite a bit the same… although there do seem to be some fortunate people who really look forward to each new day. On the surface at least, it seems that these people are never sad, down or depressed. Most of the time we just cast this off… as a few people being of "a different breed"… as though they might be from a different planet or something. Are we confused? Could we be missing something? What in the world is going on here in the midst of a thriving economy and good times?

Taking an honest look at our lives, we can begin to see some of the sources of discomfort and frustration. Getting objective advice is rather like going to the doctor to get a check-up after feeling rather lousy. An appointment with the doctor isn't much fun, because we know that he might point out some of the reasons we are short of breath, over weight or depressed, for example. Yet we still know the importance of going to the doctor's office, even though we know it'll "cost us" in more ways than one. In the long run, we recognize we will get the help we need to function the way we know we should be able to function. As little cogs in the wheel of our steam rolling society, we can't avoid some tense and irritable times. That's why we figure we can use a little tender care or lubrication whenever we get the chance. But let's get back to the point. There are many irritants in our daily lives. In fact, we seem to be dealing with an increasingly weakened social fabric. As time goes on, there are more bad days than good days, and the reality is that there are good explanations for this being the case. Like when we go to the doctor, it would be nice to hear that the sources of our problems come from outside of our control or have infiltrated our bodies through some "foreign agents." As is usually the case, we can't get that kind of break. Getting right down to it, we've got some damaging aspects of our lives that are causing us grief. We have to face the facts that until we understand the roots of our problems and perceive that the symptoms we feel have indisputable causes, there won't be much relief from the troubles we've seen. Consequently, the following four detrimental factors to our overall wellbeing are worth contemplating. The upside is that we can do something about them.

One of the detriments to the smooth running of our society is the glaring exclusiveness that has developed in recent years. It may have originated to some degree from our competitiveness or it may have come from the individualism that pervades our activities. "The rich get richer and the poor get poorer" has also become a significant factor in the feelings many people have toward others in society. Obviously the rich and the poor end up having very little in common and so become more and more exclusive in their priorities and activities. It's pretty easy to imagine the consequences of such things within a society meant to function cooperatively. Our exclusiveness undoubtedly means that groups like the rich and poor, blacks and whites, conservatives and liberals, big car people and little car people and other such groups look at their competitors or rivals with some serious doubts, criticisms and questions, to put is mildly. It shows up in common things -- in the attitudes people have toward others on the highway, how justice should be implemented, what social programs should accomplish, the purposes of work and leisure and even spiritual concerns. As exclusiveness increases, tension and friction builds to the point where serious breakdowns occur... and once in a while even make us all pause in horror. A "society of exclusive groups" eventually is no more healthy or even workable than a society in the midst of revolution or chaos. Extremes tend to push people into becoming even more extreme. The extreme symptoms usually lead to a bad prognosis -- pain, convulsions and finally death for all the parts of a once robust society. Nobody wins in the end.

Another detriment to our present social fabric is the aggressiveness that's on the rise... from the home to the entertainment center to the school. To be aggressive is the opposite of being submissive. It has to do with starting fights or quarreling and is closely associated with being bold, active and pushy. For decades most parents in our society have been actively training their children to be aggressive and not submissive. We say to ourselves... we all know it's only the aggressive ones that get ahead in the jungle of life. So who or what isn't teaching aggressive behavior these days? Who in the world wants to be a servant... or a loser... or a non-qualifier? What sport or video game is passive in nature -- in its rules and goals? Even the Church (with a servant Lord) wants to appear to be in the fast lane and strut it's stuff for public consumption. It's no wonder that aggressiveness has taken over and dominates. We don't even want to think about the long term consequences to such behavior, however. Parents want to either cover up or ignore the fact that their children have learned their aggressive lessons almost too well. Even knowing the system, it can get uncomfortable when some kids show they even know how to push around their parents and teachers... privately and publicly. Is this hard to take? Not when a society gets used to it. Don't fans get extremely excited when one team can really "blow out" another team? The only answer for the losers is to do the same to the other team at a later date. Parents, teachers, coaches and friends all encourage the same approaches to success -- use whatever you have at your disposal to conquer or overwhelm your opponent. What happens if your opponent might be your friend? The common wisdom is that mere friendship shouldn't hold you back -- not at least in an era when "winning is everything." Might there be some drawbacks to aggressiveness in our society and culture? Only everything from infant quarrels to mass murders... from stealing drugs to making billions... from speeding in a car to terrorizing a school... from divorce courts to military bombing runs... and on and on. It's fairly obvious there's some credible explanation for the fact our social fabric is getting some rips and tears.

A third detrimental characteristic within our present society seems to be a rather harmless blemish at first. It could be classified as simple "near sightedness." However, as many of us know from experience with our own eyes, a severe case of near sightedness can affect how we react to all most everything else in the world. This "eye problem" has to do with how we look at ourselves. Essentially, we only want to (and in effect can) see the world subjectively -- from our own point of view. The toys we get are ours. Rules for people to live by are subject to our own interpretation. The money we make or the rewards we get are for our own personal use. The moral standards we live by have to do with our own choices. In other words, within our society, each of us as individuals is pretty much limited to seeing the world through our own, personally adapted, rose colored, near sightedness. We really haven't tried to walk in anyone else's shoes, we don't want to and we shouldn't have to. It's very close to "everyone for himself or herself"… because no one else will do the job. That being the consensus of opinion within our society, it's very difficult to break out of the mold. What are the consequences to a culture caught in the grips of near sighted people? Problems far away don't get much attention. They might get a temporary glance and a little concern, but the general response is that we've got our own pressing interests. Tensions are highlighted among people who insist on seeing things in their own way. Security is also a never ending concern as long as the individual has to remain in charge. The environment that everyone depends upon for life and health is basically always left to someone else's care or responsibility. There's a lot that goes unseen in a culture or world that hold's out ultimately for purely individual rights. The really sad consequence is that we may never know what we could have done to even "save ourselves," if our vision had been more far sighted and concerned about our own long term interests as well as those of our neighbors on spaceship earth.

A fourth and last detrimental condition to note within our society has to do with our divisions. We have heard that a house divided against itself cannot stand. We know what divisions mean between male and female, north and south, east and west, black and white, rich and poor. Of course, the goal is always to heal the separation between the sides. But what happens when the mediators depart or no longer exist? The culture or society crumbles. Now it's true that individual uniqueness, talents and interests are important to society and even to the world. They are part of the wonder and abundance of the whole creation. The divisions or separations that hurt are those where serious conflicts break out and hurt important relationships. Beautiful diversity in healthy, productive, creative harmony enhances all of life, while destructive divisions can disrupt the whole balance of nature. It's critical that every society carefully protects its diversity, while being very cautious about permitting divisions to develop that hurt stewardship and carefulness. Our stewardship of human and material resources has been hurt by our need to focus our attention on divisional disruptions. Our carefulness of the creation has been hurt by the distractions of our social divisions. Unfortunately, individual lives are lost and harmony is sacrificed when we get caught trying to patch up what should never have been divided in the first place. Certainly careless activities in our culture have increased the opportunities for divisions within our ranks and have made us a sensitive and nervous people.

These four detrimental characteristics of our social life together are clearly interrelated in many ways. Movement to correct any one of them might do wonders to begin to erase the other three. The major point is that positive change is critically necessary to eliminate some of the disturbing and irritating symptoms we experience daily. If we are unwilling to change toward a more caring path, however, and in apathetic self-centeredness let the causes of our symptoms advance to even greater trauma, then we will have permitted our own demise as a so-called "advanced society."

An illustration of our present condition might be appropriate for insight into the importance of change in our lives. This illustration comes from Philadelphia -- called "The City of Brotherly Love." Not so very long ago, a news report from NBC told about a lone man sitting on a long bridge... high over a 500' river in Fairmount Park. At first, not many people noticed the man on the steel structure of the Falls Bridge. It was a nice day and people were filling the paths in the Park. One couple,

Tara Johnson and her boyfriend Garrett Cupples who were rollerblading, noticed the man sitting by himself, but at first they were not concerned. Then they spotted police closing the bridge and a rescue truck arrived. As their attention focused more on the solitary figure more police and fire rescue people showed up. Quite a few spectators began to take notice and a man with a video camera started to take pictures. Fifty feet above the river, the man named Matthew Beaufort seemed to be threatening to jump. By now maybe 50 officers were on the scene -- all not far from a local firehouse just down the block overlooking the river. The man threw his wallet to police and leaned out over the river. A spectator yelled "Don't jump!" It was surprising to Tara and Garret that no rescue boat was yet in the water. Then Matthew Beaufort began banging his head against the bridge. Still, no boat appeared and even more suprising was the fact that there didn't appear to be any rescuers down by the river's edge. Garret, a lifeguard and medical student trained in CPR, was trained in water rescue and began wondering if he might need to go in after the man.

By now it had been about 25 minutes since police had arrived, and people were watching from both sides of the river. Suddenly Matthew Beaufort jumped from the bridge and came up treading water. No boats appeared in the river. It wasn't long before people noticed that he was having trouble and couldn't swim. Then he went under. Garrett Cupples was gone in a flash but clearly there wasn't much time. Police, rescue officials and most spectators were watching. Garret, in spite of his ability, was having some difficulty of his own since the water was murky and his contact lenses were giving him blurry vision. One hundred yards... then fifty yards... but Beaufort who had surfaced went under again. The video camera scanned the water for a sign of life but found nothing. Meanwhile, Garret was not giving up. Under the water he was searching, until suddenly he was face to face with the drowning man. The human brain has about four minutes without oxygen, so after pulling him to the surface, the struggle to save his life was just beginning for Garrett. Matthew Beaufort made a sound as though he was attempting to breath and Garrett called for a life buoy to help bring Matthew to shore; but still Matthew wasn't breathing and his lips were getting blue. Taking another serious risk, the lifeguard decided to give him mouth to mouth and scanned the shore for help. There was no direction as to where to go or what to do. By this time one other man -- just another person in the park -- went into the river and was swimming out to help. Mr. Steven Loyd was a registered nurse and also trained in life-saving CPR but he was not a strong swimmer. By the time he was close to Garret and Beaufort he was exhausted. The two began the tough job of trying to bring Beaufort to shore while also giving him air. Garret shouted for help on the shore, but by the time he brought Beauford in and gave him a couple of breaths, only two or three fire rescue were there to begin chest compressions. Steven Loyd began shouting at them to ventilate him. As the two rescuers climbed up the bank of the river, the crowd applauded their efforts. However, time ticked away while "precautions" were taken. By the time Philadelphia rescue personnel got him to the hospital, Matthew Beauford was dead. It turned out that this man was not a homeless person but a troubled man with a steady job and a family. Garrett Cupples and Steven Loyd felt he could have been saved with the proper equipment and medicine. Mr. Beauford's sister said he was swimming, was yelling for help and wanted to be saved. As for answers from the city's authorities -- they didn't have any comments... because of litigation.

This illustration from real life in our contemporary society doesn't need much analysis from anyone, say nothing about from outsiders. Yet it does suggest that we all do some serious thinking about the urgent need we have to change priorities and policies. Don't we all tend to suffer a little bit as we begin to ask ourselves the questions only we can answer. What would we have done? What are we doing for troubled people? Are we happy with the choices we are making? Are we happy with the condition of our feelings, emotions and spirits? Is there any cure for this "sickness" that causes concern, uneasiness and sadness? What part do we play and what responsibility do we have in the larger society? If we do not have regrets or second thoughts about the direction we are heading in our lives and in the society in which we live, we certainly do not need to reassess our activities and go about changing direction. But on the chance we can begin to see the roots of our frustration and deterioration, then it's compelling for us to look into proper remedies.

Learning how to change is not a difficult thing to do if we have some basic understanding about how we think and act as human beings. Nor should change be something we are afraid of trying to accomplish. On the contrary, once we (individually or corporately) recognize there is some new direction we want to take in our lives, we should feel gifted or blessed in receiving the insight or inspiration to change. As we already know, change is always taking place in our environment... as well as within ourselves and especially within our society. It's rather discouraging, however, that change is often down hill and out of our control. Being unaware of what's happening to us, we go with the flow and ultimately take our lumps. The "powers" at work within our culture are usually short sighted and unconcerned about the best long-term benefits to humanity as a whole. Generally these powers look for quick and self-seeking results which usually bring heartache for many. That's why it's so spectacular that individuals sometimes see more healthy ways to live and decide to take charge with change for the better... and for the common good of all. When people begin to clue in one another and help one another begin to change toward higher and greater goals, then more rapid change can take place. We should not lose sight of the fact that even a single person beginning personal, uplifting change can initiate what can eventually change the world.

Society can reap unimaginable benefits when common people learn how to care for others and consequently improve the good of all. Think of the ripples outward when one person dives in to rescue a troubled soul. Think what could happen if even a few criminals switched sides to become crime fighters. Think of the benefits to society if food, shelter and medical care were extended to everyone willing to work for the common good of all people. Think about what small changes could do to make a big difference in everyone's quality of life. Think about a world with less exclusiveness, aggressiveness, near sightedness and divisions. We all need to look into what life could be like if certain changes were made. In doing this we could come to understand the large gap or separation between our present dead end destination as a culture and a much more positive one with regard to our human destiny on earth. This has the potential to inspire nearly every single person toward revolutionary insights and efforts concerning change. Together our efforts could become joyful and meaningful undertakings, which could be honestly appreciated by future generations. They could live to tell about it because of our actions. Many more diligent efforts in areas like peaceful coexistence, environmental protection and population control could make the world a sustainable garden, helping to take care of the total needs of all species.

When we think about cheering on change, we need to get into "the mood" for we definitely are talking about an emotional issue. Certainly cheering is often present within an exciting atmosphere. New life, victory, awesome beauty, surprising gifts, forgiven debts and good predictions are all the kinds of things that inspire cheering. If we really begin to think about it, the positive changes we would like to have in our lives are very close to these words and phrases. The change which will put our culture into a hopeful process evokes thoughts of new life, beauty, peace, goodness, forgiveness and victory. So we most certainly should celebrate and cheer when we begin to get on track toward those excellent goals. Maybe we haven't been accustomed to cheering on change in the past, but with a little mind and spirit adjustment we certainly can. The first step may be to just "do it" -- cheer -- whether it feels right at first or not. After all, that's what it takes to change and do something contrary to what has been done before. We all need to become good cheer leaders (and we can) regarding our own re-creative actions and the rehabilitating actions of those around us. Acting inspired and leading the way to celebrating change can do wonders for our own spirits as well as for encouraging our neighbors -- even in far distant places.

The Christian Church's rightful role in dispensing "inspiration" should be to highlight and cheer on change. There's no need for Christ followers to do a lot of cheering for new churches calling attention to our material wealth, no need for how beautifully we can sing and make music to the unseen Gods, no need for feel-good, entertaining sermons overlooking and catering to our addictions, no need for crumbs scattered to the world's most destitute and hopeless peoples, no need for self-serving politicians who cater to our worst self-centered fears while trying to look religious, no need for military might to protect a faithless, addicted nation, and no need for us as children of God to use up and waste what we have not created or protected. On the contrary, Christians can and should cheer on heartfelt change in people who are taken up with The Servant's humble message of love, forgiveness, peace and hope. That's truly worth cheering about, because The Lord promises abundant living here and now and forever. He just calls people to believe it… and to act on change for the sake of eternal life for all. Now that's truly worth "sacrificing" a bunch of trinkets, shallow personal security, egotistical worship, proud nationalism and inner turmoil to attain. What's the chance of change? We should not kid ourselves into thinking that this way of looking at life in our world is apparent to everyone or even those closest to us. It takes "being inspired" and a humble spirit to be willing to head out in a new direction. "Father Abraham," the great example of faith in the Bible's Old Testament was led by God to venture out and leave all the familiar things behind him. He was willing to be led by the Almighty into a different land. He was willing to change. It's surely expected by "The Savior" of all people (who join hands at the foot of the cross) that we too should be inspired to move out into unfamiliar territory for divine and re-creative purposes. Our uplifting undertaking with fellow convicts and addicts was intended to do nothing less than turn the whole world upside down.

Convicts changed into crime fighters would be a revolutionary development for our culture and the world. Imagine "Church people" fighting for their own freedom from addiction and for the freedom of those caught in our justice and prison systems. Then imagine those "freed convicts" working together to liberate our culture and the world from certain deterioration and death. Church and prison convicts would have much to offer each other in their personal attempts to find wholeness... as well as in their individual attempts to help others. Of course, no "con jobs" -- no deceptive words or actions -- would be beneficial for rehabilitation within either the Church or the prison. On the plus side, from the Heavenly perspective, there would be no greater partnership than that found in a revitalizing mission among empathetic "soul mates" from these two lowly and humble institutions. Such change would be true inspiration -- change inspired by the Gods for extending abundant life to the whole creation. Could we contemplate anything more inspiring than cheering on change... for heaven's sake?

To be sure, there is a certain "craziness" in even contemplating an alliance between rebellious prisoners and pious Christians. Who could realistically speculate that such apparently divergent parts of society could accept one another, say nothing about work side by side for the same purposes -- freedom, peace and renewal? Still, isn't this precisely what the world hopes for in the daily grind of life -- the lion laying down with the lamb, guns turned in for garden plots, the dictator coming to see the light of democracy, communism finding common ground with capitalism, east and west sharing historical humanitarianism and enemies celebrating their own change? These goals and ideals are worth the effort in our new millennium. Individuals with optimistic, confident and believing hearts and minds in all ages and in all places should be able to envision such great goals. The ultimate step is to begin to achieve them. And that usually means some change in direction.

People around the world yearn for daily happiness, enduring peace and significant meaning in their lives. The only hope to attain these illusive objectives is to take part in a process that moves toward their fulfillment. There can be special joy in "the process" of reaching for such goals as happiness, peace and meaning in life. When it comes right down to finally achieving great goals or possessing something strongly desired, attaining the end result too quickly can actually reduce the satisfaction. This might seem strange. Yet most of us recognize that we can receive a lot more joy, satisfaction and pleasurable anticipation in working a long time to purchase a new car… rather than simply possessing it one day off the car lot. We can understand that there actually are benefits to gradually moving in a steady process toward lofty goals. So it's just fine that we spend time preparing ourselves for a more caring and sharing world. We can understand the increasing benefits of good choices, as well as enjoy the steady, meaningful steps of going after those exalted goals that some people never see. Isn't it really quite a nice thing, as well as an honor, to be inspired toward greatness? Clearly, we shouldn't belittle people for going after "the best" within their capability, because basically, each person yearning for what is just a bit better uplifts us all. When all is said and done, we help the world immensely by cheering on beneficial change.

There is terror on the imaginary cruise ship that is swiftly heading toward Niagara Falls. Realizing that no one understands what's happening may be the worst fear. Are we drifting without insight into the danger before us? Are we out of control with no time left? Individually we can be in the same situation. A person drifts toward a fatal moment -- a severe heart attack, a horrible auto accident, a monstrous terrorist attack, a natural calamity or disaster, a drug, bullet or poison in the wrong place at the wrong time -- and never has a chance to do what needs to be done. He or she never sees it coming. It's all rather horrifying. Yes, we all know that real, thinking, feeling people wish to end their lives gracefully and with honor. We all want our lives to have meaning and a proper ending. We all want to be satisfied in our final moments. The most glorious and earth-shaking news we could ever receive... can give us everything we need for life in the present and future as well as for whatever ending we might face. In this very moment or in any coming moment, we can choose to turn our face in a new direction and begin to move toward new life... new life even rippling outward into the whole world. Instead of being a detriment to ourselves, others and the environment around us, we can begin the process of change toward unimagined blessings for all people. Maybe we have already started down the road of favorable change. Maybe in the reading of this book we have decided to break free from our old path. Maybe we need to focus on one particular aspect of our lives that's hurting us. Maybe we can talk to someone with the intention of building a bridge over a hurtful relationship. Maybe we could commit ourselves to freeing convicts cheering change. Or maybe we feel like opening the doors of our hearts and minds to new possibilities for caring and sharing. Whatever any one person does to make some small change for the wellbeing of this small planet, that action will count as a divine blessing for healing, health and wholeness of the entire universe. As we go from the small step to the really big picture -- let's be heard and seen in the process of "cheering on change." Certainly uplifting change will do us good... and self-giving change will bring us blessing!